# PRAISE FOR *THRIVING AS AN EMPATH*

"Judith Orloff, a psychiatrist from UCLA, advises physicians on improving their intuitive powers. Her simple but powerful message is 'Listen to your patients.'"

**NEW ENGLAND JOURNAL OF MEDICINE**

"In *Thriving as an Empath*, Dr. Judith Orloff shows you how to embrace your empathic gifts and share more love and caring with the world. It's a book of inspirations for sensitive people who want to learn how to lead empowered lives and savor the joy of being alive."

**DEEPAK CHOPRA**
author of *You Are the Universe*

"*Thriving as an Empath* supports you in honoring yourself each day of the year as a sensitive person so that your gifts of empathy and intuition will flourish. Practicing loving self-care is the key to your empowerment. This book shows you how."

**IYANLA VANZANT**
#1 *New York Times* bestselling author and host of *Iyanla: Fix My Life*

"*Thriving as an Empath* is a wonderfully written book of daily wisdom that offers profound insights and practical tools to free your mind, body, and soul. This book is the true manual for anyone who wants to keep their heart open in life and thrive while doing it! Judith Orloff, MD, teaches you how to master your inner empathic world."

**DR. JOE DISPENZA**
*New York Times* bestselling author of *You Are the Placebo: Making Your Mind Matter*

T0034523

"Sensitive people aren't weaklings or victims. Dr. Orloff, an empath herself, shows you how to be sensitive, strong, and clear—and to say 'no' to the energy suckers in your life. Read this book every day to stay centered in your personal and spiritual power."

CAROLINE MYSS
*New York Times* bestselling author of *Anatomy of the Spirit*

"Lovely and wise daily prompts for tending your life."

JACK KORNFIELD
author of *A Path with Heart*

"Powerful daily readings to free empaths from limiting beliefs so they can re-take control of their lives. This book is a precious resource and companion to keep nearby and refer to again and again."

BRUCE LIPTON, PHD
cell biologist and bestselling author of *The Biology of Belief*

"We take on so much as empaths! This inspiring day book helps us navigate the stress we absorb from the world and to set boundaries."

ROSANNA ARQUETTE
Emmy® Award–nominated actress and film producer

"Dr. Judith Orloff succeeds again, in her unique and inimitable way, to present empowering and practical tools for radical self-care. She blends a psychiatrist's logical training with the heartfelt sensitivity of the empath. This book is the key to success inside and out. It reminds us, 'I recognize authenticity. I thrive on kindness. I cultivate a graceful lifestyle. I am the power of love itself.'"

MARGOT ANAND
author of *Love, Sex, and Awakening*

# Thriving
## as an
# Empath

# Thriving
## as an
# Empath

## 365 Days of Self-Care
## *for* Sensitive People

## Judith Orloff, MD

**sounds true**
BOULDER, COLORADO

Sounds True
Boulder, CO 80306

Published 2019, 2022

Cover design by Lisa Kerans
Book design by Karen Polaski
Author Photo © Bob Rhia

Printed in the United States of America

BK06550

978-1-64963-010-0

The Library of Congress has cataloged the hardcover edition as follows:

Names: Orloff, Judith, author.
Title: Thriving as an empath : a daily guide to empower sensitive people /
    Judith Orloff.
Description: Boulder, CO : Sounds True, 2019.
Identifiers: LCCN 2019002632 (print) | LCCN 2019981035 (ebook) |
    ISBN 9781683642916 (hardcover) | ISBN 9781683642923 (ebook)
Subjects: LCSH: Sensitivity (Personality trait) | Self-actualization
    (Psychology) | Empathy.
Classification: LCC BF698.35.S47 O76 2019 (print) | LCC BF698.35.S47
    (ebook) | DDC 158.2—dc23
LC record available at https://lccn.loc.gov/2019002632
LC ebook record available at https://lccn.loc.gov/2019981035

10 9 8 7 6 5 4 3 2 1

For Ann Buck

**Nothing is more precious than
being in the present moment.
Fully alive, fully aware.**

Thích Nhất Hạnh

# CONTENTS

# Reclaiming Your Time: The Art of Self-Care for Sensitive People

Self-care is essential for all empathic people. When you mindfully and lovingly practice it each day, your sensitivities will flourish.

The self-care practices, perspectives, and meditations I present as daily offerings in this book will support you in being a compassionate, empowered empath without shouldering the suffering of others or trying to "fix" them. All people deserve the dignity of their own paths. Day by day, I'll offer gentle reminders about how you can be loving without becoming codependent or a martyr.

As a psychiatrist and empath, I am fierce about my own self-care practices and teach these principles to my patients. I feel so strongly about them because I want to keep enjoying the extraordinary gifts of sensitivity—including an open heart, intuition, and an intimate connection with spirituality and the natural world. Shallow emotional waters don't appeal to me. I love going deep—and my sensitivities take me there.

Still, a big challenge for all sensitive people is how to be compassionate without absorbing the stress of others and the world. We don't have the same filters as most people. We are emotional sponges who feel everything and instinctively take it in. This differs from "ordinary" empathy, where your heart goes out to others in pain or happiness, but you don't take on their feelings.

We empaths are helpers, lovers, and caretakers who often give too much at the expense of our own well-being. Research suggests that our mirror neuron system (a part of the brain responsible for compassion) is hyperactive, which can burn us out. This is not how I choose to live. I want to be loving, but overhelping or absorbing someone's distress just puts me on sensory overload, which is painful to my sensitive body and soul. It also doesn't serve the other person in any lasting way.

To stay healthy and happy, you must be prepared with effective self-care practices so that you're ready to deal with stress. Throughout the book, you'll learn to keep yourself balanced and whole by trusting your intuition, setting boundaries, and protecting your energy.

The secret to an empath's well-being is to break the momentum of sensory overload before it consumes you. The strategies and attitudes that I'll share, which have been lifesaving for me, will quickly bring you back to center when you are overwhelmed or emotionally triggered.

## THE SACREDNESS OF TIME

Time is precious. How you spend your days profoundly effects your energy level and well-being. Time gives us an opportunity to grow. It's up to you to use it well. I urge you to open your arms to the flow of time rather than fearing or ignoring it. Being mindful of time lets you reclaim it by being proactive in your choices.

The average sixty-year-old has lived for about 2.2 billion seconds. Every moment we've been given is holy: the pain, the bliss, and all that lies between. Framing time this way helps you experience the wonder of life, whether you're folding laundry or meditating on a Himalayan mountaintop. It also allows you to be discerning about who you spend time with so that you can choose nurturing relationships.

The ancient Greeks had two concepts of time—Chronos and Kairos—which can help you wisely channel your sensitivities. Chronos is clock time, which is measured in seconds, minutes, months, and years. This is the material realm of to-do lists, deadlines, nine-to-five jobs, and social obligations that can feel overwhelming if you don't have skills to override stress. But Chronos is also a place of amazement, beauty, and fun if you manage your schedule well and create room for those incredible experiences.

In contrast, Kairos is sacred time, a nonlinear awareness that is an empath's truer home. It is the infinite realm of the soul, the zone of divine timing where everything happens in perfect order. You can reach this state through intuition, meditation, silence, observing synchronicities, and other practices I'll offer. *Thriving as an Empath* will help you balance your time-bound and timeless selves so you're not cornered by the clock.

## TIME, NATURE, AND CYCLES OF LIGHT

A secret to making the most of each moment is to be aware of the phases of nature and cycles of light. This will increase your energy and connect you with the pulse of life. The following four strategies, which I highlight in this book, will help:

- Experience the power of the seasons
- Note the solstices and equinoxes
- Observe the phases of the moon
- Tap into the elements

### Experience the Power of the Seasons

The seasons are markers and containers for our lives. They influence weather and crops but also your mood and vitality. You may feel happier and more energized during one time of year than another. Some empaths may experience seasonal affective disorder, a depression related to reduced light, for which I offer self-care practices. Noticing your responses to seasonal changes connects you to the rhythms of your body and the Earth. This more powerfully aligns you with your own needs.

Each season has unique changes and patterns of light and dark that affect your body. For instance, during winter, when the Earth's axis tilts away from the sun, it is darker and colder, with turbulent weather in many locations. So we may instinctively take refuge in our homes and our inner lives. During summer, when the Earth's axis tilts toward the sun, the days are longer and warmer, and we're more outer-oriented.

In the spirit of welcoming and attuning to the seasons, this book is divided into four parts, each of which focuses on the unique qualities of each season starting in midwinter on 1:

Winter: Going Inward, Sensing Truth
Spring: Rebirth, Growth, and Rejuvenation
Summer: Passion, Play, and Abundance
Autumn: Harvest, Change, and Letting Go

What's amazing about these cycles is that rebirth always follows darker periods. Nothing stays the same. Though the seasons aren't as dramatic in some places, having less or more daylight can affect your mood, energy, and schedule. Being aware of seasonal changes (even here in California where they are subtler) grounds you and lets you flow more effortlessly each day.

Sometimes, your body's rhythms may conflict with the reality of your schedule. For example, during winter, your body may say, "Slow down," but holiday commitments increase your stress and activities. At those points of tension, the practices in this book, including boundary setting, will support you in replenishing yourself more quickly.

### Note the Solstices and Equinoxes

The solstices and equinoxes aren't just ordinary days. They are special times for you to recharge and find balance. On each solstice and equinox, I'll offer a meditation for you to experience this vital energy. The winter solstice, the shortest day of the year, is a perfect point to be quiet and ignite your inner flame. The summer solstice, the longest day of the year, is your opportunity to take in this abundance of light. During the spring and fall equinoxes, when day and night are equal length, you can draw on this balance in nature to enhance your own emotional, spiritual, and physical balance.

### Observe the Phases of the Moon

In my twenty-five years of Taoist practice, I've faithfully paid homage to the phases of the moon by engaging in special meditations and rituals to connect with the power of these days. In Taoism, we learn from the harmony in nature and are revitalized by it. The moon, the tides, our bodies, and the cosmos are interconnected. Being in touch with this enlivens me as an empath.

You may want to observe the phases of the moon too. I've done this since I was a child. The moon has always been my beloved companion. The new moon represents fresh starts—many empaths experience it as calming. The full moon signifies the peak of a pattern in your life, an intense time for some empaths who feel overwhelmed or agitated. It's good to know if you are sensitive to the full moon so you can ground yourself. Mark the dates of the full and new moon each month in your journal or calendar. Let these cycles inspire you to reclaim your most ancient self who was devoted to watching the heavens, the sky, and the moon—and bowed in wonder to Creation.

### Tap into the Elements

Sensitive people often love the primal experience of tapping into the elements: fire, air, water, and earth. I'll share ways to do this through simple activities and rituals such as luxuriating in a hot bath, lying on a boulder to feel its strength, or warming yourself by a fire. The Greek physician Hippocrates taught that attending to the balance of these elements in our bodies can improve our health. Each has distinct qualities that can energize you and clear negative energy: fire ignites passion and burns away resentments, water is cleansing and dissolves remnants of stress from the day, earth is grounding, and air represents the lifting of burdens, lightness, and spaciousness. Each season is associated with an ele-ment: winter with water, spring with air, summer with fire, and autumn with earth. Throughout these pages, you'll find ways to draw on both the power and pleasure of the elements.

## HOW TO USE THIS BOOK

The daily passages in *Thriving as an Empath* provide a practical kind of prescience. Reading them sets the tone for how you face each day and outlines ways to attract positivity and deflect stress. For instance, to offset overwhelm at critical times (such as before an intense meeting), insert a self-care practice in your schedule. Even a few minutes of meditating can center you. A little self-care goes a long way. Honoring your sensitivities is an act of self-love.

Try any of the following approaches to using this book. Whichever you choose, set your daily intention to focus on grat-itude and the magic of the moment.

*Read in sequence for a year.* To receive the full benefits of practic-ing self-care for a year, start at the date you obtain this book and continue to read it chronologically. Each morning, allow a few minutes to sit quietly and reflect on or journal about the message. Apply its teachings throughout the day.

*Intuitively turn to a page for guidance.* Take a few deep breaths to quiet yourself. When ready, let your hand randomly turn to a page; this will offer a perfectly timed message for you. Also, inwardly ask a specific question like, "How can I have a health-ier relationship?" Then let your intuition pick the page with the answer and put the practice into action.

*Keep an empath self-care journal.* I've created *The Empath's Empowerment Journal* as a resource and companion to this book. In it, you can record your feelings and realizations and expand on topics that move you in these pages. Use this journal or any other that you love to chronicle your experiences.

I invite you to take an incredible journey around the sun with me. I'm excited that we can gather as empathic souls on a daily quest to be more loving with ourselves and to empower our sensitivities. I hope this book will be a friend to you and that you draw on its daily readings to thrive.

This book of days, this book of seasons, is my tribute to an empath's loving heart and to the sacredness of time. My greatest purpose is to be in service to the goodness of empathy and love. As sensitive people, let's marvel at our lives and our many openings to grow. Every day the mystery unfolds. No matter what: keep loving, keep taking deep breaths, and keep looking at the starlit sky. Allow time to help you remember your timelessness.

Holding a light-hearted awareness of the comings and goings of all things lets us feel gratitude for every moment.

# Treasure Your Sensitivity

The first day of the year is a magical twenty-four hours. It's a wide-open portal into new beginnings and new possibilities about how you view yourself as a highly empathic person. Take some quiet moments to reflect on your empathic gifts: your intuition, depth, creativity, compassion, and desire to better the world. Let yourself experience their worth.

The new year is a perfect time to recommit to your self-care. Ask yourself, "What lifestyle changes can I make to better support my sensitivities? How can I be a caring person, but not burn out? What practices can I use to replenish myself?" Clarifying your goals sets a positive tone for change.

I love the Zen concept of "beginner's mind." It allows you to see yourself with new eyes—not through the lens of old ideas or preconceptions. Starting at this moment, make it a priority to treasure your sensitive soul and the power of your loving heart.

---

**SET YOUR INTENTION**
Today and throughout the year, I will embrace my
empathic gifts. I am proud of who I am.
I want to grow into my strengths and become
an empowered empath. I will practice self-care
techniques to protect and nurture my sensitivities.

# The Gift of Being Different

Like many empaths, you may feel as if you don't belong in this world. You experience life so intensely, and love so deeply, it's sometimes hard to find kindred souls to whom you can relate.

As a child, I always felt "different" from my peers. Other kids loved going to crowded parties and shopping malls, whereas I preferred climbing trees with my best friend or writing poetry. As an only child, I was alone a lot and found companions in the moon and the stars. Often, I felt like an alien on Earth, waiting for a spaceship to take me to my true home.

Similarly, Albert Einstein said, "I am truly a 'lone traveler' and have never belonged . . . I have never lost . . . a need for solitude."

As I've grown as an empath, I can appreciate the gift of being different. I am moved by this anonymous quote: "If you feel you don't fit into this world, it's because you're here to create a better one."

Sensitive people are meant to bring light into the world. Empathy is a strength, not a weakness. I applaud everyone who looks different, feels different, or thinks different. The world needs the difference you will make.

**SET YOUR INTENTION**
I will honor the gift of being "different." I will
fully be my unique self and not let anyone take
my power away. I will shine my light brightly.

# I Am Not "Too Sensitive"

Many of us have received messages from parents, teachers, friends, or the media that being sensitive is a fault or weakness. It's important to gently reevaluate old ideas about yourself such as "I'm too sensitive," "There's something wrong with me," or "I must develop a thicker skin." *These shaming messages are not true.* You are a strong, compassionate person, a blessing to others.

Empaths often have low self-esteem because they believe society's putdowns. *Whenever someone criticizes your sensitivity, don't believe them.* You might even respond with kindness: "I value my sensitive side. Please respect this." Or, if these critical voices arise in your own head, take a breath and regroup. Simply say to them, "Stop bothering me. Go away!" Then immediately tell yourself, "My empathy is a strength." Saying no to these inner and outer negative voices will build your self-esteem.

**SET YOUR INTENTION**
I will not buy into any belief that doesn't
affirm the worth of my sensitivity, compassion,
and love. I will be empathic in my own life
and advocate these values in the world.

# Intuition Is an Empath's Best Friend

Intuition is the still small voice inside you that tells you the truth about life. It manifests as gut feelings, hunches, ah-ha moments, knowings, dreams, and sensing energy. Also listen to the messages that your body sends. Ask yourself, "How does my body feel around someone? Am I energized or tired? Does a decision feel good or tense in my gut?" Empaths can have strong intuition so it's vital that you follow it.

You may find that you second-guess your intuition or that your logical mind tries to talk you out of it. For instance, you're offered a high paying job but your body feels exhausted around your new boss. Or you are attracted to this "amazing person" but your gut says "beware." If you are unsure about how to proceed, at least go slowly and observe what unfolds. To make the best decisions, always factor in your intuition. It wants you to survive and thrive. Learning to trust it is crucial to your self-care.

**SET YOUR INTENTION**
Today I will pay special attention to what my inner voice is communicating. I will be aware of the messages my body sends. I will follow my intuition's advice and notice the results.

# Carve Out Alone Time

A secret to an empath's happiness is creating adequate alone time. This soothes your neurological system and reduces sensory overload so you can feel more inner peace. Taking a break from the busyness of life is good medicine. After you decompress, the world won't seem as overwhelming and you can have more fun when you're with people.

Reflect on what kind of alone time appeals to you. Do you want to relax in a comfortable chair, in silence? Would you like to close the door to your bedroom and journal about your day or meditate? Would you prefer taking a slow walk in nature? During cold weather, do you like curling up by the fire with a cup of hot tea? Reflect on how much alone time you need to feel replenished.

If you have a hectic schedule, be creative. Sometimes I meditate in public bathrooms if that is the only retreat space in my day! Even a few minutes of alone time can quickly restore your energy.

**SET YOUR INTENTION**
Today I will plan some alone time to wind down.
I will take a break from daily demands and be quiet
and still. I will commune with myself and the universe.

# Be in the Now

Being fully in the present is a way of slowing down time so you can savor it. The moment, the eternal now, is the miracle we've been given. You can find safety and comfort there.

Still, we may get trapped in obsessing about the past or the future, which causes us to suffer. Why did I stay in that job for so long? Will I be healthy? Will I find a soul mate or have enough income to feel secure? Also, you might conjure worst case scenarios about some area of difficulty in your life—a psychological process called catastrophizing. Recognizing this pattern and gently redirecting your thoughts to more positive ones will lessen your tension.

Mindfulness, which is the practice of consciously being in the moment without judgment, is about focusing on what's happening in the here and now. If your attention drifts, mindfully bring yourself back by refocusing on the rhythm of your breath. Also focus on your senses. Being aware of the sights, sounds, smells, and beauty around you gets you out of your head and into the Now. As D. H. Lawrence wrote, "The living moment is everything."

**SET YOUR INTENTION**
I will breathe slowly and deeply to calm stress.
I will not focus on the future. I will tell myself,
"I can handle anything one moment at a time."
Staying in the Now is my path to freedom.

# Divine Timing

There is a flow to life that you can intuitively tune in to. When you surrender to this, you will be carried toward the people, places, and situations that you were meant to experience and learn from. Divine timing happens when you stay in touch with this flow.

Sometimes, though, divine timing may differ from your ego's timing. If, according to your ego, a goal isn't materializing quickly enough, be patient and trust the rhythms of your life. Trying to force matters or pressure people will usually backfire.

Empaths sabotage their goals with anxiety. When you are anxious or overwhelmed, it's not the best time to make decisions. Once you've done everything to further a goal, for instance, in your career or a relationship, let go and be open to divine guidance. Take a sacred pause. You simply wait and watch for signs on how to proceed. With an open heart, you are inviting the universe to work its magic.

---

**SET YOUR INTENTION**
I will identify a situation in which I may be pushing
too hard. For the next week, I will just let things be.
I will become a loving witness to my life rather than
pressing forward. I will see what the flow brings.

# The Beauty of Sensing Energy

Empaths speak in the language of energy and can sense its subtle force around people. It's exciting to frame your interactions and the world in this way.

We are all composed of vibrantly colored energy fields that penetrate our bodies and extend inches to feet beyond them. Though they are invisible to most people, you can feel them with intuition. To Hindu mystics, this is called Shakti. Chinese medical practitioners call it "chi." In Western health care, the subspecialty of energy medicine recognizes our bodies and spirits as manifestations of this energy, which transmits information about our thoughts and emotions.

It's fun to practice sensing energy around various people. Throughout the day, pay attention to what positive energy feels like. Does your vitality increase around certain people? Do you feel relaxed or uplifted? Then notice what negative energy feels like. Ask yourself, "Do I feel tired, anxious, sick, or overwhelmed?" Get in the habit of noticing the energy people emit. Factor this into your choices about work, relationships, and all areas of your life.

**SET YOUR INTENTION**
I will be aware of how subtle energy affects my mood, body, and well-being. This is a way of respecting my intuition and how I empathically perceive the world.

# Is This Emotion Mine?

Emotional empaths are able to sense other people's feelings and become a sponge for both their happiness and their stress. It may be hard for you to distinguish someone else's emotions from your own. They are a form of subtle energy that we all give off, and they are contagious. You may unknowingly take on a loved one's moods. Or in crowds, you can suddenly feel anxious, depressed, or happy without knowing why.

A wonderful way to clarify this is to get into the habit of asking, "Is this emotion mine or someone else's?" Many empaths get confused and overwhelmed because they're not used to framing their exchanges in this way. That's why practice is important.

Start by asking yourself this question about three people today. Prior to interacting, notice your own mood to get a baseline of your emotional state. Are you peaceful? Anxious? Excited? Then observe how your mood changes after the encounter. If you feel different, either subtly or dramatically, most likely you are picking up their emotions.

---

**SET YOUR INTENTION**
I will empower myself by becoming aware of my emotions. Being mindful of the feelings I absorb from others enhances my self-knowledge as an empath.

# Dealing with Overwhelm

The secret to reducing overwhelm is to notice it quickly. Many empathic patients have come to me saying, "I've felt overwhelmed for years." They live in the persistent, uncomfortable state of sensory overload or else have become exhausted, burned out, or sick. Happily, you don't have to let this experience get the best of you.

Each day, treat yourself with kindness. If too much is coming at you too fast, make time to decrease stimulation. Notice when you first start feeling overwhelmed. Did a colleague or family member ask too much of you? Did you overcommit yourself? Most importantly, catch the feeling as fast as you can before it gathers momentum. Then take at least a few minutes to unplug from stimulation. I often retreat to a room without sound or bright light. I rest or meditate to recalibrate myself to a more balanced state. You can use these strategies too.

**SET YOUR INTENTION**
To prevent or reduce overwhelm, I will plan short
or longer periods to reduce external stimulation.
Learning to deal with feeling overwhelmed is
an essential part of my empath's tool kit.

# Cultivate a Meditation Practice

Meditation is a powerful way for sensitive people to recenter themselves and release stress by going inward. This practice lets you quiet your mind's chatter and put aside your to-do lists to connect with your heart in a timeless, loving state. Think of it as taking a vacation from mundane demands. Whether you're doing a walking meditation in nature or meditating indoors, it returns you to the Now and quiets sensory overload.

You may find it comforting to create a sacred space at home in which to meditate—a safe refuge from the world. This can be a simple table with candles, incense, and flowers. I meditate at my sacred space first thing in the morning and before I go to sleep. It always connects me to my heart and energizes me.

Whether you are feeling off-center, tired, or simply want a peaceful break from your day, use this meditation.

*Sit in a comfortable position. Allow your body to relax and your heart to soften. Bring your attention back to the Now. When negative thoughts intrude, let them float by like clouds in the sky. Keep refocusing on the rhythm of your breath. Invite the feeling of serenity to permeate your being.*

---

**SET YOUR INTENTION**
I will develop a regular meditation practice as a part of my self-care routine. This will help center me and restore my energy. My goal is to meditate daily.

# It's Not My Job to Take on the World's Pain

As an empath, you have an open heart. You don't have the same emotional guard up that many others do. You feel people's pain—both loved ones and strangers—and you instinctively want to take it away from them. In fact, many of us have been taught that being compassionate means it's our job to remove other people's pain.

*This is not true.* You can hold a supportive space for someone without absorbing their distress in your own body. Finding this balance is the art of healing. Inwardly you can say, "This is not my burden to carry." It is impossible to fix someone, and it is really none of your business to try. More than twenty years of being a physician has taught me that everybody deserves the dignity of their own path.

**SET YOUR INTENTION**
I will be compassionate without becoming a martyr
or taking on another person's pain. I will respect
someone's healing process without trying to "fix" them.

# Overhelping in Social Situations

Do people like to share their innermost feelings with you? At parties, do you often end up listening to someone's life story? Sensitive people frequently magnetize others who want to confess their problems, including strangers, as if you're wearing a sign saying, "I can help you." Others sense your loving nature and flock to you for advice.

Empaths often don't know how to shift into "unavailable mode," an invaluable skill to learn. For instance, if I want to be quiet on airplanes, I picture an invisible cloak around my body that insulates me, and I draw my energy inward. I don't make eye contact or start a conversation. I do this lovingly, not with meanness. But others can feel that I'm uninterested in engaging. You can try this technique too.

It's okay to be unavailable at times. In fact, it's necessary for your well-being. Whether you say, "Excuse me, I must go to the bathroom," or else set a limit on how long you talk on the phone with someone, being discerning about who you listen to is empowering.

**SET YOUR INTENTION**
I will practice self-care in social situations. It is my
choice to limit the time I interact with others. I don't
have to be available to everyone who wants to talk to me.

# Tune in to Nature

Sensitive people are drawn to nature and feel at home there. You may get refreshed among the trees, flowers, meadows, or mountains. You may love being close to bodies of water. I can relate to the poet Wordsworth when he writes about times in which "the world is too much with us" and about the peacefulness of nature. The natural world is an ideal place to retreat to and rejuvenate yourself.

Nature cleanses toxic energy. You don't have to "do" anything other than slow down and absorb its beauty. Keep putting yourself in the presence of green growing things. Notice how they move and breathe. Plants infuse the air with oxygen and remove carbon dioxide, which purifies our environment.

Nature is also sensual. Notice the delicate way the sunlight falls on leaves, the pure white snow, even the bare trees in winter that lie dormant until their rebirth in spring. Each phase of nature can renew you. Regularly tune in to the natural world for solace. It is the touchstone to the essence of life.

---

**SET YOUR INTENTION**
Today I will look up at the stars, the moon, and the sky.
I will savor the beauty of trees and of the land. I'll rest
in the grace of the natural world and allow it to fill me.

# Lessons of Water

In many healing traditions, the four elements—fire, air, water, and earth—possess unique, nurturing qualities and are linked to different seasons. Water has often been associated with winter. It represents tranquility, conserving energy, flexibility, and flow. Since our bodies are two-thirds water, it's understandable that many sensitive people are drawn to it.

Water in motion emits calming negative ions that increase serotonin, your body's natural antidepressant. That's why the ocean and waterfalls feel so soothing. Water purifies any unwanted emotions you may have absorbed. During a busy day, even washing your hands or drinking water helps clear stress.

Observing water can teach you how to maneuver around obstacles. Even glaciers, which are rivers of ice, eventually flow to the sea.

You can reduce tension by being yielding like water—especially during a conflict, whether you're arguing with your spouse or stuck in traffic. When a wave is about to crash on you, it's wise to dive beneath the turbulence rather than hurt yourself by struggling. The lessons of water remind you to glide like a Zen warrior through adversity toward serenity.

---

**SET YOUR INTENTION**
I will learn flexibility from observing the
motion of water. I will practice flowing around
obstacles rather than forcing a confrontation.

# Practice Self-Compassion

Self-compassion means directing loving-kindness inwardly. Instead of beating yourself up, give yourself a break and acknowledge that you did your best in any circumstance. When you become your own champion, you will feel more protected in the world.

Research shows that people who are compassionate toward their own shortcomings experience greater well-being than those who harshly judge themselves. We all make mistakes, but the larger lesson of love is how we treat ourselves at those times.

Still, it's often easier to have compassion for others than oneself. Over the years, many psychotherapist friends have lamented to me about this issue. Don't worry. This is an area of growth that loving people must address so they can be more compassionate with their own struggles.

Compassion can be learned. Start by planning at least one act of kindness toward yourself daily. For example, turn off your computer and enjoy a walk or tell yourself, "Good job," or "I'm happy that I didn't react nastily to a controlling friend." My Taoist teacher says, "Beating yourself up a little bit less each day is spiritual progress."

---

**SET YOUR INTENTION**
I will be my own best friend. I am not perfect,
nor are any of us. I will not beat myself
up. I will treat myself with kindness.

# Reclaim Your Inner Child

Each of us has a precious inner child who deserves to be loved. However, you may have not been raised in a family where this sensitive soul was seen or supported. Instead, your inner child might have been shamed for being "weak," a "sissy," or a "cry baby." This is wounding enough for girls, but it's especially brutal for boys who may get bullied and rejected by more macho kids.

By the time you're an adult, your wounded inner child could have retreated so far within, you may have forgotten about it. Nevertheless, their pain is still alive—even if you're not conscious of it—and can wreak havoc in your relationships. This can manifest as fear of intimacy and a reluctance to set boundaries or be your authentic self.

It is crucial to retrieve your inner child. Here's how. Visualize your childhood home where your inner child was not seen or cared for. Then extend an invitation to this darling girl or boy to reemerge. Acknowledge, "I'm sorry you were hurt. I know how painful that felt. But now, I vow to protect you. I won't let anyone hurt you again." Then bring that sweet child home with you where he or she can become the amazing, creative being that Spirit intended.

**SET YOUR INTENTION**
I will reclaim my inner child, a vibrant,
sensitive part of myself. I will always nurture
and protect this adorable being.

# Set Healthy Boundaries

Your relationships will improve when you can set clear boundaries. A boundary means communicating your preferences about how you want to be treated. For instance, "It would be great to see you tonight, but I only have an hour." Or "I'm sorry, I can't take on another commitment now." Or "Please stop raising your voice." If you are wishy-washy you won't be taken seriously. To successfully express a boundary, be kind but firm. Then others will know you are serious and will be less likely to feel offended.

If you are reluctant to set boundaries, what holds you back? Is it low self-esteem? Are you afraid of being rejected or hurting others' feelings? Maybe you didn't feel safe expressing yourself in your family. Some of my sensitive patients initially start psychotherapy feeling too timid to speak up in their lives. Before they were able to set boundaries, they'd always been the designated doormats or victims in their relationships.

To shift this pattern, practice the adage "Feel the fear but set the boundary anyway." Start with easier people, such as a telemarketer or a supportive friend. (Don't begin with your mother!) Learning this protective skill will help you thrive.

---

**SET YOUR INTENTION**
Today I will firmly and kindly assert a boundary
with one person. This form of self-care will
allow me to have healthier relationships.

# "No" Is a Complete Sentence

If someone has unrealistic expectations of you or asks you to do something you are unable to take on, remember: "No" is a complete sentence. The way to say no, and have it be received well, is to come from a centered, neutral place. Being curt or reactive will have negative results. You don't need to defend yourself or get into an involved conversation. Simply be clear and say no with love.

I am moved by what Mahatma Gandhi says: "A 'No' uttered from deepest conviction is better than a 'Yes' merely uttered to please, or to avoid trouble." Kind but firm limit setting is healthy. It's not your job to fix anyone. Enabling always backfires. Without limits, a relationship is on unequal ground. No one wins.

Compassionate people don't always say yes to every request. Buddhist nun Pema Chödrön warns against what she calls "idiot compassion," using kindness to avoid conflict when a definite no is required. There's a right time to give and a right time to say no. Keeping this balance protects you from being drained and supports honest, caring relationships.

---

**SET YOUR INTENTION**
At least once today, I will say no with love, even
if it initially feels uncomfortable. I will assure
myself that this will become easier with practice.

# Recognize Inauthentic People

Your intuition lets you sense when people aren't as they appear. It may tell you, "Something isn't right. I'm not sure if I can trust this person." Empaths have been called "human lie detectors" since their inner radar is excellent at sensing inconsistencies in others.

When your intuition alerts you that someone may be inauthentic, there can be a range of reasons, from the person feeling insecure to express their true feelings to misrepresenting the truth. To find out, simply observe the person over time to see if their actions match their words. Also, as you get to know them better, you'll gain greater insight into their motivations so that the truth will become clear.

**SET YOUR INTENTION**
I will listen to my intuition about people. I will not
second-guess myself. I will be cautious if someone
feels inauthentic and stay observant to discover why.

# Befriend Your Body

Befriending your body is necessary for your empathic gifts to flourish. Your body is a sensitive intuitive receptor. It is wired to help you survive and thrive.

Still, it isn't always easy for empaths to be in their bodies. For years, I wasn't comfortable in my own skin, nor did I feel safe in my body. It seemed like I was in too small a container. So many intense emotions overwhelmed me that I floated numb a few inches above myself. However, once I learned to stop absorbing other people's stress, my body became a safer, much more fun place to be.

Your body is the sacred temple that houses your spirit. Listen to its guidance, as you would an inner guru. To center yourself, focus on your breath. Tell your body, "I will treat you like a friend and pay attention to your signals. When I'm overloaded I will be quiet. If I need a break, I will play." Treating your physical self well makes you feel more energized and alive.

**SET YOUR INTENTION**
I will settle into my body completely by
taking a few deep, slow breaths. I will enjoy
my sensuality and notice how good it feels to
walk, breathe, eat, and smell the flowers.

# Listen to Fatigue

Fatigue is one of the first signs to notice when you start feeling overwhelmed. Even so, you may keep pushing to complete your to-do list, work projects, or other activities. Then you become chronically tired, which puts you at greater risk for exhaustion. This leads to sensory overload, adrenal burnout, anxiety, and depression.

Sadly, our society rewards toughing out adversity. We commend overachievers who ignore their body's signals. We are conditioned to live from the neck up. These choices are especially harmful to sensitive people who have delicate systems that require more rest and alone time to thrive.

I advise my patients to consider fatigue a voice of wisdom. It is telling you, "Take a rest, even for a few minutes." Meditate. Nap. Or simply sit quietly. These mini tune-ups, along with a good night's sleep, will help restore you. Listening to your fatigue level lets you treat yourself with love by practicing self-care.

---

**SET YOUR INTENTION**
Today, I will ask myself, "Am I experiencing
either acute or chronic fatigue?" Then I will
identify one compassionate action I can
take to rest and restore my energy.

# Breathe Out Stress

During a hectic day, paying attention to your breath will center and relax you. In Hindu traditions, the breath is revered as prana, the sacred life energy. You can tap into this vitalizing force to reduce stress.

I always observe my new patient's breathing patterns to determine how much they're clenching or letting go. Sensitive people may unconsciously hold their breath or breathe shallowly, which constricts energy. Just as animals slow their breathing when they don't want a predator to notice them, you may also hold your breath as a form of protection.

Your breath cleanses toxicities from your body by inhaling oxygen and exhaling carbon dioxide. You also can exhale harmful emotions. Conscious breathing will anchor you in your body and release stress. Try this exercise:

*Take a few quiet moments to relax with your eyes closed, focusing only on your breath. As you inhale, slowly breathe in calm. As you exhale, breathe out any stress you might have absorbed. Then inhale serenity and exhale worry and fear. Finally, breathe in contentment as you feel a sense of well-being permeating your body.*

**SET YOUR INTENTION**
I will practice conscious breathing. If I notice I'm constricting my breath, I will begin to breathe slowly and naturally again. With each inhalation and exhalation, I will feel my life force growing stronger.

# Manage Your Time Wisely

I am fierce about my time management. I want to have a balanced life in which I'm not rushing, overcommitted, or stressed out. As an empath, if I overcommit myself, I will quickly manifest physical symptoms such as a stomachache or back pain. Or I will become irritable and exhausted. I want to do everything possible to avoid this.

It is a radical act of self-care to manage your time well. Reflect on how you currently organize your days, weeks, and months. Are you happy with your schedule? Do you have a comfortable balance of work and play? Or does overcommitting or rushing make your life feel tiring? Compassionately evaluate your situation. It's helpful to journal about positive changes you can make. Identify ways you can better prioritize your daily activities, delegate responsibility, or eliminate distractions. Then put these changes into action. Strike a balance between demands that can drain you and activities that energize you.

**SET YOUR INTENTION**
I will mindfully manage my time. I want to
have a balanced life in which I am passionate
about work and also passionate about play.

# The Search Is Over

There comes a time when, after trying so hard for many years to "make things happen" and seeking answers on the outside, you just give up the search. This doesn't mean that you don't still follow your dreams. Rather, it signifies that deep inside, you know you've already arrived. I'm not referring to external accomplishments such a fantastic job or money in the bank—though these may exist. Even more significantly, you have a sense of heartfulness within that you feel proud of. You find ongoing refuge there. The heart is a place to warm yourself in the cold of winter and always.

My dear eighty-something Buddhist friend Ann placed the following saying, which she created, next to her meditation altar. I also have it in my home. I hope it brings you peace on your path toward growth and self-realization. You have already arrived, though you may not realize it. Home is the abiding loving-kindness that is within you.

> Nothing to do
> Nothing to be
> Nothing to have
> Rest in your own natural
> Perfection
> As is
> Calling off the search

**SET YOUR INTENTION**
I will feel at home in myself. I will experience
my own perfection and the joy of who I am.

# Positive Self-Talk

Your thoughts affect your energy level and trigger biochemical reactions in your body. Positive attitudes boost well-being by producing endorphins, the "feel good" hormones. Negative attitudes deplete it by increasing stress hormones.

Positive self-talk is a powerful form of affirmation that stops you from focusing on negative or fear-based thoughts. During winter, when there's less daylight, sensitive people may be more prone to depression. (More on seasonal affective disorder on December 16.) Positive self-talk can help you through this. For instance, if you are burned out from interacting with too many people, tell yourself, "It's okay to take alone time to decompress," instead of beating yourself for declining invitations. Or say, "It's great that I went to a fun movie," rather than criticizing yourself for being lazy.

Positive self-talk reprograms your tendency to focus on fear or negativity. The more you practice, the more natural it feels. You may not be able to control all the events of your life, but you can control your attitude.

---

**SET YOUR INTENTION**
I will be grateful for what is working in my life rather
than obsessing on what has gone wrong.
I will focus on seeing the best in myself and others.

# Feeling Loneliness and Isolation

I've worked with many sensitive patients who feel isolated or alone. They often become overwhelmed by the world's stress and retreat into their homes where they feel safe—a habit that blustery winter weather can intensify. Since many of us feel like we don't belong, we may also be lonelier in groups than by ourselves.

If you can relate, I understand your loneliness and your desire to retreat, having experienced it for much of my life. But you don't have to feel alone anymore. You are part of an empath tribe. There are so many of us who understand you. Worldwide, empaths are coming out of the closet and are owning their power. Though we might not have met personally, we can draw on one another's strengths.

Connecting with other empaths can quell your loneliness. One way to do this is to form an empath support group, a process I discuss in *The Empath's Survival Guide*. Also you can check out groups such as Dr. Orloff's Empath Support Community on Facebook where you will meet kindred spirits.

---

**SET YOUR INTENTION**
I will locate other empaths by searching the internet
for information, articles, or supportive groups.
I will also identify other sensitive people in my life.

# Find Comfort in Spirit

Tuning in to a higher power can calm your anxieties. It shifts you out of fear and into love. Spirit has many names: God, Goddess, love, nature, the great Mystery, a universal intelligence. Tuning in to spirit takes you beyond your small self, what Buddhists call "the monkey mind" of whirling thoughts, fears, and worries. You're transported to an expanded version of yourself and can hear your intuition's wisdom more clearly. Spirituality is the unlimited vastness that surrounds your smaller, fear-based identity.

When you're tired, worried, or on sensory overload, set aside a moment to pause. You are not hostage to those feelings. Slow everything down. Take a few deep breaths and inwardly request to feel the expansiveness of Spirit. Stay open to the sublime love, the peacefulness, and the sense of being cared for that Spirit brings. Allow all that positive energy to permeate your being and reassure you that, in this moment, all is well.

**SET YOUR INTENTION**
I will regularly connect to Spirit to overcome
my fears. I have a choice to shift out of
fear and into love at any time.

# Make Time for Silence

Creating periods of quiet allows you to recover from the intensity of our fast-paced world.

You may not realize how much the toxicity of noise drains you. Sometimes you can barely hear yourself talk, let alone listen to your intuition. Loud restaurants. Sirens. Jackhammers. Incessant talking. In response, you may unconsciously wall off your sensitivities for protection and walk around defended or shut down.

Silence offers you a reprieve. For me, it is a relief. Quiet and nonverbal periods can renew you. Buddhist teacher Thích Nhất Hạnh says, "If our minds are crowded with words and thoughts, there is no space for us." The slower rhythm of winter encourages us to go within and mimic nature: You can be silent like snow or as still as a dormant forest prior to spring bloom. In the stillness, your intuitive voice becomes clearer.

Plan at least five minutes of silence a few days a week. This is sacred time when no one can intrude. You can be quiet in your office or home or out among the trees. In the sublime absence of noise, you can reconnect to your Spirit.

**SET YOUR INTENTION**
As part of my time management, I will plan regular
periods of silence. Even if I'm not used to this, I will be
open to the experience of how quietude can renew me.

# Choose Contentment

To fill your emotional well, focus on feeling content in your life. Contentment is a choice. It comes from accepting what is, even though it may not be perfect. Contentment means feeling good about yourself whether you're flourishing or falling apart. In both situations, you can say, "I love myself."

Contentment comes from your heart, not your head. You experience a sense of compassion, happiness, and warmth in your chest that is self-soothing. Being content doesn't make you passive. You still pursue your goals, while simultaneously being grateful for what you have. Though it's tempting for your mind to obsess on what still needs improvement, creating periods of contentment lets you temporarily set aside the pressure of all striving and simply bask in the splendor of life.

---

**SET YOUR INTENTION**
I will allow myself to feel content for at least a few minutes every day. I will not focus on imperfections or shortcomings in myself or others. I will appreciate my life and be satisfied with what I have been given.

# Create a Life You Love

Thriving as a sensitive person means creating a mix of energy, balance, and passion in your life. Start by making choices that are aligned with your soul. It's fine to use logic but also keep intuiting what feels on center for you. Don't assume that what worked a year ago will be right for you now.

Evaluate your happiness level by assessing different aspects of your life: alone time, people time, play and creativity, health, love, and work. Start by modifying one area. Then address others. Ask yourself, "How can I gain more energy, balance, and passion here?" No need to make giant shifts unless you are moved to do so.

Begin with small changes, the tiny magical steps to freedom. Perhaps meditate a few minutes more each day, plan longer breaks between appointments, or imagine a new inspiring project at work. Gradually, keep adding satisfying elements to your day. Over time, reenvision the different aspects of your life to feed your energy and soulfulness.

**SET YOUR INTENTION**
I will try something new that makes me happy.
Creating a life I love comes from making
one small change at a time. It is never too
late to start on this beautiful endeavor.

# Pace Yourself

Pacing yourself is key to loving your life. You can't expect to be serene if you are constantly hurried and pressured. Rushing is especially toxic to your sensitive nature because it puts you in a chronic state of anxiety, sensory overload, and burnout. It also speeds up time so it's harder for you to enjoy every moment.

When you rush, your stress hormones rise and serotonin, the body's natural antidepressant, decreases. You may push too hard because you're overscheduled or because you judge yourself as lazy or inadequate unless you accomplish certain goals. Plus, if you are a people pleaser, you may become overcommitted because you're afraid of disappointing others.

Pacing yourself boosts your vitality and prevents burnout. Does your daily schedule support your energy level? If so, great. If not, consider what pace suits you better and gradually set out to achieve it. Even if you are busy, taking short meditation or rest breaks between appointments is a quick way to gain stamina. Even making micro-shifts in your pacing will improve your energy. It's wonderful to be productive. However, you will feel better if you have intervals of taking it slow, even for a few minutes, throughout the day.

**SET YOUR INTENTION**
I will take a mindful look at the pace of my
life and create a more balanced routine. I will
avoid rushing and overscheduling myself.

# Physical Movement: The Fountain of Youth

Regular exercise helps you thrive because it releases stress and grounds you. It also boosts endorphins, your "feel-good" neuro-chemicals. When you're grounded and calm, you can be more empathic and avoid sensory overload.

Movement keeps your body and immune system robust and helps you to look and feel younger. You will stay strong and flexible so that your muscles don't stiffen with age. A sedentary lifestyle stops the free flow of energy, but the more you move and stretch your body, the younger and more vibrant you will feel.

I depend on exercise to balance me and expel stress I have absorbed. I do a combination of aerobics, yoga, and weights. I also enjoy hiking in the canyons and walking on the beach. Just moving and breathing hard feels pleasurable and primal.

Similarly, find an exercise routine that appeals to you. If you are just starting out, doing simple yoga stretches once daily is a gentle beginning. Since empaths love water, swimming may also feel divine. Pilates, dancing, or riding a bicycle are other alternatives. Go slow. Experiment with different forms of movement to determine what feels good.

---

**SET YOUR INTENTION**
I will move my body every day to strengthen myself and release stress. I will view exercise as a mindful meditation rather than a competitive sprint to the finish line.

# The Sacred Ritual of Bathing

After a busy day, immerse yourself in a bath or take a shower to wash away the day's stress. Make bathing a sacred ritual rather than simply a functional act. It's inspiring to place candles and crystals nearby to illuminate and empower your space. You can add a touch of lavender essential oil in the water to calm you.

Water is a potent element for empaths to restore themselves. In ancient Rome, bathhouses were often used for healing. After a battle, wounded soldiers convalesced there by working with the finest healers. In Judaism, the mikvah is a spiritual cleansing tradition. Similarly, in Christianity, ritual immersion in water, called baptism, is purifying.

One birthday, I had the privilege of visiting the Tassajara Zen Center in a remote part of Northern California, away from phone coverage and the internet. At the entrance to the mineral springs, a variation of the following prayer is posted to invoke the sanctity of bathing. You can use it too before stepping into a shower or tub.

I wash my body and mind
Clear and shining
Free from dust
Free from stress
Free from fear
Pure and shining
Within and without

### SET YOUR INTENTION
I will immerse myself in water and be cleansed of all toxic emotions or stress. I will let water take all my cares away. I will relax into this rejuvenating experience.

# Simplicity and Minimalism

Simplicity is a central principle of my Taoist path. It helps me notice the simple beauty of how the light falls on trees, of cooking an artichoke, or smiling at a friend. Many empaths are drawn to simplifying their lives to decrease stimulation and reduce sensory overload. Plus, it just feels liberating to not be so busy or have so many possessions.

You can find happiness more in life itself rather than in accumulating things. A few years ago, in the midst of a move, I gave away most of my furniture and clothes and took only necessities. Traveling light felt amazing! Less can be more. It was a way of clearing physical and psychic space as well as eliminating excesses.

Streamlining your life helps you reclaim time. Instead of being jammed with appointments or possessions, you find a resting space, a sacred pause, and open-ended periods to imagine what is possible and savor the magic of simple things. As Henry David Thoreau wrote, "A [person] is rich in proportion to the number of things [they] can afford to let alone."

---

**SET YOUR INTENTION**
I will feel how freeing it is to simplify my life by planning fewer activities and letting go of some possessions. I will observe how this opens up time and space so I am better able to enjoy the moment.

# Feeling Things Intensely

Empaths have sensitive neurological systems that react quickly to input. It's as if you're holding an object with fifty fingers instead of five. Since you don't have the same filters that non-empaths have, light, tastes, smells, sounds, and emotions often feel incredibly intense. You experience life passionately, and you're more unguarded.

I used to be afraid of being "too intense," of turning people off (especially the men whom I was dating) with my strong emotional responses. So I would try to hold in my feelings and be someone I wasn't. However, as I've grown as an empath, I can see how beautiful living with passion and intensity is. I never want to change this about myself.

Still, self-care is critical to support your intensity and open heart. If violent movies or newscasts are too painful to watch, limit your exposure. Always plan adequate time for quietude to balance your intensity with calm. Once you embrace your ability to feel deeply, you will attract others who value this quality in you.

---

**SET YOUR INTENTION**
I will not pretend to be someone I'm not or
repress my emotions. I will accept that I have
strong feelings. I will seek out people and
situations that support my sensitivities.

# Being Alone Versus Being Lonely

Taking regular periods of alone time is an empath's salvation. Being alone lets you stop interacting with people and responding to their needs. You can regulate the sound, light, temperature, and other aspects of your environment to suit yourself. Alone time lets you enjoy your own company without any intrusions. You can meditate, breathe, stretch, and reattune to your natural rhythms.

But being lonely feels different from being alone. It is a painful separation from a nurturing source, whether that is self, Spirit, or community. Sometimes, when you are alone, loneliness will arise. Don't resist it. We all feel lonely at times. I feel homesick and lonely for myself when I get too busy! You can also feel lonely with people. Whether you experience loneliness a little or a lot, this emotion alerts you to reconnect with a wellspring of love.

You are never really alone. Spirit is always with you. So if you're lonely, focus on your heart and on Spirit. Also try reaching out for support rather than simply retreating from the world, as empaths tend to do. Love will help your loneliness subside.

---

**SET YOUR INTENTION**
I will make room for alone time each day to
rejuvenate myself. Feeling lonely reminds me
to reunite with love. At those times, I will
connect more deeply with Spirit and friends.

# Soul Friends

I am moved by the concept of *anam cara*. It is Gaelic for soul friend, someone with whom you have a special affinity and share your deepest feelings. Your bond is so close that this person may feel more like family than your biological relatives.

Growing up, I always had one best soul friend. We did everything together. This felt better than socializing with lots of people. You might relate. Empaths typically have one best friend or a few good friends, rather than a large social network.

Identify your current soul friends. Value these special connections. Relationships of this caliber encourage your growth and will help you feel understood as an empath. Also stay alert to finding new soul friends—even if this concept is something you hadn't considered. At your first meeting, you might experience a sense of déjà vu, as though you've known each other before. It feels like a reunion rather than an introduction. Soul friends are devoted allies to cherish. In the course of your friendship, you can offer each other mutual support.

---

**SET YOUR INTENTION**
I will be open to finding soul friends with whom I feel
a special connection. Even if I don't have one now,
holding this desire in my heart will help draw them in.

# An Empath's Open Heart

Empaths are blessed with open, loving hearts. You care deeply about others and the world. Your heart goes out to humankind, the flowers, the Earth, and the children. You also may have a special love for animals and all sentient creatures. Your emotions run deep, as does your intuition.

Thriving as an empath means learning to care about yourself as much as you care about the world. This includes realizing how profoundly important your empathy is in our overintellectualized society. Your caring provides the crack of light in the darkness that will get us all through. Though loving so much can hurt too, your heart makes you strong and bright and pure.

As part of self-care, you must become the protector of your open heart. How? Say no to anyone who wants to make you small. Practice positive self-talk to reverse your negative thinking. For instance, if you tell yourself, "I'm not enough" (which many empaths do), you can learn to quickly counter this false statement by reaffirming, "I am enough. I am loving. I am growing stronger and more confident." Then you've brought yourself back to the realm of positive energy and kindness.

---

**SET YOUR INTENTION**
I will value and protect my open heart and choose
relationships that support it. My ability to love
brings light into my life and the world.

# Marry Yourself

The most important relationship you will ever have is with yourself. Nurturing this bond will keep you healthy, happy, and whole.

I adore the idea of marrying yourself, also known as a "self-uniting" marriage. It's a way to formally commit to love, honor, and cherish your own growth and empathic gifts. It has nothing to do with narcissism or being self-absorbed. The vows to yourself can include, "I will treat you with compassion. I will not abandon you or let anyone hurt you. I will listen to your needs. I will always be loyal to your well-being."

How do you marry yourself? First, formulate your own unique vows, which are a love letter to yourself. Write them in your journal to refer to. Next, create a simple ceremony such as reciting your vows in front of a flower-laced altar or at a magical location in nature. This can be in private or with friends and animal companions as witnesses. It's also okay to say your vows inwardly without any ceremony. In addition, you can wear a ring, bracelet or pendant as a symbol of this sacred union with yourself, if that appeals to you.

Marrying yourself is possible whether you are in an intimate relationship or single. In either case, cherishing yourself magnetizes and deepens love. From this place, you can attract and sustain the right partnership that honors your sensitivities.

---

**SET YOUR INTENTION**
I commit to love, honor, and cherish myself. I
will be devoted to my self-care and growth always,
whether or not I am in an intimate relationship.

# Attracting Love

A basic law of energy is that you attract who you are. The more love and positivity you emit, the more you will bring to yourself. We are all subtle energy transmitters. We are constantly sending out signals that others on similar frequencies receive.

Since your energy reflects your beliefs, it's crucial that you feel worthy of love. This may not come naturally if you were raised in a dysfunctional family that didn't "see" you or support your sensitivities. Or perhaps you had narcissistic or alcoholic parents who couldn't give you the love you deserve. If so, your healing work is to acknowledge your own worthiness. Then you can attract people who are capable of loving.

Intimacy is as much about what you bring to a partnership as what you receive. You can't expect others to treat you better than you treat yourself. The self-care practices throughout this book will support your sense of worthiness and align you with the frequency of love. When your goal is to treasure yourself and heal any fears that close your heart, love will open its arms to you and satisfy what you have been yearning for.

---

**SET YOUR INTENTION**
I am a loving person. I am worthy of love. I will attract
the kind of love that supports my body and soul.

# I Want Love and I Want to Be Alone

Do you feel comfortable when you're in an intimate relationship? Or are you conflicted? Do you want companionship but also want to be alone?

Until recent years, I've spent much of my life being single. Too much togetherness seemed suffocating to me. When I was in a relationship, I'd get overwhelmed and long to escape. When I was single, I'd long for a soul mate. My desire for connection conflicted with my desire for solitude, a push-pull feeling you might identify with.

I've learned that intimacy becomes possible for empaths when they can authentically express their needs. Bottling up your emotions will not make you happy or at ease. When the pressure builds, you may want to bolt. A core part of self-care is identifying your intimacy needs and expressing them to your partner.

To start, it's helpful to journal about what would really make you comfortable in a relationship and highlight your top five priorities. Do you need more alone time? Less noise and clutter in the house? Fewer visitors? More walks in nature with your mate or time for sensuality? Being authentic paves the way for conscious communication.

**SET YOUR INTENTION**
I will honestly express my empathic needs in a
relationship, including my need for downtime and to be
alone. I deserve to feel relaxed and happy with a partner.

# Don't Get Seduced by Someone's "Potential"

Recognizing a person's positive qualities is wonderful. However, to have clarity in your relationships and avoid choosing the wrong people, try to see others for who they are, not who you hope they can become. It's easy to be seduced by someone's potential, especially for empaths who are thrilled to find the best in others and who think, "My love can bring out this person's highest self."

However, the reality is often quite different. Although you may be intuiting the real potential in a prospective mate such as a desire for an intimate relationship, you can't force them to commit. Don't obsess about how connected you feel to this person or indulge the thought "With time, they will come around." They need to have some emotional awareness and desire for introspection so they can do the ongoing inner work of relationships. Releasing the fantasy of what could be will keep you from losing years trying to improve someone and being hurt in the process.

**SET YOUR INTENTION**
I will not get fooled by someone's "potential."
I will not keep hoping that someone will change or
get lost in a fantasy of who they could become.

# Feeling Safe to Open Your Heart

Opening your heart to someone is a vulnerable act. How do you know it is safe to do so?

First, observe a person's behavior toward others. Is it consistently caring? How do they treat friends and family? Are they respectful to strangers, children, or elderly people? Or do they lash out impatiently at the store clerk for "going too slow"? The way someone treats others reflects how they will treat you once the bliss of the honeymoon phase fades. Behavior is more trustworthy than words.

A common mistake that my sensitive patients make is to get emotionally involved with someone too quickly. Like them, you might feel the euphoric rush of hormones that comes from attraction — then prematurely jump into sharing intimate aspects of yourself. Especially if you've had previous betrayals, it's wise to take it slow.

Spend time journaling about what makes you feel safe around someone. One patient wrote about a man she'd been seeing: "He listens to me. He is dependable. He likes that I'm sensitive and isn't afraid of my emotions." In the same way, defining your own criteria will help you determine how quickly you can open your heart or if it is appropriate to do so. You want a relationship to be a secure container for your love.

---

**SET YOUR INTENTION**
I will be open to a positive relationship with someone who can reciprocate my caring. I will be with someone who can both give and receive love.

# The Sacredness of Commitment

One of the most sacred actions you can take is to commit to the power of love. Valentine's Day is an auspicious opportunity to do this. Whether or not you are in an intimate relationship, I'm talking about love in the most expanded sense that includes romance and much more. In that spirit, I suggest taking the following commitment vows from your heart. (Feel free to modify this list to include all of your beloveds.)

- I commit to living a life based on love, not fear.
- I commit to being loving with myself.
- I commit to my own spiritual growth and to honor the divine.
- I commit to loving my partner.
- I commit to loving my children.
- I commit to loving my friends.
- I commit to loving my animal companions.
- I commit to loving the Earth and all of her creatures.

---

**SET YOUR INTENTION**
I will not be afraid to commit to what I love.
I will let my love flow freely. I want to be
totally present for the moments of my life.

# The Three-Minute Heart Meditation

To calm stress and sensory overload, as well as to connect with love, I suggest practicing this heart-focused meditation. Begin by doing it once daily. Then you can increase the frequency. I depend on this heart meditation to center myself between patients and throughout the day. To relieve emotional and physical discomfort, act quickly and use this meditation.

*Close your eyes. Take a few deep breaths to relax. Then place your hand over your heart chakra in the middle of your chest. Focus on an image that makes you happy: a sunset, a daisy, the ocean, a dolphin. Begin to notice a growing sensation of warmth, openness, and loving-kindness build in your heart area and flow through your body. Let this feeling soothe you and remove all discomfort. Toxic energy leaves your body as you become purified by love.*

**SET YOUR INTENTION**
I will practice the Three-Minute Heart Meditation
each day to center myself, release stress, and
cultivate loving-kindness. It is a practical form
of self-care that I can use many times a day.

# Boundaries and Intimacy

Setting boundaries draws a line between you and someone else. For example, you say, "I need this," "I'm not able to go there," or "Please don't do that." However, you might feel that you don't have the right to stand up for yourself. Perhaps it wasn't safe to do this in your family. Even so, this skill is essential for healthy relationships.

Boundaries protect you and help you feel safe. Without them, you might start resenting a behavior that annoys you about your partner, or you might get exhausted from giving too much to a friend. Internalizing stress is a setup for developing physical symptoms, depression, and anxiety.

Creating boundaries is good for your health and your relationships, but it takes practice. Do it with kindness, without being confrontational. For example, say, "It would be wonderful if you'd help me wash the dishes." Consider what other types of boundaries you'd like to set. Be specific. Do you want your partner to spend more quality time with you and less on the computer? Is it okay for family to visit for two days but not a week? Set one boundary at a time rather than tackling many at once. Speaking up will create a more honest and happier relationship.

**SET YOUR INTENTION**
I will practice setting a boundary today. I will begin with an easy issue rather than one with an intense emotional charge. I will also start with a supportive person rather than asserting myself with my father or my boss.

# Suffocation Versus Abandonment

Do you often feel suffocated in intimate relationships? Then at other times abandoned? One moment, you wish your partner would give you more space, but when they are gone too long, you get anxious. Flipping between these two feelings is a common dilemma for empaths.

Most of our parents were clueless about how to respect our boundaries or personal space. Thus, to some degree, you probably felt overstimulated, even suffocated by them. Or you were left alone too much, which made you feel abandoned. These early experiences can affect your relationships now. For instance, my mother was extremely loving but intrusive. So, as an adult, I am sensitized to personal space intrusions such as someone entering my office without knocking. Once my partner knew this about me, he could better respond to my needs.

Review your own history. Honestly assess where you stand with these issues. Then, with kindness, discuss them with your partner. Don't make him or her wrong. Say, "These are my issues that you can help me with." Speak in "I" statements such as "I feel smothered when I don't get enough alone time" or "I feel anxious when you forget to call." Then you can find the right balance of togetherness.

**SET YOUR INTENTION**
I will appreciate the fine line between feeling
suffocated and feeling abandoned. I will convey my
personal space needs and how much interaction feels
good. This will help me have closer relationships.

# The Difference Between Lust and Love

As a psychiatrist, I've seen how intense sexual attraction can destroy common sense and intuition. To make mindful rather than painful choices, learn the difference between lust and love.

Lust is driven by the primal urge to procreate. Studies suggest that the brain in this phase is much like the brain on drugs. MRI scans show that the same area lights up when an addict gets a fix of cocaine as when one experiences lust. Also, early in a relationship, when sex hormones are peaking, lust is fueled by idealization and projection. You see what you hope someone will be rather than the real person.

In contrast, love can involve physical attraction, but you also want to get to know someone. This intimacy keeps deepening and leads to better sex. You listen to each other's feelings and priorities. Love is about genuinely caring for someone and becoming good friends rather than simply a physiological "high."

At the start of a relationship you may feel lust along with the beginnings of love. However, enduring love isn't based on idealization or projection. Real love is proven over time. It's something you must live into.

---

**SET YOUR INTENTION**
I will know the difference between lust and love. This will protect my sensitivities and keep my expectations of a potential partner realistic. I will always ask myself if my tender heart feels safe in a romantic situation.

# There Is No Such Thing as Casual Sex

When you touch someone, energy is communicated. Even if you have limited emotional involvement with a sexual partner, some merging occurs between you. This can affect your emotional and physical well-being.

For women, oxytocin, the bonding hormone that surges when mothers are caring for their newborns, also rises during lovemaking. So women tend to become attached to a partner. (Some drug companies have marketed oxytocin as Liquid Trust.) Since most men don't have the same oxytocin response, this attachment may not be reciprocated. Many of my women patients have felt hurt and disappointed about this when they became intimate with someone too quickly.

Since empaths are so sensitive to energy, there is no such thing as casual sex. You can absorb a partner's stress, fear, and happiness into your own body. You may also receive intuitions about their thoughts and feelings. Sex is always an energy exchange. A lot of nonverbal information comes through physical contact.

**SET YOUR INTENTION**
I will remember that intimate contact
conveys powerful energy. I will make wise
choices about my physical relationships.

# Sleeping Alone or Together

In traditional relationships, couples sleep in the same bed, but some empaths never get used to this. Perhaps you are a light sleeper or are awakened by snoring and movement. Or, to claim some quiet time, you may like staying up late when your partner or kids are asleep. No matter how amazing your partner is, to get a good night's rest, you may prefer sleeping alone.

I enjoy the unencumbered energy of sleeping alone. Because I am an avid dreamer and remember my dreams every morning, I need the silent time upon awakening to record them in my journal. However, I also love sleeping with my partner. It's a way for us to feel close and be intimate. So we've compromised by sleeping together a few nights a week, though we snuggle often at other times.

Consider your options. Would you prefer a king-size mattress? Or types that don't register movement, such as memory foam? Would you opt for separate rooms? Would ear plugs work to block out sounds? Would you like to push two twin beds together? Honestly and lovingly, discuss your sleep preferences with your partner to find a solution that feels good to both of you.

**SET YOUR INTENTION**
I will create sleeping arrangements that feel comfortable to me. I will not suffer silently when sound or movement disrupts my sleep. I will honestly discuss this issue with my partner.

# Release Your Partner's Stress

Inevitably, there will be times when your partner is stressed or in a bad mood. Perhaps a promotion fell through, there are money issues, or intense traffic put your beloved over the edge. You might absorb their stress and feel upset or depleted too. Or if you are already tired, your mutual discomfort can morph into more aggravation for both of you.

At these points, train yourself to recognize what's happening. Don't panic. Simply notice: "The person I love is under stress. I need to center myself." Draw a boundary. Tell yourself, "This is him or her, not me." The fixer in you might want to jump in to solve the problem (whether or not help is requested) but stop yourself. This impulse makes you work too hard, will drain you, and probably won't be appreciated — or make a difference. Instead, before you listen to your partner, practice these visualizations.

*Go into a private area, even your car, where you can be alone. Slowly inhale and exhale to calm yourself. With each breath, feel stress dissipate as you visualize it floating into the sky. You can also imagine a shield of white light around your body that repels tension and negativity. Then you can reenter the situation feeling more positive, protected, and genuinely supportive.*

---

**SET YOUR INTENTION**
I will have a plan for dealing with my partner's
stress. I will be prepared to center myself
and hold a loving space for them, but I don't
see it as my job to fix their problems.

# Stop Controlling People

Trying to control people is painful and exhausting.

It's a relief to let go of control, particularly if you tend to be a caretaker or an overgiver. The truth is, the only person you can control is yourself. The minute you try to control how others behave, what they do or don't do, you are in territory that's none of your business. What causes us to be overcontrolling? Fear, anxiety, and ego. For instance, do you feel that unless you personally handle something, it won't be done right? Or if you don't control the decisions of a family member, they will fail at a goal?

A way to let go of control is to detach with love. You can hold loving thoughts for someone but allow them to live and learn at their own pace, including making their own mistakes. Don't nag, repeat yourself, or offer unsolicited suggestions. It's fine to express concern about an issue once. But, other than life or death circumstances, it is not your job to step in and control the people you love.

### SET YOUR INTENTION
I will let others lead their own lives. I will address my own anxiety when I become overcontrolling. I will let go and turn the results of a situation over to Spirit.

# Soul Mate or Cellmate?

A soul mate is a meant-to-be relationship with someone for whom you feel a strong connection. When you meet, something in you awakens. You want to support each other's souls and are each other's safe place to land. You can take each other further than either of you could go alone.

Still, soul mate relationships aren't always peaceful or without conflicts. You mirror each other's light and dark sides. Seeing the union in this way helps you open your hearts even more.

However, your soul mate can become your cellmate without a mutual commitment to grow. Once the honeymoon phase ends, suddenly this idealized person is irritating you and has so many flaws! Your fears, anxieties, and other unresolved emotional triggers surface. Try to embrace these triggers as opportunities for spiritual growth. Your soul mate is not your savior or your therapist but rather someone whom you can love and learn from. When both partners are on the path to spiritual growth, your relationship will be a portal into the mysteries of intimacy.

---

**SET YOUR INTENTION**

I will have realistic expectations of a soul mate
and not think of them as my savior. I will take
responsibility for my own growth. I want to heal
anything in myself that keeps me from loving.

# Living Comfortably with Unresolved Problems

In all relationships, some issues take time to resolve. You may be unable to reach a perfect solution immediately. You must grow into it. In such circumstances, try to accept that there is no answer yet. I've had patients who kept working too hard to "fix problems" with their partner, friends, or other relationships when the time wasn't right. This only generated more anxiety, confusion, and arguments.

Sometimes the wisest tactic is nonaction. This can mean being the mountain and waiting for a solution to arise rather than forcing the issue to lessen your anxiety. Mutually agree to take a time-out. Create some breathing room so you're not rehashing a subject that isn't quite ready to resolve. Practice patience. During meditation, tune in to your intuition to discover creative solutions to overcome this obstacle.

---

**SET YOUR INTENTION**
If I reach a block in communicating with
someone, I will take a rest rather than forcing
the topic. I will have faith that my intuition
and the universe will help us find the answers.

# Communicating with a Non-Empath

It's a revelation to discover you are an empath. A light bulb flashes. Suddenly how you respond to life makes complete sense. But, it may take some time for you and others to acclimate to this new information.

Non-empaths have different neurological systems than we do and perceive life in other ways. They neither absorb people's stress, nor share the deep sensitivities and tendency for sensory overload that we're wired for. You don't have to be the same to get along. Respecting each other's differences will create a wonderful relationship.

Gently and patiently, educate your loved ones and others about what an empath is and how they can respect your needs, including alone time or quietude. Recommend books or articles for them to read. Many people have never heard of an empath before! If they think the concept is "woo-woo," use the term "sensitive person," which may be easier for them to hear. Since some people will never understand, it may be wiser to back off with them. But many others will appreciate you sharing this aspect of yourself, so they can have a more meaningful relationship with you.

---

**SET YOUR INTENTION**
I will educate my loved ones about my experience
as an empath. I will be patient and not overload
them with too much information at once. I will
answer their questions and let them assimilate
what I'm sharing in their own time.

# A Light Touch in Relationships

Empaths tend to work too hard in relationships because they may give more than they receive. You want everyone to be okay, to be satisfied, to be happy. You work overtime to solve their problems, and you may become anxious when that's not possible. The difficulty with this approach is that you take issues so seriously that pressure builds in your relationships and in yourself.

*You don't have to try so hard.* It brings great relief to realize that you are not alone. Spirit is always with you. It can inspire you to handle problems in ways that are beyond your good intentions or problem-solving capacities.

When you notice yourself getting overly serious about life and making a big deal over smaller issues, take a breath. Say to yourself, "I want a lighter touch in relationships. I don't need to make situations into a pressure cooker or let my anxiety disturb the peacefulness of my relationships." Then watch how answers fall into place in their own elegant time and rhythm.

**SET YOUR INTENTION**
I don't have to work so hard in relationships.
I don't have to be overly serious. I will breathe
more and ask Spirit for assistance.

# You Don't Need to Be Perfect

The goal of spiritual development is to cultivate compassion and wisdom. It's also to expand your heart so that you can more fully awaken. The goal is not to be perfect. The traditional Japanese art of *wabi-sabi* views imperfections such as asymmetry, roughness, or cracks as beautiful and part of the nature of all things.

I agree with the saying in twelve-step programs, "Strive for progress, not perfection." Release the notion that you must be without flaws. Perfection is boring and impossible to achieve. Your imperfections are what make you interesting. So aim for excellence — not perfection — and to be the best person possible.

Human beings are imperfect and messy and wondrous all at the same time. As part of self-care, reprogram the messages you might have received from family, friends, or society to have a perfect body, mate, or job. You are perfect just as you are, though you will also continue to evolve as you become more awakened. In all areas of life, seek love. Listen to your intuition to guide you to the people, places, and situations that are right for you.

### SET YOUR INTENTION
As I keep growing, I will appreciate my
progress. I will not be fooled by the illusion
of perfection. I will accept my whole self and
know that I am a fantastic work in progress.

# Navigating Social Situations

Socializing can be fun, but you must know your limits. If you are an introverted empath like me, you may become overwhelmed by too much socializing and you may dislike small talk. Noisy restaurants or loud parties can be overstimulating for my sensitive system. Also, you may end up staying too long at gatherings just to be polite, though you are tired and want to go home. In contrast, extroverted empaths may be energized by socializing and small talk, though afterward, they also need quiet time to decompress.

It's liberating to have self-care strategies in place for navigating social situations. For instance, ask yourself: "What is my ideal time limit to socialize?" Mine is typically three hours, though I might leave earlier if I'm tired. Do you prefer smaller gatherings to large groups? Do you prefer going to an event with others, driving yourself, or taking an Uber, taxi, or Lyft? If your partner or friends like to stay longer, you may want to arrange your own transportation so you're not stuck. Clarifying your needs will strengthen your self-care program and help you feel more comfortable in the world.

---

**SET YOUR INTENTION**
To relieve the pressure in social situations,
I will recognize my empathic needs and
act on them. I don't have to be stuck in
situations that I'm uncomfortable with.

# Balance Your Personal and Social Needs

You might experience a fine line between needing to be alone and maintaining social connections. To thrive, you can learn to meet both needs.

Like many of my sensitive patients, you might go to extremes. You either hide out and feel isolated and lonely, or you become overwhelmed by excessive people contact. Intuitively check in with yourself each day so you're not trapped by obligations that could easily be shifted. You don't want to feel like a hostage to your schedule.

Make sure you plan enough alone time and quality social time. Each will feed you in a different way. If you prefer taking a walk with a friend instead of going to the mall, respect that. If you want a day alone at home with your animals, honor that too. Keep tuning in to your intuition about what kinds of interactions energize you and feel right.

**SET YOUR INTENTION**
I will be mindful of balancing my alone time with socializing. Whenever possible, I will modify my schedule to respect my energy level and empathic needs.

*This day only occurs once every four years.

# Be Mindful of Your Energy Level

Would you like to wake up with energy and feel vibrant throughout the day? Since being energized is central to your health, keep intuitively checking in with how your body feels. In the morning ask yourself, "Is my energy level high, medium, or low?" And throughout the day ask, "When does my energy peak or dip?"

Perhaps you're more sluggish in winter when there are fewer hours of daylight. But, now, as days start to grow longer, your vitality may be increasing. Noticing how your energy fluctuates in response to light will help you practice extra self-care if necessary.

Our major energy sources include food, exercise, rest, relationships, meditation, and nature. Write in your journal about where you stand. Are you receiving the maximum energy from each area? If not, what specifically can you improve? Eating purer foods? Interacting less with draining people? Meditating more regularly? Resting when you're tired? Enjoying your garden? Being mindful of your energy in these ways will increase your quality of life and help you take loving care of your sensitivities.

### SET YOUR INTENTION
I will train myself to be aware of my energy.
I will listen to my intuition about activities
and people who drain or nurture me.

# Manage Your Emotional Triggers

Emotional triggers are those super-reactive places inside you that become activated by someone's behaviors or comments. When triggered, you may either withdraw emotionally and simply feel hurt or angry, or respond in an aggressive way that you will regret later. You react so intensely because you are defending against a painful feeling that has surfaced.

Your emotional triggers are wounds that need to heal. We all have them. As you identify what they are, be gentle with yourself. Reflect on the top five triggers that set you off. If someone says, "You're just too sensitive!" or "Darling, you're putting on a little weight" or "You're too old to find a relationship," use these comments as prompts to heal your insecurities. You need to compassionately address the part of you that feels flawed or has self-doubts about your body image or your worthiness to find a partner.

Healing your triggers is liberating because you won't be thrown off or drained by people's inappropriate comments. They may still be annoying, but they won't have the power to zap you.

**SET YOUR INTENTION**
I will identify my emotional triggers and make a loving commitment to heal them. When I'm triggered, I will pause rather than simply react.

# My Past Doesn't Control Me

Many sensitive people have had challenging upbringings, early trauma, and difficult relationships. Growing up with the sense of not being "seen" by your family may have injured your self-confidence. Perhaps no one ever stood up for you or said, "This sensitive soul deserves to be appreciated." Also, getting used to feeling alone and unsupported might have spilled over into your adult relationships. So you choose difficult partners such as narcissists who are incapable of giving unconditional love or respecting your sensitivities.

No matter what has happened in the past, now is your time to shine and thrive. Each day brings new opportunities. Seek out positive people and situations. It is never too late to create a wondrous life that supports you in every way.

**SET YOUR INTENTION**
When negative stories from my past resurface,
I will tell myself, "My past doesn't control me.
I am in my power now. I deserve to be happy."

# New Possibilities

The poet Walt Whitman wrote, "I am large, I contain multitudes." These words have had such meaning to me, especially when I am overtaken by fear and retreat into my "small self." They can remind all of us that we are larger than our fears so that we can reclaim the infinite, timeless power of the heart.

Each morning when you open your eyes, it is a new day. The promise of personal change, of growing larger than your fears and creating a life that feeds you is always there.

As spring approaches, if you listen carefully, you can intuit that the Earth is about to awaken with life. Though the dormancy of winter is still present, it's thrilling to welcome the first inklings of fresh growth in the natural world and within yourself. No matter your age, health, work situation, or relationship status, new possibilities are about to emerge. This is a time for great optimism. Be willing to let the universe miraculously unfold for you.

**SET YOUR INTENTION**
Each day has a new promise. I will stay
open to all opportunities. I invite my life
to change in positive and surprising ways.

# Ground Yourself with Gemstones

When you feel off-center or overloaded, experiment with holding different gemstones to ground yourself. Since ancient times, they have been believed to contain healing properties that help you feel healthy, energized, and protected. Many of my empathic patients are sensitive to their beneficial effects. You can also use them as part of your self-care grounding practices.

The best way to discover if you respond to the qualities of a particular gemstone is to hold one or wear it and see how you feel. Crystals are gorgeous. Each one has powerful attributes. For instance, amethyst is used for protection and peacefulness. Some healers recommend sleeping with amethyst under your pillow to relieve insomnia. Other stones to ward off negativity include black or pink tourmaline and black obsidian. I love wearing a jade pendant of the goddess Quan Yin who is associated with protection, compassion, and health. Some smooth polished gemstones are "worry stones," which have a thumb-sized indentation. You move your thumb gently back and forth over the stone for anxiety relief.

It's fun to experience gemstones and choose the ones you are drawn to. Many spiritual bookstores and rock and mineral shops carry them.

**SET YOUR INTENTION**
When I am stressed or if I'm around a toxic person,
I will hold a gemstone to ground and protect myself.

# Cooking with Love

Food is life-giving, especially when your love infuses it. That's why food cooked with love is more healing than food cooked without it. When you prepare a meal, bless it with love. Doing so infuses it with positive energy. This is very different than say, when, in a restaurant, a server slaps down your plate in frustration or even anger. These toxic emotions saturate the food too. When you're preparing a meal for yourself or loved ones, use your intuition to choose the perfect spices and ingredients. The care you put into these decisions is transmitted through the food. To express reverence and gratitude, say a prayer before you eat. Thank Spirit and the Earth for this meal's nourishment and contribution to your survival and well-being.

**SET YOUR INTENTION**
I will cook meals with consciousness and love.
If I am at a restaurant or eat prepared food,
I will bless it with a prayer and direct my love
into the meal prior to partaking of it.

# Healthy Eating

Food is medicine. Imagine how alive your body would feel if you ate high-energy, healthy foods and eliminated those that deplete you. High-energy foods are fresh, organic, non-GMO, unprocessed, and free of preservatives and antibiotics. Homegrown and local products contain the most vitality and can improve your health and clarity.

Your sensitive system is highly responsive to anything you put into it, especially food. You want to stabilize your physiology and moods with the right nutrients. In particular, notice how you react to sugar. White processed sugar causes mood and energy swings that can burn out your system. Cacao is a better natural replacement for sugar if you are craving something sweet.

Thoughtfully review your diet today. Evaluate which foods give you sustained energy and which cause brain fog, sluggishness, or erratic highs and lows. You may need to experiment with one food at a time. This useful information will help you make the best dietary choices that harmonize with your system.

**SET YOUR INTENTION**
I will be aware of how different foods
affect my body. I will choose those that are
healthy, balancing, and energizing.

# Shed the Armor of Excess Weight

Sensitive people unknowingly overeat when they feel emotionally overwhelmed. You become a sponge for everyone's stress and take it into your body. When you are thin, you have less padding and may be more vulnerable to absorbing emotions from others. Early twentieth-century faith healers were known for being obese to guard against taking on their patients' symptoms, a common trap I've seen many modern empaths fall into unconsciously.

Consider whether you use overeating to protect yourself. Some of my patients gain weight to ward off stress at home or at work. If you can relate, energy may be at the root of your hunger. To cope with stress without overeating or consuming the wrong foods, try putting a meditation pillow near your refrigerator as a reminder to center yourself before you reach for the door. Use this technique and other protection strategies in this book to fortify your self-care by strengthening your center.

**SET YOUR INTENTION**
I don't have to use excessive weight as
armor. Instead, I will practice meditation and
visualizations to ground and protect myself.

# Conquer Cravings

When you feel cravings to overeat, breathe and center yourself. Then use the following meditation.

*I will let all thoughts of craving gently float by like clouds in the sky. No matter how intense these feelings are, I will not attach to them. Instead, I will keep returning to my breath and focus on the gentle movements of my inhalation and exhalation. I will ask Spirit to lift my cravings. As I feel them dissipating, I will repeat this mantra inwardly: "I am safe. I am whole. I am protected." I will focus on the loving energy in my heart and allow it to flow throughout my body. Nothing can harm me. Love is all there is. My body is solid, connected to the earth, and filled with the infinite compassion of Spirit.*

**SET YOUR INTENTION**
I will consider cravings as messages to ground myself.
I don't have to act on my cravings. I can release
them into the infinite, universal matrix of love.

# Self-Soothing

Self-soothing means being able to calm yourself during trying circumstances or when you are emotionally triggered. Like many of my empath patients, you might not have learned to self-soothe. When stress hits, you have no defense or way to find comfort.

If we're fortunate, soothing is an experience we first had as infants and children. Ideally, your parents held you and rocked you in their arms when you were upset. This unleashes oxytocin, "the cuddle hormone," which makes you feel safe. Then they would reassure you, "Don't worry, darling. Everything will be fine." You learn to self-soothe from them and begin to do it yourself. However, without this, the world might have seemed unsafe. So instead of expecting the best, you imagine worst-case scenarios.

But now, as an adult, you can learn tools to self-soothe by becoming your own nurturing parent. When worries arise, tell yourself, "All is well. We will get through this together." Simultaneously, place your hand over your heart to activate unconditional love, the greatest self-soother of all.

**SET YOUR INTENTION**
Each day, I will practice self-soothing techniques
to relieve stress. I will offer myself ongoing
words of reassurance and understanding.

# The Gift of Drinking Water

Water is rich in life force and is a gift from the Earth. It is essential for health and hydration. Water also flushes toxins and negative energy from your system. If you are feeling overloaded or stressed, immediately drink a glass of water. You can also splash water on your face and wash your hands.

You require more water than you think. Many people only start craving it when they are dehydrated, but it is better to drink water before you reach a point of thirst. You need six or more eight-ounce glasses daily. Do not substitute with coffee or sodas. Bottled and filtered water are best. Glass containers are preferable to plastic, which leaches chemicals into the water that you consume.

Water heals and detoxifies you. It composes two-thirds of your body and has a sacred resonance in our cells. As the poet Rumi wrote, "We know the taste of pure water."

**SET YOUR INTENTION**
I am grateful for water. With each glass, I will
say thank you to the Earth to acknowledge
water's healing role in my life and our planet.

# Afraid to Speak Up

Are you overly polite because you fear offending people? Do you stay in a draining conversation because you believe the other person will feel bad if you leave? Do you place their needs above your own? Sensitive people often squelch their own voice in an attempt to please others. Notice if this is true for you.

Speaking up allows you to begin to heal any low self-esteem issues or fear of rejection. It also opens your throat chakra, the energy center responsible for communication. You can speak your mind politely and lovingly, without snippiness or anger. Even if this new behavior feels uncomfortable, simply act "as if" and try it out. Start with the easier people in your life. Making yourself heard protects you from becoming an emotional doormat or martyr.

**SET YOUR INTENTION**
If I am afraid to speak up, I will practice expressing
my thoughts and needs. This is empowering
and will help my energy to flow freely.

# The Three-Minute Phone Conversation

Some people may call and talk for hours about their problems. You want to be a good friend, but these long conversations exhaust you. Of course, you would like to lend support if a friend is in crisis. However, if someone starts playing a victim with a "poor me" attitude or keeps going around in circles, it's healthy to set limits.

The three-minute phone conversation is a useful solution. Listen briefly. Let the person know that you care. Then calmly but firmly tell them that unless they want to discuss solutions, you can only listen for a few minutes. You might even suggest that they seek therapeutic support to help them work through their issue. Limiting your conversation is a loving way of saying no to enabling nonproductive behavior and yes to being available when your friend is ready for solutions.

**SET YOUR INTENTION**
I don't have to listen endlessly to friends, family,
or coworkers who are indulging in a poor-
me mentality. I can kindly set a time
limit for how long I speak to them.

# Break the Rescuing Pattern

Sensitive people may want to help those who are struggling or in pain, including strangers. It may be hard to step back and refrain from rescuing them. This is where it is useful to understand the difference between empathy and being an empath. Empathy exists when your heart feels for someone, but being an empath is when you reach out to take away another's pain. Healthy empathy is what is necessary to keep your center.

Naturally, you do what you can to assist loved ones. But there comes a point when they must do the work themselves. I know it is frustrating and painful to see someone you care about struggling. But getting caught in their frustration or offering unasked-for suggestions is counterproductive for them and draining for you. To tolerate being in intimate relationships, you have to sometimes step back. Will the other person ever resolve the problem? You must live with that uncertainty. But always hold good thoughts and prayers for them while giving them space. In addition, a mantra I find helpful is "I am not responsible." As you repeat this, you will feel less of a need to rescue others.

**SET YOUR INTENTION**
It is not my job to rescue anyone or fix their
problems. I will learn the balance between
healthy empathy and stepping back.

# I'm the Only One Who Feels This Way

Since I was a little girl, I've been frequently told, "You're the only one who feels this way." It is a crazy-making comment for any sensitive person to hear. When I didn't know better or mistrusted my reactions, I would question myself and think, "If no one else has felt this way, then what I'm experiencing is not real." As I matured as an empath, I realized that it was irrelevant if anyone else responded as I did. If I felt something, it was real.

I want you to value the importance of your own reactions too. If you take a medication and experience a side effect that no one else has ever reported, your reaction is real. If you are drained around someone who everyone else raves about, your reaction is real. If you feel that a job is right for you, but your parents or other authority figures don't approve, trust your instincts. It is often wise to evaluate the merit of healthy criticism, but the bottom line is that you must have faith in yourself.

**SET YOUR INTENTION**
The way I perceive life may be original and unique.
Even if I am the only one who experiences something,
my reaction is valid. I will not question my own truth.

# Recognize Limitations

Sometimes you might be unable to go any further with a person, a project, or other situation. You have reached a temporary or permanent impasse. It's wise to recognize that no amount of pushing or cajoling will be effective. You can't make your spouse want to express emotions. You can't force a friend who is a full-blown narcissist to feel empathy. You can't make an unavailable person commit to your relationship.

In the I Ching, the ancient Chinese Book of Changes, some limitations are described as troublesome, but others are necessary. For example, in nature, there are fixed limits for the length of the seasons, as well as day and night. The I Ching says that if you live economically now, you will be prepared for times of want. So some limitation is smart and helpful. It also describes a situation in which you want to undertake a goal but are confronted with obstacles. Then you must know when to stop. During a rest period, you accumulate more energy, which then enables you to act with greater force at the right time.

**SET YOUR INTENTION**
I recognize that limitations are a natural
part of life. I will flow with them rather
than force a premature outcome.

# Reading People: Trust Your Gut

Intuition is nonlinear knowledge that comes through gut feelings, flashes, and dreams rather than strict logic. Research shows that we have a brain in the gut called the enteric nervous system. It contains neurotransmitters, similar to those in the brain, that relay information. Your gut is a central hub of intuitive intelligence. Listen to the wisdom it conveys about people and decisions.

Today, pay special attention to what your gut tells you. Choose a coworker, friend, or family member to focus on. Then notice what your gut says. Does it feel relaxed, comfortable, and energized around this person? Or is it queasy or tight? Do you get a sinking feeling? Factoring in the intuitive messages your gut sends helps you read others more accurately. Then you can create a circle of people your gut feels good around.

**SET YOUR INTENTION**
I will let my intuition guide my life. I will trust
my gut and not let my analytic mind override
the information my intuition conveys.

# Clearing Family Karma

Empaths are often the bearers of light in a family. As you awaken to your sensitivities and heal, you may find that you're the one chosen to break generational family patterns of dysfunction or abuse. Part of being an empowered empath is building your confidence and self-esteem. You learn to set boundaries when someone treats you disrespectfully. By saying no to family members or others who don't support your sensitivities or highest self, you are helping to stop ongoing negative patterns.

In Buddhism, karma is the destiny you earn through actions and behaviors. What you give is what you get. Though you may not have consciously volunteered to change your family's karma, it only takes one courageous person in a lineage to stop repeating harmful patterns. This monumental decision will benefit your life and also the lives of generations to come.

---

**SET YOUR INTENTION**
I will accept my role in clearing unhealthy generational patterns. I will be the change I want to see. My personal growth will positively affect my family lineage.

# New Light Emerging

On this eve of spring, feel the power of new light emerging in yourself and in the world. Winter is receding as the marvel of fresh growth is imminent, and greater illumination will grace the sky. The period right before rapid transformation is thrilling. You've been waiting so long, perhaps all of winter and longer, to come fully alive. Feel this rebirth approaching. You're about to shed layers of yourself that no longer serve you. At age ninety, former United States poet laureate Stanley Kunitz talked about how he was not done with his changes yet. No matter your age or circumstance, positive change can occur. Let yourself open to the coming of spring's promise and the breathtaking experience of new light emerging.

---

**SET YOUR INTENTION**
I will be ready for my renewal. I will anticipate
spring with excitement and embrace the ongoing
transformation of my mind, body, and spirit.

# SPRING

## Rebirth, Growth, and Rejuvenation

Everything comes alive in spring. As the cold and darkness recede, days grow longer. The natural world emerges from dormancy and hibernation. Flowers blossom. We're graced with their sweet scent, radiant colors, and joy. Spring is symbolized by the element of air, representing lightness, spaciousness, and the release of burdens.

Empaths come alive too. You can feel the positive energy of hope, innocence, and nature's beauty. Empaths love gardens, birdsong, rainbows after the showers, and fresh green grass. The streams are high and filled with rain. Fertility abounds. It's mating season for many creatures.

Spring offers you a fresh start. It's a season for makeovers, second chances, creative ideas, graduations, and weddings. You follow your dreams with restored enthusiasm. Spring is a fantastic opportunity to ignite your creative impulses. You can also create new habits and clean out clutter. Rather than focusing on previous obstacles, keep refocusing on the brightness of a spring day and of your future.

A challenge for empaths is that you may get swept up in the momentum of the season's energy and lose your balance. You jump into new relationships, romance, and projects too quickly. You may become overly idealistic or take on too many commitments. Without enough alone time, you can become overwhelmed.

Balance is key to your well-being. On the spring equinox, nature provides a sublime demonstration of balance, when day and night are of equal length. Let this day inspire you to center yourself and find equanimity.

# An Empath in Bloom

Spring is the time to plant the seeds of happiness and hope. Stay in touch with your intuition as it blossoms in sync with the awakening of the natural world. There's a freshness in the air, and your creativity is sparked. Reflect on what aspects of your sensitivities you'd like to cultivate this season. Your intuition? Compassion? Connection to nature? A deeper capacity for intimacy? All this is possible as we transition from the interior focus of winter to the flowering power of spring.

Take in the glorious rebirth occurring. Observe the landscape transforming. Are there tiny buds on the trees? Flowers? Can you hear birds chirping or gentle raindrops? What scents are you aware of? Luxuriate in the lushness. Also, during meditation or quiet reflection, focus on the sense of balance created by the spring equinox, when day and night are of equal length. It is peaceful, stabilizing, still, yet full. The power of the equinox heralds the emergence of spring in yourself and on the Earth.

---

**SET YOUR INTENTION**
I will be aware of the coming of spring
and feel its vibrancy rejuvenating me.
I will let my sensitivities blossom.

# Renew Your Purpose and Passion

Renew your commitment to manifesting your dreams. Make a vow to let go of any "shoulds" and replace them with "My passion is . . ." Your passions are based on a deep instinct within that moves you. Sit quietly with yourself until you find this. Set aside all the voices in your head, including those of your parents, that keep telling you what they think is right for you. Their opinions must not sway you. Your passions need to be based on what's in your heart.

I believe our primary purpose on Earth is to develop our souls. Everything else is in service to this goal including work, relationships, and finances. Life has its ups and downs. When you can ride these waves of emotions and changes—and stay true to yourself—you fulfill a vital purpose, which enhances all of your choices. The greatest achievement in life is to develop your heart and use it to elevate your own life and the world.

---

**SET YOUR INTENTION**
I will listen to my intuition to find my purpose.
I will follow what's true and deep within myself.
I will stay on course with what my intuition advises.

# Phoenix Rising

In Greek mythology, the phoenix is a huge multicolored bird that is reborn out of its own ashes. The phoenix symbolizes strength, perseverance, and renewal, even when all seems lost. It is about prevailing over darkness to become successful in your endeavors.

Spring is the season that supports the phoenix rising in your life. We all go through cycles of change. Now is the time for your goals and endeavors to be reconstituted. It's important that you release any voices that tell you this profound regeneration is impossible. Even if, despite your efforts, you haven't been able to manifest a passionate goal, spring offers you additional energy to draw from.

The form the phoenix takes when it rises may be different than you imagined. Be open to the shape-shifting it presents. A relationship may be over, but a new one appears. A job you thought was out of reach is offered to you again. If you've felt exhausted or depressed, a burst of vitality now flows through you. Stay aware of how the many types of rebirth present themselves to you.

**SET YOUR INTENTION**
I will be hopeful. I will not dwell on past
difficulties. Even if I've gone through a
difficult period, I will be open to my dreams
manifesting in new or different forms.

# Clean Out Clutter

In traditional spring cleaning, you refresh your home after the winter season. As the days grow warmer, open your windows to let in fresh air, sweep or vacuum the floors, and remove clutter from countertops or in closets and drawers. As you do this, it's natural for emotions to arise including anxiety about loss or change. Let your feelings flow but don't let them stop you.

Research shows that disorder in your environment increases stress and impairs your ability to focus. Like me, you might think more clearly when your counters are neat. Piles of papers on my desk or objects strewn around the room feel overwhelming. Empaths do better around minimalism and simplicity.

Physical clutter clogs energy flow. Along with counters and closets, clean your refrigerator, donate old clothes, and toss magazines or papers. Also tackle your purse and wallet, removing old business receipts, cards, or shopping lists. Washing windows so they sparkle can sharpen your perception too. Through this cleansing process, your energy and spirit will grow lighter and clearer.

---

**SET YOUR INTENTION**
I will address the clutter in my life. I will remove
it at a comfortable pace. This clears old energy
and allows new possibilities to enter my life.

# Second Chances

Just because you went through a hard time and situations didn't work out the way you wanted, don't give up hope. Spring is a time for second chances. Whatever door was shut before may open now. Be ready for the miracle of second chances, whether it's in your life or if you're giving someone else a second chance.

When you can feel the possibility of grace offering you new opportunities to move forward, they may come to you. Grace is the action of Spirit working in your life, a gift of good fortune. Grace does not hold grudges. Perhaps you've made mistakes in the past or unwittingly hurt others. If so, evaluate how to change now. Be sure to make amends to those you have harmed. Doing so clears the way for a fresh start.

---

**SET YOUR INTENTION**
I deserve a second chance. I will open to the
forces of grace intervening to assist me. I will also
be open to giving other people second chances,
too, if my intuition guides me to do so.

# The Joy of Being with Positive People

Positive people look at life as a glass that is half full, not half empty. They are authentic, caring, and willing to learn from their mistakes. They radiate a sense of warmth and lightheartedness that makes them a joy to be around. Positive people aren't phony or only concerned with themselves. They have empathy and tolerance and can accept you as you are. Of course, no one is perfect or positive all the time, but they try to lead a compassionate, optimistic life.

Today, choose to spend at least a few hours with positive people who are energizing for you and whom you laugh around. Do not invite exchanges with anyone who makes you unhappy or drains you. Being mindful about those you spend your time with will increase your energy.

---

**SET YOUR INTENTION**
I have choice about my relationships. I will identify
some positive people in my life and reach out to
them. I will appreciate how valuable they are.

# Every Breaking Wave

With every breaking wave there is
new inspiration in the world.
With every breaking wave there is
freshness and rejuvenation.
The tides are ancient and rhythmic.
The sound of the surf connects us
to the water in our bodies.
We feel the pull and our physiology responds.
Our dreams also respond
as the breaking waves fuel our
imagination and sense of wonder.
Your life force is alive and well.
Spring is your chance to start again.
Let every breaking wave, every cycle of
life you experience, take you deeper into
your own heart and the Mystery.

**SET YOUR INTENTION**
I will allow myself to feel fresh and new.
I will be ready for the rebirth of spring in my life.
My life force will keep getting stronger.
I will be confident in my choices and path.

# Color Power

Colors emit different energies that can affect your mood and physical well-being. Notice which colors you naturally respond to. Which ones do you feel calmer around—green, blue, or violet? Which ones energize you? You may feel an energy boost from red, orange, or yellow. Do you prefer bright colors or earth tones? Spring is associated with bright, bold pastels. I'm most attracted to the first luminous green of new grass. It feels like it bursts with happiness!

Once you find colors that align with your sensitivities, weave them into your home and dress in the tones that feel good to you. Knowing how you respond to colors balances you and creates calming environments that uplift your empathic soul.

---

**SET YOUR INTENTION**
I will notice how various colors affect my
mood and energy. I will incorporate those
I resonate with into my home and wardrobe.

# Commune with Animal Friends

Animals are teachers of unconditional love. They heal us in many ways and lessen our stress. Perhaps you are an animal empath who feels a special connection to Earth's creatures. You can commune with animals and know their needs. You want to protect them and support their natural habitats.

I was madly in love with my soul mate dog named Pipe, who emotionally got me through medical school. After being on call in the psychiatric emergency room every third night, I would come home exhausted—but she made it all okay. I would talk to her and share my problems, and she would sleep on my bed. Having such a devoted companion was comforting.

Many sensitive people love animals too. Spend some time enjoying your animal companions today. Snuggle with them. Play together. Share some love. If you don't have animals at home, smile at those going by on the street or in a park. Or play with a neighbor's animal. Some empaths have therapy dogs to lessen their anxiety while out in world. Sensitive people can benefit from interacting with animal friends or being near them in natural settings.

**SET YOUR INTENTION**
I will let animals bring out my playfulness.
I will feel their unconditional love and
enjoy their trusted companionship.

# Experience Earthing

A research breakthrough in the field of environmental health reveals this new and surprisingly overlooked aspect of wellness: reconnecting with the vast supply of electrons on the Earth's surface can improve sleep, reduce pain, and enhance your overall well-being. You can experience the benefits of earthing by walking barefoot outside and also by sitting or sleeping on the ground. This allows the transfer of the Earth's electrons into your body.

When you're on sensory overload, tired, or just want an energy boost, you can reap the benefits of earthing. Take off your shoes and walk or lie on the grass or on the beach. Feel yourself melting into the ground and releasing any toxic emotions. You may even bring your computer outdoors and work sitting on the ground. Creating a garden, even if it's a simple window box, and tending to it is a divine way to experience earthing too.

**SET YOUR INTENTION**
I will walk barefoot on the grass or simply place my
hands on the ground to soak up those healing electrons.
I will tune in to the energy of the Earth to stay centered.

# Guided by Dreams

Dreams are a potent form of intuition that can help guide your life. Highly sensitive people whom I call "dream empaths" are often fascinated by them and feel at home in that world. Dreams bypass your ego so you can be wide open to intuitive guidance. They have always been sacred to me. First thing in the morning, I write my dreams in a journal and see how their messages apply to my life. If you'd like to remember your dreams too, here's how:

> *Record your dreams in your journal. Put it beside your bed with a pen. Before you fall asleep ask one question, such as "How can I find the right job?" or "How can I settle a disagreement with my son?" Upon awakening, remain quiet for a few minutes in the hypnogogic state between sleep and waking. That's where you retrieve your dreams. Then record the information you remember and look for your answer.*

**SET YOUR INTENTION**
For the next week, I will ask a question of my dreams and write down whatever I remember in the morning, even if it's just one scene. With practice, my ability to do this will improve.

# Bursting Through

As a tribute to your new growth, you can repeat this statement of empathic empowerment whenever you like:

I am ready to have my love and joyfulness burst through.
I am about to bloom in ways beyond
my wildest imagination.
I am strong and smart.
I know how to flow around obstacles.
I know how to keep my center.
I open to Spirit and all the wild,
compassionate forces of the universe
to open my heart,
to make my soul ready for all the blessings ahead.
I am bursting through all the barriers
that have stopped me in the past.
I will let spring awaken my power
and allow my spirit to soar.

**SET YOUR INTENTION**
I will allow myself to expand into new dimensions
of my inner and outer life. I will break through
all the barriers of the past and achieve a new
level of success and satisfaction with what is.

# Your Path Is Perfect

Your life is uniquely designed for your own development. Every person and situation you encounter is meant to help you grow.

Society relentlessly urges us to compare ourselves with others. We may wonder: Who has the most money? The highest social status? The perfect body? The most friends? Our habit of comparing comes from our small self, the part that is run by fear and has difficulty seeing the bigger picture. If you want to gain a larger, more enlightened perspective, rise higher in your consciousness. Look at yourself, and all of us, from the mountaintop rather than from the ground. Then you can see that more isn't necessarily better.

Everyone, no matter what they've accumulated, is struggling dearly with something. Though some people's burdens may not be obvious to you, everyone is doing the best they can.

Have compassion for yourself and others. Be grateful for the custom-designed human package you've been given. There is no one like you. I appreciate you and hope you can appreciate yourself too.

---

**SET YOUR INTENTION**
I will focus on the rightness of my own path. I will not compare my life with anyone else's. I will stay in my own lane and make it the best it can be. I will take my eyes off other people and put them lovingly back on myself.

# Release Worry

Worry comes from the Old English wyrgan, which originally meant "strangle." It is a form of anxiety. You may worry about money, health, your family, or whether you'll find love. You also may worry that if you don't worry, something bad will happen—a form of superstition that I grew up with in a Jewish family. Having a legitimate concern, such as your child undergoing surgery, is natural. However, worry takes concern into the realm of suffering.

Chronic worry is your attempt to control something that is out of your control. Liberate yourself from worry by repeating this mantra:

> May I be free of worry.
> May I be free of stress.
> May I not project my fears into the future.
> May I stay in the Now.

**SET YOUR INTENTION**
I will ask the suffering of worry to lift so I can face adversity with clarity and faith. I will do what I can in the moment to better a situation and request spiritual assistance as well.

# Be an Open Window

The element of air can help you to clear stress by removing emotional toxins and other energetic pollutants. The breath, the breeze, and the wind are not just random movements of molecules. They are powerful purifiers.

When you've taken on the world's stress, or if you've encountered a difficult person, try this visualization (which I use frequently) to release any negativity you might have absorbed. As you do this, keep gently breathing stress out of your body.

*My body is a large open window.*
*I can feel a fresh, soft breeze blowing through every cell.*
*It is gently removing stress.*
*It comforts and heals me.*
*It clears all stagnation, fear, and toxic emotions.*
*I breathe deeply.*
*I allow myself to be purified, cleared, and restored.*

**SET YOUR INTENTION**
I will practice this visualization to increase the spaciousness of my being and let the gentle flow of air cleanse my energy. I will utilize my breath to expel stress.

# Go Beyond Your Comfort Zone

Sensitive people often prefer life to remain the same so they can stay in their comfort zone. You set up your home so that the furnishings, bedding, sound level, and scents all feel good to your body. You get used to the routine of work, exercise, or family activities. This predictability may help you feel safe.

Still, sometimes it's good to shake things up. As much as I appreciate comfort, I also know that my soul longs to evolve. It's an important balance for all sensitive people to find. Ask yourself, "How can I go beyond my comfort level to grow?" Perhaps it means looking for a more fulfilling job but risking being unemployed for a while. Or deepening intimacy with your partner by moving beyond fear. Or even going on a vision quest in nature to gain clarity about a decision. Choose one area to explore. Then stay open to the unexpected benefits of transformation.

**SET YOUR INTENTION**
I will identify an area in which I'd like to stretch
beyond my comfort zone. I am willing to risk
feeling some discomfort in the process.

# Set Limits with Anger

When someone dumps anger on you, you may feel like you've been slimed. It's a shocking invasion of your boundaries. Often the outburst happens so quickly you don't have time to protect yourself.

Have a strategy in place for addressing people's anger. I have a strict "no yelling" rule in my vicinity. Yelling is unacceptable to my body: it is loud, painful, and drains me as adrenaline, the fight-or-flight hormone, burns through my system. If a loved one is angry with me, I request that we arrange a mutually agreeable time to discuss the issue, so I'm not taken by surprise. This helps protect my sensitive system. When I am prepared, and the problem is respectfully addressed, I can more easily handle the person's emotions.

Set a limit with anger. If someone is unable to honor this, you can either remove yourself or request that they leave. This may be difficult, with, say a rageaholic boss. Even so, try to make a graceful exit as soon as possible and seriously consider getting another job. You deserve to be with people who respect you.

**SET YOUR INTENTION**
As part of my self-care, I will set consistent limits
with angry people. I will hold firm and protect myself.
I will remove myself from a situation if it feels too toxic.

# Say No to Drama

Living with drama can be overstimulating and exhausting. You may get hooked into drama and become overinvolved because you're a caring person. You want to rescue the person in distress, which sets you up for frustration and depletion.

The first step in limiting the drama in your life is to recognize the people who generate it. Identify them at work, at home, and with acquaintances such as hair stylists or store clerks. Because of your giving nature, expect that drama queens and kings will be attracted to you.

To deflect their antics, never ask them how they are doing or look deeply into their eyes, which indicates interest. Then, in a kind but firm tone, tell them, "I am so sorry this happened to you. I will hold good thoughts." This approach discourages their bad behavior. When you cut off their supply of attention, they will move on to someone else.

**SET YOUR INTENTION**
I will seek low drama in my relationships.
I will not feed into drama or give away my energy
to histrionic people if they are draining me.

# Private Time with Spirit

Make a date with Spirit at least once a week to tune in to your intuition and higher self. Take a short break from chores, work, and your routine just to be with Spirit. You may choose to connect at your sacred space, during a walk in the woods, or at a church, synagogue, or other place of worship. Then quietly meditate and invite in the presence of Spirit by saying, "I want to feel you. I want to know you. I am open to your guidance and care." In stillness, and with reverence, allow yourself to be touched by Spirit's grace. Take in the compassion that is being transmitted to you.

A beneficent force is at work and at play in the universe that is so much larger than your logical mind. You are not alone. Spirit is always present and available to connect with.

**SET YOUR INTENTION**
I will schedule time to simply be with Spirit
and experience the light and hope that is within
and around me. This is a way to replenish
my energy and restore my calmness.

# The Promised Land Is Within

The source of happiness and peace is within you. Many people look for external solutions to their feelings of discontent. They go after power in the world to feel significant rather than first connecting to an inner base of strength, which is a much more solid position. No amount of wealth, sex, power, or prestige will sustain your sense of happiness. It grows from the inside out. As Buddha says, "There is no external refuge." The promised land is within you. This is extremely good news because it will motivate you to discover your inner world. Start with healing and strengthening yourself—then outer accomplishments will follow.

**SET YOUR INTENTION**
I will focus on loving myself and developing my
connection to Spirit. I will stop looking to any
person, place, or situation to fix me. First, I will look
inward for the answers before I seek outer advice.

# Overcome Adversity

When you can commit to living a life based on love, not fear, you have the foundation for dealing with adversity. Obstacles are a part of living. Learning how to overcome them with grace instead of frustration is an essential self-care skill.

As we go through the Passover and Easter season, meditate on the power of liberating yourself from emotional slavery and oppression. Sometimes we have to be lost so that we can find ourselves. We all have our own deserts to wander through in order to be liberated. What would you like to free yourself from? A toxic relationship? Shame about your body? Reluctance to express your needs? Isolation? Depression? Anxiety? In this inquiry, be kind to yourself. Inwardly request that any fear-based beliefs be lifted. See every obstacle in your life as a spiritual prompt to grow.

The Tao Te Ching, an ancient Taoist text of wisdom, says:

> He [or she] is ready to use all situations
> and doesn't waste anything.
> This is called embodying the light.

---

**SET YOUR INTENTION**
I will be strong. I will be compassionate.
I will be capable of handling whatever life
brings with patience and kindness.

# Practice the Ho'oponopono Prayer

If you're upset with someone or judge an aspect of their behavior, use this Hawaiian forgiveness prayer. It allows you to take ownership of the exact qualities that you criticize in another and heal them in yourself. This, in turn, sets you free from judging yourself or them. The prayer is based on humility, not ego. There's a saying that when you point your finger at another, you lovingly point three back to yourself.

Recite this prayer to release judgments about others or yourself:

I'm sorry.
Please forgive me.
I love you.
Thank you.

Here's how to apply this prayer. Let's say you're irritated with a controlling friend. Ask yourself, "In what ways am I controlling too?" Then inwardly say, "I'm sorry for trying to control others. Please forgive this behavior. I love myself, even with my shortcomings. Thank you for the opportunity to heal my tendency to overcontrol."

The Ho'oponopono prayer helps you accept others and yourself with more kindness and understanding. Finding fault with people drains your vital energy, which you could channel in more creative ways.

---

**SET YOUR INTENTION**
I will use this prayer to heal in myself the qualities
that most disturb me about others. I will take
responsibility for my own emotional issues.

# The Goddess of Compassion

Quan Yin is an East Asian bodhisattva who is known as the "goddess of compassion and mercy." In Chinese her name means, "one who hears the sounds of the world." According to legend, at one time Quan Yin was a generous, kind woman who suffered tremendous abuse by her father. When she passed on, the angels said, "You are such a good person. Where would you like to go?" She answered, "I want to return to Earth to help other human beings." And so, Quan Yin is here for us all if we call on her for protection.

I revere the goddess Quan Yin. Her statue graces my meditation altar, my home, and my office. I also wear a jade pendant of Quan Yin that I rarely take off. I feel inspired by the loving-kindness she represents.

You, too, can call on Quan Yin. Whether you consider her an archetype of goodness or an actual spiritual being, connecting with her helps you embody compassion. This will heal your wounds and support your empathic nature.

**SET YOUR INTENTION**
I will read about the goddess Quan Yin. I will be
open to ways that compassion can manifest in my
life. I will be of service to others in healthy ways.

# Spirit Rising

Resurrection is a primary force in nature, as exemplified by spring. During this season, you can bring back to life precious aspects of yourself that you may have forgotten or pushed away. What have you lost faith in that can be revived? The yearning for love? For optimism and hope? For success? Sometimes trauma or hurt can suppress your heart's desires. Now is the time to reawaken your dormant longings. Rise up from adversity. Rise up from pain. Rise up from old patterns that no longer serve you. Feel your own aliveness. Let your sensitivities shine. Inwardly say, "I will be a beacon of light for myself and others. I will not let anything squash my spirit or keep me small."

**SET YOUR INTENTION**
I will be a vessel for goodness and hope in the world.
I will resurrect the values and dreams that are truly
important to me if I have forgotten them along the way.

# The Martyr Syndrome

Throughout history, martyrs have been killed for their beliefs. In your own life, you may become an emotional martyr too. The martyr syndrome describes people who feel it's necessary to sacrifice their own well-being for others and to suffer. Empaths are prone to this when they haven't learned to protect themselves or set boundaries.

Martyrs can have a "poor me" victim mentality and believe that the world is against them. Or they may never complain and be perpetually stoic. They also may feel guilty when they aren't behaving as martyrs. The problem is that they see their job as taking on the discomfort of others. They regard giving as a form of self-sacrifice and an obligation rather than a joy.

If you feel this way, I invite you to reevaluate. You can be loving and compassionate without shouldering the burdens of others. If you tend to be a martyr, ask yourself, "Did this belief come from my family? My religious views? Or from myself?" As an empath, you want to have a long, happy life that honors your sensitivities. You can be a giving person and also practice self-care.

**SET YOUR INTENTION**
I don't have to be a martyr to be compassionate.
I can give in healthy ways while protecting myself.

# Let People Be Who They Are

It's a sign of respect to accept people for who they are. It feels terrible to be judged. Reflect on how you've reacted when a friend or loved one judged you. Unless someone asks you for help, it's generally better to back off or just offer a suggestion once. Except under dire circumstances, have faith that the person can handle the situation in their own way.

Imagine what kind of relationship you would have with a family member or friend if it were based on supporting their own strengths rather than fixing them. Like many sensitive people, you may believe that if you stop trying to "improve" others, the relationship will disappear, or the person will fall apart. The opposite is usually true. When a relationship exists between equals interacting with each other, it can thrive. Focusing on someone's strengths, especially in the midst of their struggles, gives them a chance to discover their wings.

**SET YOUR INTENTION**
In my relationships, I will practice acceptance rather than seeing it as my mission to improve others. I will focus on people's gifts rather than their shortcomings.

# Take Mini Breaks

A secret to having a healthy, productive life is taking mini breaks throughout the day to replenish yourself. Instead of pushing nonstop, day after day—which is a recipe for exhaustion—plan short times to regroup. Study your schedule and see where you can fit in these moments of respite. Leaving it up to chance probably won't work. But if you program yourself to stop, even for a few minutes, you're telling your subconscious mind that there will be relief. In these free periods, take a walk. Breathe in the sweet scents of spring. Or do some yoga stretches to unwind. Planning mini breaks takes the pressure off so you can have a more relaxed life.

**SET YOUR INTENTION**
I will be mindful of scheduling mini breaks
throughout the day. This is a way of nurturing
my sensitivities and rejuvenating my energy.

# Go Off the Grid

Periodically escape the mundane world and your daily routine to go off the grid for a while. Find a location where no one can reach you, except perhaps for emergencies. Think of it as an empath mental health and restoration period, whether it is for a few hours or a few weeks.

Picture where you would most like to go. Perhaps it is simply escaping to a movie and shutting off your phone for a few hours. Or taking an exotic vacation or a backpacking trip. I love visiting monasteries where there is no internet. You may even want to go on a silent retreat at a mindfulness meditation center. Whatever you choose, this is your time to reflect and just be. It may take a while to quiet your busy mind but by living in slow motion, in a more meditative state, your mind will be grateful for the rest and your body will thank you.

When you're off the grid, you will drop into a more timeless state. There will be more silence. Your intuition will open. In dreams or while awake, you might even receive visions or guidance about aspects of your life. You can put them into action when you return to the world of people.

---

**SET YOUR INTENTION**
I will plan to go off the grid for at least an hour this
week and envision ways to also do this for longer
periods. I don't have to be on call all the time for others.

# Plan Technology Fasts

In our fast-paced world, too much can come at you too quickly. You're inundated by information overload from the internet, voice mail, social media, texts, and the news. The effort to assimilate it all can sap your energy. Many of my sensitive patients slip into a state that I call "techno-despair." How do you know if you have it? After exposure to technology, you experience some depression, anxiety, a numb, zombie-like feeling, or sensory overload. Relief comes from limiting your contact with computers or the cyber world. Technology can make life easier, but it is often a chronic source of energy drain, especially for empaths.

To center yourself in the present moment, get in the habit of taking regular technology fasts. Go for a half hour without checking emails. Eat a delicious lunch instead. Or shut down your computer and electronic gadgets early in the evening. This will help you feel more peaceful when you go to sleep.

**SET YOUR INTENTION**
I will notice if I have symptoms of techno-despair.
To counter this, I will take regular breaks from
technology to clear my mind and nourish my soul.

# Make Your Home a Sanctuary

Your home is a sacred space where you spend much of your time. Make it a safe haven to be in and return to after a busy day. A tranquil environment soothes your sensitivities. Choose calming or fun brighter colors for painting the walls and for decorations. Maximize the light and allow fresh air to flow. Place sacred objects in various rooms as touchstones to your spirituality.

Home can be a retreat, not merely somewhere to drop onto the bed exhausted. A quiet environment brings the most peace. However, if you live in a city where the noise level is high or share space with family or roommates, try noise-canceling headphones or a white noise machine to block out disturbing sounds like traffic or talking. Also, you can request that others use headphones when watching television or listening to music.

Home is where the heart is. When you put your loving awareness into all aspects of your living space—and set limits with noise or other intrusions—you will feel nourished there.

---

**SET YOUR INTENTION**
I will create a home that is my sanctuary. It will
be in harmony with my sensitivities. I want to
live in an environment that feels wonderful.

# Create a Sleep Temple

Your bedroom needs to be a quiet, restful, and safe place to retreat to. Empaths love their beds. In fact, mine is one of my favorite places. Select soft cotton sheets with a high thread count rather than scratchy ones, which sensitive people can't tolerate. Consider your mattress to be a healing tool. You sleep there, make love there, and sometimes escape from the world under the covers there. To get a good night's rest, choose a mattress that supports your spine. Also, have a fresh flow of air in your bedroom. Lingering odors from the day such as food or perfume can keep your mind from switching off because they remind you of previous activities or tension.

Make your sleep temple free of stress. Your bed is a chariot into the dream realm and supports the replenishment of sleep. Ban any upsetting activities on your bed, such as arguments, paying bills, or watching the news, and set up a time to stop working on or reading from your computer. Its blue light interferes with sleep patterns. Adorn your bedroom with crystals, candles, and sacred objects. Flowers, incense, and aromatherapy create a tranquil mood too.

**SET YOUR INTENTION**
I will make my bed into a sleep temple,
a sacred place where I can relax and revive myself.
No stressful activities will be allowed there.

# Smudge Your Home

If you're stuck or depleted, there may be stagnant energy at home. Smudging is a sacred Native American and aboriginal practice of burning plants such a sage, cedar, sweetgrass, or palo santo to remove negativity and purify the environment. Various emotions accumulate in a space including tension, anger, and anxiety—as well as joy. Empaths can sense these lingering feelings, both positive and stressful, though others may not.

To clear your space of any energy that doesn't support your well-being, experiment with burning different plants. See which ones appeal to you and aren't too strong. Abalone shells are lovely containers in which to burn the plant. Be in a meditative state when you smudge. As you walk around your home with the burning plant, let the smoke purify the corners of the room, as well as the central areas. In addition to reducing bacteria in the air and increasing calming negative ions, smudging can energetically cleanse your home, office, or other location.

**SET YOUR INTENTION**
I will smudge my home and notice how the
mood in the space lightens up and feels clearer.
I will experiment with different herbs and
scents to find ones that I resonate with.

# Decrease Stimulation

Empaths have sensitive neurological systems. You may react strongly to sound, taste, odors, and textures. Also, your senses are activated by the many tones of color, light, and weather. To enjoy optimal well-being, regulate the level of stimulation in your life. Excessive input, such as bright light, loud noises, or crowds, can overload you. But just the right amount of stimulation and beauty can feed your soul.

As soon as you notice signs of sensory overload such as anxiety or fatigue, reduce your stimulation level. I sometimes retreat into a dark, quiet room to meditate and calm myself. Or you may be soothed by reading poetry or listening to Mozart. Simply lowering stimulation may be all that you need to come back to your center.

---

**SET YOUR INTENTION**
I will notice when I start feeling overstimulated.
I will take steps to decrease the sensory input from my
environment so I can calm down and feel peaceful.

# Center Yourself with Healing Music

When you are feeling overloaded, the right music can elevate your spirit. Music therapy has been used to treat depression, anxiety, and chronic pain. Neuroscientists have found that tranquil music increases positive emotions and stimulates dopamine—the brain's pleasure hormone—and that highly sensitive people may respond to music similarly to how they experience empathy.

Over the years, certain songs or musical artists might have helped you through breakups, disappointments, and periods of self-doubt. Other music may be linked with happy times such as when you first met your beloved, graduated from college, or visited an exotic place. Songs are markers for our lives and are also therapeutic.

Which music has comforted you? I associate Simon and Garfunkel's "Scarborough Fair/Canticle" with my first love and also the painful experience of him leaving me. Listening to it makes me feel melancholy, but rich, raw, and so real. When I'm stressed, I turn to devotional music such as Enya, Tina Malia, Wah!, or Bach. Music is a balm for sensitive people. Let it wash over and nurture you.

---

**SET YOUR INTENTION**
I will listen to music that uplifts, inspires,
and soothes me. I will allow the power
of music to heal my body and soul.

# Living in the Zone

The zone is the place where everything flows, where you don't have to force events to occur. You listen to your intuition and feel tuned in to yourself and others. You can live and let live. You're not struggling with the natural flow of life.

Living in the zone is something to aim for. You can arrive there by simply asking your intuition, "What feels right for me today? How is my energy level? How can I take care of myself, even though I may be busy?" The more compassionate you are with yourself, the more in the zone you will be.

Stay aware of synchronicities. These are moments of perfect timing when the pieces of a puzzle seem to fall into place. You were just thinking about an old friend and suddenly run into her on the street. Or someone mentions a doctor he respects who specializes in the exact physical problem you are experiencing. Albert Einstein said, "Synchronicities are God's way of remaining anonymous." When you're in the zone, synchronicities abound, and you are attuned to the intuitive rhythm of living.

**SET YOUR INTENTION**

I will begin my morning in the zone by
tuning in to my intuition. Throughout the
day, I will watch for intuitive signs such as
synchronicities and be open to their meaning.

# Beware of Narcissists

Narcissists and empaths have a toxic attraction. Narcissists can be charming, seductive, smart, and fun. They are also self-absorbed and become cold and punishing if you don't do things their way. Research shows that full-blown narcissists have an "empathy deficit disorder," which means they are incapable of empathy as we know it. (See November 17 for more on this.) They are unable to give you unconditional love. It's hard for many empaths to realize that they cannot heal narcissists with their compassion.

Life is fleeting. As part of your self-care, you must make a fundamental decision about whom you want to spend your time with. When you can't avoid narcissists—say it's your boss or a family member—you must lower your expectations and safeguard your heart around them. Though people who simply have narcissistic traits are capable of some empathy, you will be better off by choosing relationships with those who know how to be a friend and reciprocate love.

**SET YOUR INTENTION**
I will identify the narcissists in my life and realize
their limitations, including having minimal or no
empathy. I know that I cannot change or save them.

# First Impressions

When you're attuned to your intuition, you may receive strong first impressions about people, places, and situations. You can experience a positive gut feeling or a danger signal.

First impressions are powerful. Figure them into your evaluation of someone. For instance, on a job interview, you want to like your potential supervisor, but you feel tired around them. When your hopes and desires don't match your first impressions, pay close attention. Then let time uncover an individual's true nature.

Be careful that you don't confuse this new person with someone you know who has similar qualities. Here's what I mean: If you meet a woman who looks or acts like your critical Aunt Crystal, you might wrongly assume that she is judgmental too. When you suspect there is an overlap, tune in again to get another read or else learn more about the person over time.

I value my first impressions. They give me important information about the energy someone emits. But I also know I may modify my assessment later. So unless I get a dramatic "Stay away," or don't feel any connection, I may wait for more to be revealed.

### SET YOUR INTENTION
I will notice my first impressions and allow them to round out the picture of a relationship or situation.

# Don't Second-Guess Yourself

Many of my patients get into trouble because they second-guess themselves. They may get a clear gut feeling about, say, a potential romantic partner that communicates, "This person isn't good for me." But since their friends are impressed with the person, they doubt their intuition and move forward with the relationship anyway. Ultimately, it doesn't work out and they return to my office saying, "I wish I had listened." The lesson here is to trust your intuition or at least give it a chance to unfold.

As I developed my intuition, I sometimes learned the biggest and hardest lessons by ignoring its messages. Intuition is not a popularity vote or a consensus. It is simply what your inner voice is advising for you. This may not be what your ego wants to hear, nor is it always good news. However, when you stop second-guessing your intuition, your decisions and life will improve.

**SET YOUR INTENTION**
Today I will tune in to my intuition about
a specific issue such as work, health, or a relationship.
I will not second-guess the message that I receive.

# Tea with a Friend

Take some time out to have tea with a friend. Just an hour. You don't have to talk about anything significant. This is a sacred pause, a break, a loving moment to be with someone whom you like a lot. Sitting across from this person is a way of sharing positive energy. You're in a restaurant or a tea house or your home. It's a simple moment of rest, connection, and happiness. Gift this to yourself occasionally. It's a small, potent way of celebrating friendship, love, and the enchantment of everyday moments.

**SET YOUR INTENTION**
I will plan to have tea with a friend and simply enjoy myself. I will savor simple acts of intimacy and pleasure.

# Declining Invitations or Canceling Plans

Extroverted empaths may enjoy social events, but introverted empaths like me prefer having more quiet time. I find that one social event weekly is optimal for me. To practice self-care, you must learn the art of declining invitations. The secret is to do it with love. "The gathering sounds great," you might say. "I wish I could join you, but I'm just too spent." If you continually over-commit because you fear hurting others, your energy will suffer. However, rather than this being a "selfish" decision or one that makes you feel guilty, "No thank you" must become a regular part of your self-care vocabulary.

At times, you may also need to cancel plans. You want to fulfill commitments, but you may be longing for alone time or are just too tired to go out. Despite your best intentions, you must cancel. As hard as it may be for sensitive people to disappoint others, it's sometimes necessary.

Evaluate how important a commitment is. Some plans can be shifted easily, though others cannot. If you are fatigued but must attend a major event, such as your sister's wedding, take special care of yourself later. Always weigh the pros and cons of how you expend your energy.

---

**SET YOUR INTENTION**
If I'm tired, ill, or just need to be alone,
I will sometimes have to considerately
decline invitations or cancel plans.

# Practice Functional Speech

When I was on a retreat at Tassajara Zen Center, the monks and residents practiced what they called "functional speech" when they were cooking, cleaning, or groundskeeping. Functional speech means saying the absolute minimum of words so as not to disturb the person working at their particular job beside you. For instance, a cook would say to a fellow kitchen worker, "Tomato," or "Set table," or "Trash," rather than get into details about the activity.

Functional speech appeals to me as an empath who loves the quiet. I don't care for long explanations or conversations. I prefer focusing my attention on an activity in silence. The simplicity of functional speech creates an open space that allows one just to be without the ordinary demands to talk.

Experiment with functional speech at home as a way of practicing mindfulness. Tell your mate or others that you will be doing this for a certain time period. Perhaps they'd like to participate too. With less talking throughout the day, it is easier to find your center.

**SET YOUR INTENTION**
I will practice functional speech and simplify
my language to express my thoughts and
needs with the fewest words. I will notice how
this affects my clarity and energy level.

# The Holiness of Simple Things

Find satisfaction and awe in the simple things in life. The delicate way light reflects on water, the rousing sound of the wind, a sweet hug with a friend, your child's smile. There is enormous positive energy and light in what is most simple and pleasing. Seeing the luminous in the everyday world can be a source of great happiness for you, as it is for me. This quiet, mindful activity has great aesthetic and spiritual reward. You don't have to look far to find beauty and light. Too often, we are so busy that time slips away. People think about the future at the expense of enjoying themselves now. Take time to notice the luminosity of what's in front of you and always present. Heaven is right before your eyes if you slow down to see it.

**SET YOUR INTENTION**
Today, I will stop rushing and striving and searching.
I will let small things bring me joy and appreciate
the aliveness of every breath and every moment.

# Always Growing

Life is a process of ongoing growth. The way to stay vibrant is to keep growing and changing every day. Celebrate your baby steps of progress and also the breakthrough ah-ha moments. Your spirit is calling out to grow larger and more radiant. Hear its call by saying yes to the adventure of life with all its ups and downs. The self-healing work you do is incredibly meaningful and supports your spirit's instinct to expand. Every moment of your life is significant, from infancy to your final passage. Each presents you with an opportunity to breathe, to open your heart, and to hone your sensitivities. See with simple eyes to find simple beauty. An undulating power emanates from all of life.

**SET YOUR INTENTION**
I will never stop growing. I will not resist change.
I am dedicated to my emotional and spiritual expansion.

# Everyone Is Your Spiritual Teacher

Everyone you meet has something to teach you. Positive people are teachers of love, friendship, companionship, and trust. Difficult people aren't as easy to deal with. Annoying or unpleasant as their behavior can be, it shines light on your wounds and emotional triggers so you can heal them. For instance, when someone criticizes your choices, see this as a chance to set boundaries with their behavior and examine the tender areas within where your self-esteem may be fragile. Or if someone throws you crumbs of love but is unavailable for real intimacy, it's powerful to say, "I deserve so much more."

This kind of self-healing, when you accept all the teachings that life offers, requires humility. Your attitude of acceptance lessens suffering and resistance by letting you flow with the learning process. Remember, life doesn't happen to us, it happens for us. Instead of wishing you could avoid problematic people, accept them as your teachers too.

### SET YOUR INTENTION
I will learn about caring from positive people. I will view the difficult people I encounter as teachers who can help me heal my emotional wounds and set me free.

# Befriend a Tree

Trees are living beings that can be companions to you. When I was a child I had a favorite tree that I would visit and snuggle up to. If I was sad, I would tell it my problems. If I was happy, visiting this tree would make me happier.

Trees shade us and cool the Earth. Trees also cleanse our atmosphere by removing toxic carbon dioxide and storing carbon in their trunks, roots, and branches. In addition, they release the oxygen that we breathe. Some trees grow very old and have witnessed centuries of the comings and goings of us humans. A pine tree in the Inyo National Forest in California has lived for over five thousand years and is the oldest tree on the planet.

One of your empathic gifts is connecting with nature. It's comforting to have a tree as a companion. To find one or more, visit the woods or a park or even notice the trees that line your neighborhood street. See which one you are intuitively drawn to. When you feel overwhelmed, you can meditate there to ground yourself. Simply putting your palm on the tree (or even hugging it!) can stabilize your mood and energy.

**SET YOUR INTENTION**
I will recognize trees as living beings.
I will set out to find my companion tree
and spend time with it to center myself.

# The Cosmic Wink

Magic comes when Spirit winks at us. Watch for signs. The wink can be subtle or obvious. When I was experiencing a creative block writing my book *Positive Energy*, I kept forcing myself to write, which only made the situation worse. Then, one night, I dreamed of a specific phone number—all ten digits. The next morning, I called it! A woman answered the phone, "UCLA Labor and Delivery Room." I smiled. There was definitely a lot of pushing going on there! A cosmic force was winking at me and saying, "Stop pushing so hard." So I listened and took the pressure off myself. I allowed my project to birth in a more natural way.

Look for the cosmic winks in your life. Maybe you avoided a car accident by a hair, and the incident could have easily been more serious. Or you synchronistically ran into your old boss, who invited you to work on a dream project in his company. Let these cosmic winks help you smile more at everything.

**SET YOUR INTENTION**
I will look for magic in my life and notice
the cosmic humor all around me. I will not
get so serious that I miss these miracles.

# Lighten Up

All buddhas laughed when they awakened. They see the humor of the universe and the folly of our ego attachments and fears. Instead of taking yourself too seriously, as empaths tend to do, see the cosmic humor in life.

I have a close, ninety-something friend who has laughed at whatever happened to her over the years, including a bout with cancer. I once asked her, "Why do you always laugh at everything?"

She smiled and said, "Why not?"

A sign of an enlightened person is the ability to laugh. You can be miserable and happy at the same time. Just because a situation is difficult doesn't mean you can't feel good about yourself too. Laugh during positive times. And laugh in the midst of hardship. Whatever you're facing, make it light, not heavy. Spirit is always close. Let this knowing help you relax.

**SET YOUR INTENTION**
I will look on the light side today rather than focus
on problems. I will see what there is to laugh about.

# The Joy of Not Overthinking

Empaths are prone to overthink decisions. Though logic has an important role in decision-making, when logic turns into obsessive rumination, you will suffer. How much thinking is too much? When you have considered all sides of an issue, but you keep mulling it over endlessly.

Einstein suggested that a problem can't always be solved on the problem's level. So imagine letting go of the dilemma for a while. Nothing more to do or consider.

To stop overthinking, practice this visualization:

*Picture yourself rising high above your concerns, above the Earth, into the vastness of open space. You're free-floating and observing the twinkling stars, the planets, and the infinite universe expanding in all directions. Say hello to Brother Sun and Sister Moon, as Saint Francis called them. Take in the incomprehensible beauty and the mystery.*

This vision will transport you to a spacious place. Focusing on it will loosen your mind's grip on a concern. When you can be in awe with all there is, you will experience the pleasure of not overthinking.

---

**SET YOUR INTENTION**
When I am stuck on a problem, I will stop, take
a breath, and enlarge my perspective. Then I can
return to it from a more creative frame of mind.

# Don't Take It Personally

This simple principle of spiritual growth is often tricky to apply. When people make rude or insensitive comments, they are often telling you untrue stories about yourself.

Why shouldn't you take things personally? If someone insults you, they are projecting onto you some pattern they've learned from their upbringing. There's a saying, "Hurt people hurt people." For that moment, you have become their punishing mother or withholding father. But it's not about you, though the person may frame it that way. In *The Four Agreements*, don Miguel Ruiz says that others bring their own poison to your interaction, but you don't have to take it in.

If someone calls you "too emotional" or "weak," you must know inside yourself that this is untrue. You only take it personally if you agree with their assessment. Otherwise, you know how off-base it is. You may not like someone's comments — and choose to set boundaries with them — but you won't take them personally. As you compassionately discard false beliefs that you carry about yourself, you will become a more empowered, confident empath.

**SET YOUR INTENTION**
I will not take other people's misguided comments
personally. I realize that they are projecting
their own unresolved issues onto me.

# Opinions Are the Lowest Form of Knowledge

Everyone has opinions that represent their point of view. These aren't necessarily true, nor are they always invited. According to novelist George Eliot, the highest form of knowledge is empathy because it requires us to release our egos and appreciate another's world. In contrast, having an opinion requires no true understanding of a situation.

When someone offers an opinion about you, it may or may not feel true. The problem is, empaths tend to take others' judgments seriously and give them too much weight. If a friend says, "You need to go to large parties to meet more people," that is her opinion. It probably doesn't take into consideration that you feel anxious or uncomfortable in large groups or that you prefer smaller gatherings. You can either buy into your friend's unrealistic assessment of what's right for you or say, "Thanks for sharing." Then find a social setting to meet people with whom you feel more attuned. Know yourself and always follow your own truth.

---

**SET YOUR INTENTION**
I know that opinions are subjective. I won't give
too much credence to other people's opinions
unless they offer some wisdom I'd like to apply.

# The Bliss of Flowers

Spirit inhabits nature and flowers. Have you ever noticed how sacred it feels lying in a field of wild flowers or watching the miracle of new life blooming in your garden? Flowers exalt in the sunlight, dew, and rain. They are never too rushed or bothered to be joyful. Flowers are beautiful, but even more, they radiate a sense of ecstasy and celebration of being alive. As Ralph Waldo Emerson wrote, "Earth laughs in flowers."

To celebrate spring's flowers, create a lovely bouquet in your home or office. Spend time admiring it and let these beauties share their joy with you. Your sensitivities allow you to absorb their freshness and optimism as they herald the promise of a new day. There's reason to be hopeful. Stay open to a multitude of blessings in your life. Let flowers be the blessings of the Now, all that you need to feel content and peaceful.

**SET YOUR INTENTION**
I will take pleasure in observing the flowers and
feeling their exuberance. Flowers can beautify
my environment and spiritually uplift me.

# Honor the Feminine

Both men and women have feminine, or "yin," energy. This is the yielding, flowing, feeling, moon-like part of you. The yin complements the masculine, or "yang," energy within all of us that wants to make things happen, solve a problem, and march forward to conquer the world. Balancing your masculine and feminine sides keeps you passionate and vibrant.

On and around Mother's Day, let's pay special tribute to all mothers and the mother within to acknowledge the power of the feminine. Be grateful for the blessings of being a parent and say thank you to your own mother. Mothers and grandmothers can be our greatest spiritual teachers. They know exactly which buttons to push in us. Let us use these prompts to grow emotionally and spiritually.

The feminine is the part of you connected to the Earth and all her creatures. She is the goddess of creation and the birth giver to life. Praise the feminine. Feel her warmth and strength in your body.

---

**SET YOUR INTENTION**
Today, I will honor the feminine in myself
and in all mothers throughout time, including
Mother Earth. I will let the feminine reconnect
me with my body and the Earth.

# I Am Not My Mother

To be fully empowered, you must realize that you are a separate person from your mother. Though you might share certain qualities that you admire in her, it does not serve you to keep repeating her negative behaviors. You are each on your own spiritual paths.

Empathic children instinctively want to help their mothers and may inadvertently absorb their anxieties or insecurities (which can still stay with them as adults). For instance, if your mother was anxious, in an attempt to lessen her discomfort, you might have unconsciously adopted her anxiety or depression too. This doesn't help her, and it only burdens you.

Journal about which of your positive qualities resemble your mother's—perhaps humor, generosity, and intelligence. Also reflect on which of her unproductive emotions or behaviors you might have taken on. Perhaps you mirror her critical voice or her fears and insecurities. Examine which traits are yours and which are hers.

Practice this mantra when you want to release any of your mother's issues that you may still be shouldering: "I am not my mother. I am on my own, unique spiritual journey. I am ready to release any negativity that is hers."

---

**SET YOUR INTENTION**
It is not my job to take on my mother's pain.
I will learn from all the lessons she taught me,
both positive and difficult. I will bless her journey
but know it is a different path than mine.

# Rebirthing: What Is Your Creation Story?

Rebirthing involves renewing an aspect of your life that is floundering or stagnant. You can go through rebirthing at many stages. Ask yourself, "What specific areas would I like to address? My spirituality? Intuition? Work? The relationship with a parent or my partner?" Then formulate a "creation story" to define constructive changes you can make.

Creation stories mark the beginning of a new phase. Reflect on what your creation story might be. One patient told me, "I want to create a solar windmill business to generate clean energy." Other patients have said, "I want to create more solitude." "I want to create a closer relationship with my mother." "I want to create a baby and become a parent." Even if aspects of your life have stalled, you can jump-start them again by developing a rebirthing plan.

**SET YOUR INTENTION**
I will construct my own creation story.
I will specify, "I want to create . . ." then fill
in the truth of what my heart tells me.

# Shielding with Family Members

Sometimes it's necessary to practice shielding with certain relatives to ward off their negativity. Many people are unconscious about the impact of their behavior or moods. Your parents and siblings may be unaware when they slip into a victim mentality or habitually criticize your choices. They may not grasp that their continual bickering drains you.

With receptive family members, share that you are a sensitive person and describe ways they can support you during gatherings like talking more softly or seating you next to a pleasant relative. Ideally, they will accommodate you.

Still, you may need to protect yourself around some people. One mother told me, "I feel guilty if I shield myself from my children," as if her job were to stay wide open to their bad behavior. Instead, think of shielding as putting a positive force field around you that centers you. Here's how:

*Picture a shield of white or pink light completely surrounding your body about five inches from your skin. It keeps out all negativity and stress but allows in positivity. Maintain this shield for as long as necessary at family gatherings or in other draining situations.*

**SET YOUR INTENTION**
As a form of self-care, I will practice a
shielding visualization when I am with stressful
relatives. I can still care about someone and
also shield myself from their negativity.

# Focus on One Issue at a Time

To get your point across, it's best to focus on one issue at a time rather than overloading someone with too much information.

As a caring, emotional person, you may have a lot of feelings and empathic needs swirling around within. You want to express yourself. You want your needs to be heard. But it is wise to communicate in a centered, simple way to get results. Sometimes, it's tempting to blurt out all the problems that are bothering you at once, especially if you're anxious or upset. In one conversation you might convey, "I need more alone time. I'll be exhausted if your parents visit us for a week. Also, please turn the television down and help me with the kids." Instead, start with the top of the list. Then, over days or weeks, address each additional issue individually. This is a respectful, effective way to communicate.

**SET YOUR INTENTION**
I will identify the main five concerns I'd like to
discuss with my spouse, friend, or others. I will
address only one topic at a time. I will not overload
loved ones with too much information at once.

# Small Talk

I do not enjoy small talk. As an introverted empath, I've never been able to do it well, and it makes me tired. Small talk feels forced to me and like it is just meant to fill up time to avoid an uneasy silence. You may agree but haven't given yourself permission to refrain from it. You may feel that opting out is rude. Or you may feel ashamed that you lack this skill, so you avoid social gatherings.

Honestly evaluate how you view small talk. Does it make you feel awkward? Do you dread it? Or, if you're an extroverted empath, is it a friendly way of relating to others? There is no right or wrong response.

How can you avoid small talk in a Zen-like way? If I attend a party, I will simply ask my mate or a gregarious friend to engage in it since they enjoy doing so. This takes the pressure off me. Then I will just listen and dive in if the conversation deepens. Or I find someone else I can more easily relate to and talk to them. Consider solutions that feel realistic for you.

---

**SET YOUR INTENTION**

I will identify my preferences about small talk
and strategize ways to cope that are comfortable
for me. I will enlist the help of friends to support
me in small talk during social situations.

# Curing Energy Hangovers

You can carry the energy of an interaction even when it is over. Have you ever had a delightful afternoon with a friend and continued to feel wonderful hours later? Or, alternatively, have you ever interacted with someone who's anxious and still carried their anxiety the next day?

Energy hangovers occur when the negative effects of an encounter linger in your body after the source is gone. Even if you set good boundaries with someone, later you may still have a stomachache or a sense of fatigue that you absorbed from them. At those times, jump into a bath or shower so that the water can wash away the lingering energy. Or smudge your space with sage or sweetgrass to clear the negative or stagnant feeling (see April 20). Also, deep-breathing exercises will expel any unpleasant sensations. When you purify your system and physical space, the energy hangover will dissipate.

**SET YOUR INTENTION**
If I have an energy hangover, I will
acknowledge that it is real and take steps
to cleanse the lingering emotions or stress.

# Feeling Emotionally Safe

Learn to interact with others in a healthy way that honors your sensitivities. Emotional safety comes from experiencing a primal place of comfort within. You can relax knowing that you aren't going to get hurt, criticized, or attacked.

Emotional safety starts within you. It means recognizing your own emotions and not repressing them. As a sensitive person, your feelings can get intense and overwhelming. At those times, be gentle and compassionate with yourself.

In intimate relationships, emotional safety means that you trust another person and can be vulnerable with them. You give each other the benefit of the doubt in a conflict. Love, acceptance, respect, and feeling desirable can allow you to feel safe emotionally.

To clarify your needs, think about what emotional safety means for you. Each of us is different. Ask yourself, "What makes me feel emotionally safe? Who do I feel safe or unsafe with?" Focus on your friends, your spouse, and your family. Write about the changes that need to occur for you to be more secure in these relationships. Taking care of yourself in this way allows you to be vulnerable and open with those whom you trust.

**SET YOUR INTENTION**
I will choose relationships in which I feel
respected and not judged. I will also create
a circle of emotional safety for others.

# Codependent or Empathic?

There's a joke that when a codependent dies, it is *your* life that passes in front of their eyes. Codependents feel overly responsible for people and pick up the slack in relationships and work. If you're a codependent, it can be hard to pull back and let others travel their own paths. You may want to overhelp or fix people, believing that if you don't intervene something terrible will happen—a habit you might have learned from living with an alcoholic or anxious parent.

Empaths can have codependent tendencies but not all codependents are empaths. The difference is that empaths absorb the stress, emotions, and physical symptoms of others, something not all codependents do.

As a highly empathic person, practice protection techniques such as shielding and meditation (see May 13) to deal with the energy absorption issue, which isn't as relevant for a pure codependent. However, for both empaths and codependents, setting boundaries and seeing others as separate, not simply an extension of yourself, is also part of healing. You are still present, but you can be a great listener and a loyal friend without taking on someone's problems.

---

**SET YOUR INTENTION**
I will stop obsessing about others and focus
on my own self-care. I can be a giving person
while maintaining healthy boundaries.

# The Power of Eye Contact

Our eyes transmit potent energies. Just as the brain emits an electromagnetic signal extending beyond your body, studies indicate that your eyes project this kind of energy too. Observe people's eyes. Are they caring? Sexy? Tranquil? Mean? Angry? Cold? Also determine from their eyes whether anyone is at home, indicating a capacity for intimacy. Or do they seem guarded, distant, or veiled?

As a caring person, you want to understand others and be empathic. So you may instinctively look deeply into a person's eyes to contact their essence. In fact, "eye gazing" is a tantric technique for lovers that helps them grow closer by maintaining longer periods of loving eye contact. However, in everyday life, be discerning about your gaze. Determine if you want to share eye contact with someone.

The eyes are windows into the soul, but not everyone wants to have their souls read. Be careful not to be intrusive with your gaze and look away if someone is intruding on you. Empaths do the dance of energy exchange all the time, but you must choose for yourself what's healthy.

**SET YOUR INTENTION**
I will make wise choices about the people I share
energy with through my eyes. I will not look
into someone's eyes if I feel uncomfortable.
In those cases, it's healthy to avert my gaze.

# Return to Sender

Whenever you have taken on emotions, stress, or any sensations that don't belong to you, clear them from your body as soon as possible. A mantra that I use and suggest to you is called "Return to Sender."

*Once you've recognized what you have absorbed from others, don't panic. Simply notice it. Take a breath. Then inwardly and confidently repeat three times, "Return to sender. Return to sender. Return to sender." Pause for a few seconds to inhale and exhale deeply. Next, feel the discomfort leave your body and completely dissipate into the infinite matrix of the universe. You are now balanced, healthy, and whole.*

**SET YOUR INTENTION**

I will use the mantra "Return to Sender" as a quick way to release unwanted energy from my body.

# Mirror Neurons

Your brain has a specialized group of cells called mirror neurons, which are responsible for empathy and compassion. Studies suggest that empaths have a hyperactive mirror neuron system, which is what places them high on the empathy scale. When someone you love is in pain, you may feel it as if it is actually happening to you. Sometimes, you even feel the pain of strangers and the world. Similarly, when someone has been compassionate, you absorb the intensity of that compassion too.

Understanding the responsiveness of your mirror neuron system reminds you of the importance of protecting yourself from discomfort that is not your own. It's a gift to be so caring, yet it's also necessary to set healthy boundaries. To conserve your resources, use your empathy well. Know when the time is right to go inward and refuel.

---

**SET YOUR INTENTION**
I have a finely tuned mirror neuron system that
is wired for compassion and empathy. I will continue
to seek balance between healthy giving and self-care.

# With Power Comes Responsibility

It's empowering to experience the gifts of intuition, empathy, and connection to Spirit. As they mature, you'll feel more centered, confident, and able to read others. This gives you greater compassion for people and the world. Your capacity to be kindhearted is a beautiful form of power that warrants respect.

Use this power wisely with yourself and others. What does it mean to take responsibility? First, be humble about your astute empathy and intuition. Never use them to boost your ego, control people, or offer unsolicited advice. Also, you are able to listen to others but also maintain your well-being. You can be giving and centered at the same time. Finally, you commit to your own self-care and to conserving your energy. Being responsible and empowered is a compelling combination.

**SET YOUR INTENTION**
I will embrace the power of my sensitivities
and the responsibilities that accompany it.
I will use my abilities with integrity.

# Graduation: Master of Your Destiny

Spring is the season for graduations, for completing one phase of your education, whether you're graduating from college or achieving a level of mastery in another area in your life. Graduation is also about recognizing the breadth of wisdom you have acquired, including the self-care practices you have learned as an empath. It marks the culmination of one period of your development and the beginning of a new one.

Life is our Earth School. There is so much for us to learn about empathy and compassion. Your achievements can range from being a devoted parent or spouse to pursuing a career or developing your emotional intelligence and empathy. There are many kinds of graduations. Today, acknowledge yours. What phase have you graduated from? What adversity have you surmounted? What new path is before you? Be pleased with all you've accomplished.

---

**SET YOUR INTENTION**
I am the master of my own destiny as I enter this new
phase of my life. I will honor how I've deepened my
empathy as well as all my achievements and graduations.

# Hypervigilance

To protect yourself from being overloaded by others' stress, you may become hypervigilant. You keep scanning your environment to make sure you are safe from being drained or entering a state of hyperarousal. Empaths are often mistaken for being aloof or snobbish, but others don't realize that the distance you seem to keep is because you're focused on protecting yourself.

If you were exposed to early trauma or abuse as an empathic child, including not feeling "seen" by your parents, you may have become exquisitely attuned to your environment to ward off threat. When your young nervous system develops without healing, you can become hypervigilant. However, once you feel more at ease with your empathic abilities and learn to set clear boundaries, including shielding yourself, hypervigilance will lessen. You can relax more. The world will feel like a safer place to inhabit.

**SET YOUR INTENTION**
I will observe how much time I spend scanning
my environment for safety. I will utilize protection
techniques to gain a greater sense of comfort.

# Plan a Short Burst of Intense Exercise

Whenever you've taken on stress from others, plan to exercise. In addition to your routine, a short interval of intense movement—from one to five minutes—can quickly purify your body. It releases endorphins into your system that block pain impulses, decrease your appetite, and produce calm or even euphoria.

Find a type of intense exercise that works for you. Take a short power walk or run. You can also try more difficult yoga postures, dancing, skipping, running, doing squats, or jumping rope. These help burn off anxiety, anger, or other uncomfortable emotions in a quick burst. Choose a safe form of exercise that also challenges your body and causes your muscles to "feel the burn."

**SET YOUR INTENTION**
I will explore what form of short, intense
exercise I can turn to when I want to quickly
release stress. This will help me expel unwanted
emotions I have picked up from others.

# Energy Work

Empaths speak the language of energy and are receptive to the beneficial effects of energy medicine. When you're on sensory overload or are feeling ill, seek out an energy healer such as a Reiki master or Healing Touch practitioner. They transmit therapeutic energy to patients through their hands, a subtle technique shown to remove blockages and rebalance you. In turn, your own healing system kicks in to improve your well-being.

Your body is a finely tuned instrument. You may be prone to experiencing mystery symptoms, some of which you absorb from others. These ailments can migrate from one part of the body to another. Unfortunately, conventional medical doctors might misdiagnose you as a hypochondriac. Energy work gently helps your system stabilize itself so you can shed aches, pains, depression, and anxiety.

If your energy is low or if you're experiencing chronic physical or emotional symptoms, I recommend getting energy work. It is a gentle way for sensitive people to feel calmer and more vibrant. Receiving energy work is a key part of my self-care.

---

**SET YOUR INTENTION**
I will consider going to an energy healer.
To achieve optimal wellness, I will be open
to balancing my body's subtle energy.

# Release Fear

Make a commitment to lead a life based on love, not fear. Be prepared to counter fear in its many forms, including imagining the worst in a difficult situation. Fears are tricky because certain ones help us survive. However, you can also take on other people's fears and inflame your own, which only leads to burnout.

As the saying goes, "Fear is false evidence appearing real." Reflect on the truth of this statement. Fear only grows when you feed it. Releasing fear and building courage are how you become strong emotionally.

In your journal, write about your top five fears such as financial scarcity or being lonely. Then decide to release one of them and turn the fear around with an affirmation. For instance, "I will find the right job that provides financial security." Or "I will reach out to friends more often so I don't feel isolated and alone." Even if you are simply acting "as if" (which is a fine first step), this mind shift begins to shrink fear and release it.

**SET YOUR INTENTION**
I will replace a fear-based thought with
a positive outcome. I will connect to Spirit
and feel its support in manifesting my goals.

# Let Loose

As the days are getting lighter and warmer, let loose, have fun, and practice surrendering your worries. Simply play. This doesn't necessarily mean going to crowded beaches or parties, which isn't always the best way for sensitive people to have a good time. Instead, find your own fun wherever you are. Make this weekend a time to be carefree. Do something enjoyable that you've been thinking about but haven't had time for during your work week. Perhaps that means hiking in nature, playing Frisbee or Ping-Pong, or doing an art project. It's healthy and inspiring to have designated days to explore in ways that your soul longs for. Set aside your daily obligations, turn off your computer, and avoid the news. Explore the splendor of life that is all around you.

---

**SET YOUR INTENTION**
I will feel the freedom in my soul.
I will open myself in joy rather than contract
in fear. I will let loose and simply be.

# The Way of All Things

There are cycles to life, the coming and going of seasons, the changes you experience in different phases of growth. Nothing is ever static. Nothing stays the same. But beneath this sense of impermanence is the groundless ground, the strength of love and of the awe-inspiring, evolving universe.

The way of all things is a great mystery, but you can depend on the ebb and flow of your feelings and circumstances. When you accept the divinity of these cycles, when you surrender your tendencies to clench or to be afraid, you can know that all is well.

The way of all things is to let the majesty of nature's changes take precedence over everything else. Love is all-knowing and illuminating. Have faith in its power to keep you safe and to shepherd you toward your highest good now and also on your journey beyond this plane.

**SET YOUR INTENTION**
I will be aware of the groundless ground supporting
me. Even when I am feeling afraid, it is always
there. I will trust the wisdom of my life's path.

# Warriors of Love

We each have a mighty warrior within. This is the part of you that will fight for what you believe is right and guard you from injustices. Empaths are warriors of love. Once we claim our power, we are neither meek nor fragile. Our greatest strengths are our empathy and our desire to bring understanding to the world.

In the spirit of Memorial Day, which occurs at the end of May each year, let us also honor our fallen warriors in the military who sacrificed their lives for the greater good. In the Gettysburg Address, Abraham Lincoln poignantly described these heroes as those who "gave the last full measure of devotion."

As an empath warrior, nourish the peacefulness in yourself and heal the parts of you that are at war. This will help create peace on Earth. As an empath community, let's pray for the day when there are no more wars. May we all join as one planet, an interconnected family. May we see the humanness in all people, show mercy for one another, and have empathy for all.

---

**SET YOUR INTENTION**
I am sensitive and as strong as a warrior. I will honor
the empath warrior within myself and all warriors
of love who fight for the forces of goodness.

# Transcendence

Your small self is the part of you that keeps you trapped in fear and insecurity. Your larger self knows you are so much more than this. It connects seamlessly with your intuition and the existence of Spirit.

Every day set out to transcend what is small inside you. Rise higher than the struggles of daily life. In meditation, tune in to the enormous power and light that is within and around you. If negative thoughts intrude, let them float by like clouds in the sky. Focusing on the positive helps you transcend what is small in yourself.

Realize that you contain suffering and also infinite light. When you consciously say, "I can be more than my struggles; I can find peace in myself," you will lift yourself above any person or emotion that wants to keep you small.

**SET YOUR INTENTION**
I am committed to transcending my fears
and small self. I will connect with my largeness
of spirit and find strength there.

# Letting Go

Letting go at the right times is a secret to success. You might think that it's counterintuitive to let go. However, it can actually help clear the way for a goal to happen. A strange and wonderful joy comes over you when you can let go. This doesn't mean saying yes to everything but instead going fully with a choice and not second-guessing yourself.

Reflect on the issues in your life where you may be pushing too hard without results. Is a project stalled? Do you want your son to go to college, but he's resisting? Are you recovering from an injury slower than you would like? Next, choose one instance where you feel frustrated and say to yourself, "I surrender this to Spirit. I will take a pause. I will take a breath. I will just let go." Then release your attachment to the outcome by shifting your focus to other areas of your life. Simply wait and watch with an open heart to see what occurs.

**SET YOUR INTENTION**
I will begin flowing in my life instead of clenching.
Rather than forcing things to happen, I will practice
letting go. I will try not to push the river.

# Elevated by Sacred Art

Sacred art from around the world can inspire and uplift you. Its power accomplishes more than the eye can see. Beginning with ancient cave paintings, awe for the heavens and earth have been conveyed through various creations. Whether you visit a holy site such as Machu Picchu, take in a museum exhibit, or delight in a stunning photography book, art can impart a sublime sense of holiness.

Recently, before one of my talks, I had the privilege of visiting a one-thousand-year-old Quan Yin statue in the Nelson-Atkins Museum of Art in Kansas City, Missouri. This goddess is more than ten feet tall and is carved from a large tree trunk. My friend and I meditated at her feet. We felt blessed by her compassion. A museum guide said that people make pilgrimages there just to be in her healing aura. This statue exemplifies how sacred art can catalyze spiritual elevation.

What types of art do you respond to? Illuminated manuscripts, ancient spiritual texts, or nature photography? What about the works of the great masters such as Monet, Van Gogh, Michelangelo, and Da Vinci? Draw solace and inspiration from the brilliance of these creations.

**SET YOUR INTENTION**
I will find art forms that move and inspire
me. I will expose myself to the positive
energy of creativity on a regular basis.

# The Heartbeat of Drumming

Drumming provides a primal sound that calls you back into your body. The beat of our mother's heart in the womb was our early link to sound. When you're overthinking or stressed, you tend to migrate up to your head. Then you are more prone to obsessive, fearful thoughts and may miss your body's intuitive signals. Participating in a drum circle or listening to drumming gets you out of your head and grounds you.

It's fun and easy to bring drumming into your life. You can buy a small drum for your home. When you want to calm down, beat it in a steady rhythm that mimics the rate of your heart. This tempo communicates, "There's nothing to be frightened of. I am the beat that is slow and true within you." Your cells recognize the regular, rhythmic sound of drumming. Let it balance you in just the right ways after a long day's work or simply for the joy of it.

**SET YOUR INTENTION**
I will experiment with drumming to ground myself. I will find the drum rhythm that is in sync with my body's natural rhythms.

# The Jaguar Meditation

Animals are powerful friends to call upon when you need healing and protection. In Native American culture, animal medicine can help, for example, by connecting you to the spirit of a lion or a snake. Each has particular strengths that you may draw on. The lion has courage, while the snake contains primal energy and has the ability to shift shape.

When you need protection from draining people or in stressful situations, the jaguar can be a trusted ally. At those times, try this Jaguar Meditation:

*In a quiet place, take a few breaths, get into a relaxed position, and close your eyes. With each breath, release the thoughts and stress of the day. When you feel settled and calm, call on the spirit of the jaguar to assist you. Inwardly say, "Brave and noble jaguar, I need your help." Then feel the jaguar's presence enter your room. Inwardly visualize this gorgeous, compelling creature with shiny eyes and a graceful body patrolling your personal space. She will keep protecting you as long as you need her. Feel how safe you are and what a devoted ally the jaguar is. As you close this meditation, express gratitude to this spirit animal for her assistance.*

**SET YOUR INTENTION**
I will practice the Jaguar Meditation when
I need protection and a circle of safety around
me. I will enlist the help of an animal ally.

# Vision Quest

A vision quest is a rite of passage in native cultures when adolescent males go into the wilderness to request a vision or dream that will guide them as they enter adulthood. Their aim is to attain personal communication with Spirit, which is induced by fasting or prayer. This ritual is solitary and contemplative.

Going on a vision quest can revive your connection to Spirit when you feel stuck in your life. This may entail taking a day or more of introspection in the mountains, forest, or desert. Programs offer guided vision quests or you can go on your own.

During this ritual, be totally present in the experience. Bring only a few clothes and necessities with you so you can leave behind materialistic concerns. You might go on a complete fast or a juice fast to cleanse your system.

Embark on this sacred undertaking with seriousness and reverence. Your vision might come while awake or in a dream, revealing a deeper truth about yourself. In either case, write it down, remember it, and apply this wisdom when you return to the world of people.

**SET YOUR INTENTION**
If I need clarity about a decision or want guidance
about any aspect of my life, I will consider going
on a vision quest to seek answers from the Mystery.

# Positive Body Image

Your body image contributes to your self-esteem and sense of attractiveness. It is shaped by your family's beliefs, media hype, and cultural ideals. It's important to free your mind from any brainwashing so that you can enjoy your physical form. It's a misconception to think that you have to change how you look to feel better about yourself. So much is governed by your own perception. I've treated thin patients who believe they're fat, and plus-size patients who carry their weight lightly and feel sexy.

How you perceive your body is up to you. I appreciate that it is important to like how you look. To reinforce a positive body image, limit your exposure to negative media images with stick-thin models or muscle-bound athletes representing some illusory ideal. Also, let go of comparisons. Instead, develop positive self-talk. It's fine to want to eat healthy food and lose weight but remember to be compassionate with yourself in the process.

**SET YOUR INTENTION**
I will say kind things about my body because
I know it hears me. I will focus on myself
and will refrain from comparing myself to others.

# Heal Your Pain-Body

Your body carries around all the painful experiences you've ever felt. The "pain-body," as spiritual teacher Eckhart Tolle calls it, is the part of your energy field that contains all these stored physical sensations and emotions.

The first step in healing your pain-body is to be aware that you have one. Then, when painful thoughts arise or when smaller situations trigger enormous reactions, this is a sign that your pain-body has been activated. Being conscious of this is key. All pain is interconnected. For instance, you injure your ankle and suddenly the anguish of not being seen as a sensitive child emerges. One painful event can subliminally activate a cascade of other unresolved distressing incidents in your body.

So when pain emerges, engage in self-observation. Eckhart Tolle says, "If you are present, the pain-body cannot feed anymore on your thoughts, or on other people's reactions. You can simply observe it . . . Then gradually, its energy will decrease."

---

**SET YOUR INTENTION**
When I feel pain, I will notice it and respond
with compassion as I also focus on healing its source.
I will practice breathing pain out of my body to release it.

# Was I Born an Empath?

Some infants enter the world as empaths. Their empathy and sense of intuition is part of their inborn temperament. You can see it when they come out of the womb. They look like little versions of Buddha and show heightened responses to light, smells, touch, crowds, movement, and noise. These babies seem to have the temperament of empaths from the start.

If you weren't born an empath, other factors, such as early trauma, may contribute to your becoming one. This includes emotional or physical neglect or abuse or being raised by narcissistic or substance-addicted parents. Such an upbringing can potentially wear down a child's healthy defenses so they feel more exposed and unprotected in the world.

Healing is possible for all sensitive people. Though positive parenting can help you develop your gifts, not all of us have had this. So you must learn self-compassion and how to set boundaries and utilize the self-soothing techniques I've presented in this book. You can also re-parent yourself in healthy ways by cultivating positive self-talk. In addition, you may want to find surrogate parents. These are caring and generous people with strong maternal or paternal instincts who will take you under their wing.

---

**SET YOUR INTENTION**
I will be my own loving parent to my inner
child and choose to be around supportive
people who make me feel safe and accepted.

# Turn Down Your Sensitivities

Sometimes it's necessary to turn down the volume of external stimulation when you're feeling overloaded. Depending on your schedule, you can do this for ten minutes or an entire weekend. Close your door. Shut off the lights. Climb under the covers to hibernate. Or you can spend the afternoon watching movies or playing with your animal friends. No talking. No news. Minimal or no interactions. No stress or too much information intruding. Simply relish the peace of being in your own company.

This period of minimal stimulation will help reset your physiological system. The downtime lowers your heart rate, slows your metabolism, and turns off the fight-or-flight stress response. Instead, your body begins making endorphins, your natural pain relievers and "feel good" neurochemicals. By decreasing stimulation, you are taking charge of self-regulating your body. Empty space, empty time, and having no people or demands is a trusted formula for rejuvenation.

**SET YOUR INTENTION**
I will be aware of when I feel overstimulated and
use this as a cue to take a time-out. As soon as
possible, I will lower my stimulation level or only
expose myself to external input of my choosing.

# Micromanaging

If you feel that a task won't be done right unless you do it yourself, you could be a micromanager. What are the signs? You resist delegating work. You look at the details rather than the big picture and lack faith that others can perform well on their own. It's exhausting for you. And, in an office or team situation, your behavior undermines morale and make others feel incompetent. If you try to micromanage your partner or family, they will grow annoyed or resentful. It will aggravate loved ones if you ask them to undertake a task and then do it yourself.

Micromanaging is a form of excessive control over people or situations. For better relationships, reflect on the question, "Why do I micromanage?" Perhaps you came from an out-of-control, chaotic family where it was your job to restore peace and order. Or you've been burned by people who didn't fulfill their commitments.

Of course, hiring a well-trained staff will help a business to thrive. But also manage your expectations at work or at home and clarify your goals with employees or family members. Conveying that you have faith in them and focusing on their best qualities rather than your disappointments will inspire them to shine.

---

**SET YOUR INTENTION**
I will notice my tendency to micromanage.
I will show people I have confidence in
them and micromanage them less.

# Mindfulness

Mindfulness is when you concentrate your attention on the present moment. At the same time, you acknowledge the feelings, thoughts, and sensations in your body without trying to alter them. Accepting life as it is, without fighting it, trying to control it, or complaining is the essence of mindfulness in action. You see yourself with kindness rather than beating yourself up or harshly comparing yourself to others.

From a mindfulness perspective, it's helpful to know and accept yourself as you are in the Now. You are not focused on the future or the past. Research has shown a connection between practicing mindfulness meditation and psychological health. It allows you to find a witness state and a center amidst chaos or adversity. When you are mindful, you can see everything—including yourself—from the standpoint of compassion.

**SET YOUR INTENTION**
Today, I will practice mindfulness. No matter
what happens, I will stay focused on the
present moment and be gentle with myself.

# The Heaven of Loving-Kindness

You can create heaven in your life by infusing every day and every interaction with loving-kindness. Of course, sometimes you may slip into anxiety, fear, or insecurities, as we all do. But keep reminding yourself of the bliss of loving-kindness and how it softens everything including anger, fear, and the most harrowing of circumstances. It is the sparkling fairy dust that heaven sprinkles on us daily. Stay open to giving and receiving it. Loving-kindness is the quality I most admire in others and seek in those I'm close with.

Practice the following meditation by directing loving-kindness to yourself. (If you'd like to send it to another person simply replace "I" with "you.")

*May I be happy.*
*May I be well.*
*May I be safe.*
*May I be peaceful and at ease.*

If you can imagine a heaven full of golden light, you can re-create it on earth by how you treat yourself and others. No matter what trials you have endured, no matter what the past has been, loving-kindness can free you from suffering.

**SET YOUR INTENTION**
I will experience the heaven of loving-kindness today
and bask in the glow of its merciful healing powers.

# The Joy of Uplifting Films

I've always adored escaping the world for an afternoon and going to the movies. In the theater, I feel safe and away from it all as I get lost in the richness and human complexities of a film. I can feel the textures, smell the scents, and empathize with the emotional trials and breakthroughs that the characters experience.

When you're feeling overloaded or simply need a break from daily demands, try watching an uplifting film. Choosing the right one will warm your heart and renew your spirit. Whether you go to a theater or stream one online, this is your time to be inspired. One of my favorite films is *Wings of Desire*. It's about an angel who takes human form (thus sacrificing his angelic superpowers) so he can marry the trapeze artist with whom he has fallen in love. My other favorites are *Ghost, Dances with Wolves, Won't You Be My Neighbor, The Lord of the Rings Trilogy,* and *The Secret of Roan Inish*. You can also include inspirational films as a joyful, creative part of your self-care.

**SET YOUR INTENTION**
I will choose an uplifting movie to watch and forget about the rest of the world for a while. I will immerse myself in the fun of storytelling, drama, and comedy.

# Explore Essential Oils

Sensitive people often have a keen sense of smell. A subtle scent can be a divine experience for us, but a megadose of perfume may feel suffocating. Scents are a very personal preference. Discover which ones feel healing for you.

Aromatherapy is a treatment that uses extracts of plants called "essential oils" to relax you, decrease anxiety, deepen sleep, and calm your system. You can breathe them in, rub them on your skin, or put a few drops in your bath water. Essential oils are derived from flowers, herbs, and tree bark. The cells that make plants fragrant are called their "essence." Always use essential oils that are pure rather than synthetic.

Lavender, chamomile, eucalyptus, lemon, and peppermint are a few types of essential oils. Each has different uses. For instance, lavender promotes sleep and relaxation, whereas peppermint is more stimulating and helps with depression. Essential oils provide a subtle infusion of healing into your body through their delicate and therapeutic nature.

### SET YOUR INTENTION
I will experiment with essential oils to find the
ones that most calm or energize me. I will focus
on the sensuality and pleasure of each aroma.

# The Difference Between Intuition and Fear

It's important to recognize the difference between intuition and fear. Reliable intuitions convey information in a neutral, unemotional way. They feel right in your gut and are compassionate and affirming. Sometimes, when you experience these intuitions, you may feel detached, as if you are in a theater watching a movie. In contrast, fears have a high emotional charge. They often convey critical messages about old psychological wounds such as, "I am not good enough."

Journaling about your top five fears will clarify which intuitions to be suspicious of. For instance, you might have a fear of abandonment or of being unsuccessful. Another fear some of my patients struggle with is that they are too emotionally damaged to sustain healthy relationships. As I tell them, even if you've been deeply wounded, you can learn to open your heart again.

True intuitions will never put you down or enforce destructive attitudes. They always support your best choices and behaviors.

**SET YOUR INTENTION**
I will practice recognizing the difference
between my fears and intuitions. I will trust
intuitions that encourage my highest good.

# Dysfunctional Family

Families are living organisms. The health and behavior of its members contribute to its overall wellness. In a healthy family, you learn to identify your needs and feelings; you receive consistent, loving messages from your parents; and your authenticity is valued. A dysfunctional family lacks clear boundaries. Their communication may be unskillful. Shaming and blaming occur. One family member may become a scapegoat, or parents may be struggling with substance abuse or their own emotional distress and trauma.

If you come from a dysfunctional family, it's wise to accept the limitations of each of the members and lower your expectations. Setting polite but clear boundaries with toxic behavior stops you from becoming a doormat. Also recognize how your relatives emotionally trigger you; then choose how to respond. At family gatherings, be calm, cool, and neutral. If someone tries to suck you into a negative interaction such as pitting you against your sister, simply refuse to get hooked. You may be unable to control your family, but you can take charge of your behavior.

**SET YOUR INTENTION**
I will not allow myself to get emotionally
drawn into my family's dysfunctional
dynamics. I will set clear boundaries with
relatives. It is not my job to fix my family.

# Self-Acceptance

One of the most liberating changes a sensitive person can make is to practice self-acceptance. This means embracing yourself as you are, including your strengths and areas which still require growth. We are all unique. There is only one of you. Instead of comparing yourself to others or trying to put on a false front to impress the world, take some time to relax into yourself. You don't have to pretend to be anyone else.

Being comfortable in your own skin is a divine feeling. Self-acceptance doesn't mean that you become stagnant or stop evolving. You just move forward in a way that emerges from your authentic core. Spirit has given you everything you need to evolve on your journey. If you deem an aspect of yourself "less than" someone else, this is a cue for you to compassionately practice self-acceptance. No one is perfect. That's what makes us all so interesting.

---

**SET YOUR INTENTION**
I will accept myself more each day. I will appreciate my strengths and smile at my foibles. I will continue to heal and grow.

# Celebrate the Sensitive Man

Since Father's Day occurs in June, let's honor all the brave, sensitive men who aren't afraid to show their feelings and can express love. They're able to give and receive without being commitment-phobic or unavailable.

A man's empathy allows him to be caring and to hold a non-judgmental space for others to be authentic. But empathic men must nurture their sensitivities while also grounding themselves and setting boundaries with negative people so they aren't drained.

In the name of all the sensitive men who were ever called "sissies" or were bullied as children, I apologize for everyone who has ever hurt you or shamed you. Your tormentors were just afraid of your strength and open heart. You are forging the path of what it means to be an enlightened man. I thank all the sensitive fathers, grandfathers, and every courageous man who isn't afraid to embody both strength and sensitivity.

**SET YOUR INTENTION**
I will express gratitude for a sensitive man in my life.
I will tell him what an incredible role model he is.

# Teachings from Your Father

Some spiritual traditions believe that prior to entering this life we choose our parents. We select those who are perfectly suited to help us grow. Their role is to provide us with different lessons from being loved and cared for to handling heartbreak and abandonment. Of course, no one would purposely choose a difficult parent, but on a greater level, that's exactly what we may need for our spirits to stretch.

With that in mind, spend some time reflecting on what your father has taught you. In your journal, make two columns: one for positive lessons and one for painful ones. In a positive light, did your father show integrity, consistency, strength, and the ability to love? If so, how did he transmit these values to you? On the other hand, was your father emotionally unavailable, hurtful, critical, or self-absorbed? Again, ask yourself, "What did he teach me through these troubling behaviors?" Perhaps you've become more present with your children or are less critical of your spouse. Whatever you have learned, let these experiences help you be more loving, empathic, and kind.

**SET YOUR INTENTION**
I will see my father as my teacher, whether or
not he was loving. I will consider what I've
learned from him and let these lessons help me
love myself and become a better person.

# Meditate on the Summer Moon

This is the special night that comes right before the peak light of the summer solstice. Tonight is the moment to savor as the powers of goodness, love, and passion are rising high and strong. Look up at this moon as the messenger of summer. Meditate on her and anticipate the new season to come. She knows that summer is near and smiles down on this time of light.

As part of your meditation, also feel the moon's strong but gentle light in your body. Let it nourish you and beam away any weariness. The moon is excited about the light-filled season to come and all the phases she will pass through. Let yourself be excited about your changes too.

**SET YOUR INTENTION**
I will gaze upon the moon tonight and
let her radiance fill me. On this summer's
eve, I will welcome in the new season.

# SUMMER

## Passion, Play, and Abundance

Summer is the season with the most light. This helps us experience our own radiance, passion, and abundance. It's often symbolized by the sun and the fire element.

Everything seems gentler, dreamier, and more sensual. The days are warm. The nights are temperate and fragrant. Baby birds leave the nest and learn to fly. Gardens are alive with bright flowers and butterflies.

Summer offers you the special gift of playfulness. Because empaths can get overly serious, summer invites you to lighten up. It's vacation time; school is out. You can laugh more and worry less. You can wear bathing suits, flip-flops, or shorts. Also walking barefoot is an energizing "earthing" practice (see March 29). Plus, it's freeing to go off the grid in nature for a while. Without the jarring input of cell phones, computers, or work demands, you can reattune to your natural rhythms.

Summer can also have challenges for empaths. Your senses may get overstimulated when it's too hot, humid, or bright. Beaches, parks, and other vacation spots may be overcrowded, which isn't our idea of fun.

Summer embodies abundance and passion. Just as crops are maturing, you, too, can advance your goals. During this time, the Earth is tilted closest to the sun. The solstice is the most light-filled day of year, the beginning of summer. It sets the tone for your personal and spiritual expansion. Throughout this season of light, making the right choices for self-care is key to enjoying its magic.

# Pinnacle of Light

The summer solstice is the longest day of the year, when the light is peaking. Around this period, you can focus on emanating your inner light too. What does this mean? Be yourself to the fullest. Speak your needs. Say no to energy vampires. Express your creativity. Go for the project you've been passionate about. Tell your partner how crazy you are about them. Laugh. Meditate. Open your heart. Feel your fire and don't hold back. Connect with the spiritual and mystical forces. Let them wash over you and cleanse you of all fear. Feel your strength building. Own your power and experience how natural and good it feels.

**SET YOUR INTENTION**
I will be my largest, brightest self today.
I will emanate my full radiance. I will see
light in everyone and everything.

# Slow Walks

During the longer summer days, plan to take slow walks regularly. These are such a luxury, a time to mindfully be aware of your body and let your thoughts wander to creative places. You're not rushed or pressured in any way. You're not hurrying to an appointment. You're not checking messages. Unlike power walks, which are an intense form of aerobic exercise, slow walks are not meant to be a strenuous workout. Rather, they can reset your physiology to a quieter rhythm and still your mind. During a slow walk, breathe in the soft summer air, feel the sun's soothing warmth, and open your senses. What do you see? What do you feel? What do you smell? Allow yourself to be uplifted by children laughing and playing. Take in the glory of flowers and hummingbirds and butterflies.

**SET YOUR INTENTION**
I will go on a slow, luxurious walk. I will
relax my pace so that I can slowly take in the
sights, sounds, and scents I encounter.

# Awaken Your Inner Adventurer

Each of us has an inner adventurer that is longing to be awakened. Perhaps you have forgotten about this daring part of yourself, or it has been dormant until now. Ongoing obligations and constant work can stifle your free spirit.

Your inner adventurer likes to explore unknown territory. It doesn't want to be constrained by a strict schedule or routine. To awaken your adventurous self, simply invite it to emerge. Inwardly say, "I am ready and excited to meet you." Then, when it appears—and it will—pose these questions: "What have I always wanted to do but have been inhibiting? Climb a mountain? Build a sand castle on the beach? Travel to Tibet? Surf the Mavericks? Dance the tango?"

Instead of holding back or finding a "good excuse" why this isn't "practical," make it happen. Start with simpler adventures such as hiking a different trail or visiting a new museum. Then stretch your comfort level by trying different activities. Don't overthink it. Let your inner adventurer guide the way to enlivening explorations and happiness.

---

**SET YOUR INTENTION**
I will get to know my inner adventurer. I will listen
to its ideas and follow through with the ones that feel
right to me. I will never lose my sense of adventure.

# Dancing

Dance can get you out of your head and into your body. Just like any good low-impact cardio workout, it boosts your immune system, stamina, flexibility, and cardiovascular health, plus it improves your mood. You can let loose and play.

If you feel inhibited, try dancing a little at a time. A gentle way to begin is to just put on music you like in the privacy of your own home and slowly start to move. Lift your arms, extend your legs, even twirl to the beat. As you dance, profound feelings might arise including sadness, frustration, or joy. Keep dancing through them and let them flow. Releasing emotions helps you clear pent-up energy.

Investigate different kinds of dance. Find the forms that feel good to your body. Possibilities include salsa, ballroom dancing such as the sexy tango, Zumba, dancing to rock music, and ecstatic spontaneous dance such as the 5Rhythms technique originated by Gabrielle Roth. Dancing allows you to become more fully embodied and in touch with your fire.

---

**SET YOUR INTENTION**
I will counter a sedentary lifestyle with dance. I will not be afraid to move my body. I will dance for fun and to feel free. I will enjoy how good dancing feels.

# Chanting

Chanting is a dynamic way to utilize sound to heal. It involves singing your prayers to balance your system. This lifts you high above your daily concerns so you can feel your largeness and bliss. As the popularity of yoga has spread throughout the world, chanting sacred Sanskrit words such as *om* has become popular. *Om* means "peace" and is thought to be a soundless sound that runs through the universe.

You can chant on your own or listen to recordings. If you're chanting alone, start by choosing a mantra to chant that comes from your spiritual tradition. These include *om* and *shalom* for "peace"; or *Thy will be done*; or *aham prema,* which means, "I am divine love"; or simply, *Let it be*. Keep repeating the mantra in a meditative state and allow yourself to sing it. You can also listen to ancient Gregorian chants or to Indian devotional music.

I enjoy Kirtan performances. This is a call and response type of devotional chant set to music. The singers open with a sacred phrase or story, then the audience repeats it. There can be dancers and drumming, as well as the ancient mystical sound of the harmonium. The audience often moves and dances spontaneously. As long as it doesn't feel overstimulating, being in a group can amplify the therapeutic effects of chanting.

---

**SET YOUR INTENTION**
I will explore chanting as a way to balance
my nervous system, decrease stress, and
joyously connect with spiritual music.

# Roaming Around

Sometimes it feels marvelous just to roam around. You don't have to set off in any particular direction. Just walk in the direction your intuition leads. This spontaneity of movement may appeal to you. You're just following your instincts and going with the flow. When empaths feel safe and are in their power, they love to be spontaneous and explore the world.

Some summer mornings, I leave my home in Venice Beach and just start walking. I have no idea where I will end up, which is part of the fun. I respond to different cues. I see a hummingbird around the corner, so I follow it. I hear the waves breaking in the distance so I turn toward the surf. I smell the scent of incense and look for its source. I never know what I will encounter or even whom I might meet.

Try roaming around too. You can do this in your neighborhood, in a park, by the beach, by a lake, or in the center of a city. You're a free agent. Roam around without a care in the world. If you can turn off your phone, even better. Be guided by your inner voice and the great Mystery.

---

**SET YOUR INTENTION**
I will take part in the delight of roaming around
to see where my intuition takes me. I will pay
attention to the people who pass by me and the
details of the neighborhood I am exploring.

# A Lightness of Being

If you tend to be overly serious, as is true of many sensitive people, use this affirmation to reconnect with the lightness of your being. Repeat it as frequently as you like and feel your seriousness lift.

I am light as a feather.
I am carefree.
I am safe and protected.
I run like the wind.
I soar like a bird.
I flutter like the butterfly.
I am the sky and the stars.
I am at one with the universe.
I am grateful.
I am watched over.
I can smile.
I am at peace.

---

**SET YOUR INTENTION**
As an antidote to chronic seriousness, I will repeat this affirmation. I will stay in touch with my lighter side and the essential spiritual lightness of my being.

# Balance Work and Play

Summer is a time of innocence, of letting go and of play. Evaluate your schedule to see how you can more skillfully balance work and fun. The last thing you want to do is be chained to your desk all summer. When you look back on your life, you probably won't say, "I wish I could have worked more weekends that June." So keep your priorities straight. Even if you have a high-pressure job, the overall pace of many businesses tends to naturally slow during this season, and some offices even close early on Fridays. Think about ways to plan afternoons or days off. If you mark these on your calendar, taking time for play can feel more realistic.

Summer is also associated with vacations. Sensitive people thrive when they get periodic breaks from mundane reality. Otherwise, they risk getting worn down, overwhelmed, and fatigued. If you're an introverted empath, you might prefer retreating to a quiet lakeside cabin in the woods. If you're an extroverted empath, you might be drawn to the excitement of big cities such as New York or Paris while taking regular breaks to moderate the intensity. The more you can balance work and play, the more your body will thank you.

---

**SET YOUR INTENTION**
This will be my summer of fun and adventure.
I will carefully look at my schedule and make
room for playful activities and spontaneity.

# Summer Clothes

The fun of summer clothes is that the fabrics are soft and light, which appeal to sensitive people. You may feel freer and cooler wearing shorts, T-shirts, light cotton dresses, bathing suits, and flip-flops. However, although some clothes can make you feel more confident, in others you may be more self-conscious and insecure.

With the warmer weather, clothes are lighter. There will be less material covering your body. Some empaths feel too exposed in skimpy outfits. If you get anxious at the idea of wearing a bathing suit (especially a bikini), revealing shorts, or baring your arms or midriff, simply make body-positive choices that help you feel good. You can wear sensual, flowy materials without showing more of yourself than you feel comfortable with. One-piece swimsuits, sarongs, or loose caftans can be playful too. In addition, you can use the many protection strategies, including shielding, that I share in this book to lessen your anxiety.

Although body image issues often arise more frequently in summer, use this season as a chance to select the clothes that suit you without shame or blame.

---

**SET YOUR INTENTION**
I will choose summer clothes that feel good on
me. I will not be pressured by people or society
about what to wear. I will stop judging other
people's bodies and also stop judging my own.

# Permission to Unplug

Give yourself permission to unplug regularly from the daily demands of life. This is so easy to forget. You get swept up in all the details of life from waiting for the plumber to arrive, to turning in a project, to picking up your kids. Your to-do list may seem endless. Don't keep trying to get to the bottom of it. This effort is exhausting and nearly impossible to achieve each day. Be at peace with doing your best. And, even in the midst of more tasks to complete, allow yourself to unplug at least for an hour.

Stop the world and get off for a while. This "me time" lets you reconnect to yourself and your dreams. Allow your imagination to float along with the clouds that drift lazily in the sky. Feel the space between your thoughts and a spaciousness in your being. If your body is assured that it can routinely unplug, it will breathe a sigh of relief just knowing that rest and release are available.

---

**SET YOUR INTENTION**
I will review my schedule and plan periodic
times to unplug from obligations and stress.
These merciful breaks nurture my well-being.

# Be a Rebel for a Day

At times it is inspiring to awaken your inner rebel. This is the part of you that is brave enough to question long-held, ingrained assumptions and fight to uncover truths about your life or the world that truly make sense to you. It is the opposite of being a people pleaser.

Today, question authority and give yourself permission to be socially or spiritually incorrect at least once. Stand up for yourself. Resist social norms if they feel wrong. How? Don't answer the phone every time it rings. Wear daring clothes. Sing aloud. Speak your uncensored views to a friend. Question the sacred cows in your life, those ideas that are considered "above scrutiny." Break a few rules. Reject any inner or outer voices that denigrate your sensitivities. Unapologetically, be an empath who is centered in your power.

**SET YOUR INTENTION**
I will let myself be rebellious and question
whatever doesn't ring true to me. My inner
rebel can spark my free spirit and passion.

# No More People Pleasing

Do you always want people to be happy? Do you frequently put others' needs ahead of your own? As a sensitive person, you are a natural giver who may try to be all things for all people. But this can lead to becoming a habitual people pleaser too.

It's admirable to want the best for others, but people pleasing takes your caring attitude to an extreme. This tendency may reflect low self-esteem, an aversion to conflict, or fear of rejection if you don't over give. Perhaps growing up you associated receiving approval with people pleasing. So you tried to win love by getting into others' good graces. Also, you may feel responsible for someone's emotional or physical state. If you're a people pleaser, you can give away too much of yourself and squash your own needs and emotions.

To shift out of this pattern, begin by saying no to something small. Also, express your opinion about an issue (start with a less emotionally charged one), even if it differs from that of friends or family. Asserting yourself will build self-confidence. You don't have to please people all the time. You deserve to be liked and respected for being your authentic self.

---

**SET YOUR INTENTION**
I will be aware of my tendency to be a people
pleaser. I will find the right balance between
expressing my own needs and supporting others.

# Interdependence Versus Codependence

We live in the world with many people. Some are heartfelt and uplifting to be around. Others are more difficult. It's important to find a comfortable way of relating to people so that you can develop a harmonious interdependence rather than being codependent.

When you're interdependent, you have a healthy reliance on others in your personal life, at work, and in the greater world. You depend on each other for support and respect and also to perform particular tasks such as collaborating on a project, raising children, participating in team sports, or hiking with a group.

In contrast, codependency is an unhealthy form of dependency. This occurs when you are more focused on another person's life and problems than your own. You are reluctant to assert your needs or set clear boundaries for fear of the consequences.

Spend some time journaling about your relationships. Which are interdependent? Which are codependent? List a few constructive steps you can take to make codependent relationships more balanced. For example, checking up on someone less often, setting a clear boundary, or letting others make and learn from their own mistakes. Then, one by one, begin to reshape your codependent relationships and appreciate your interdependent ones.

**SET YOUR INTENTION**
I will thoughtfully examine and heal my
codependency issues and seek a healthy
interdependence in my relationships.
I will not get consumed by someone else's life.

# Celebrate Freedom

Freedom allows you to make your own choices, live in a fulfilling way, and express your empathic voice. Emotional freedom grows as you liberate yourself from dysfunctional relationships and negative thoughts.

This is one of the most social days of the year with barbeques, picnics, and parades. Although our country celebrates its independence today, you may need to take it slowly. The fireworks display, parties, heat, and crowds can feel like "too much" for empaths. There may be more noise, drinking, and loud voices than you can tolerate. Both animals and sensitive people often prefer to retreat indoors to reduce stimulation.

Take special care of yourself today. You may be delighted to join family and friends for good food, comradery, and laughter. Or you can choose quiet "sensory friendly" activities without fireworks such as a concert or a museum. Practice saying a loving no to invitations or limit the time you socialize so you don't feel trapped. Also, it's okay to stay home. Watch a movie, cuddle with your animals, meditate, cook a delicious meal, listen to music, or simply rest. Holidays let you stretch time out by slowing your pace.

---

**SET YOUR INTENTION**
I will take good care of myself today and
make wise decisions about my energy. I will
acknowledge how I have freed myself from negative
relationships, emotional patterns, or situations
of hardship. I will be happy for my progress.

# Liberation from Your
# Parents' Negative Voices

A child's brain is still growing and is so impressionable. Many children get brainwashed by their parents' beliefs and critical voices. What you learn early on can stick with you forever unless, as an adult, you do the healing work to discard beliefs that are not your own.

Deprogram those voices so you can be free. Today, journal about the negative messages your parents transmitted and how you took them in. Write down the top five beliefs or voices that you'd like to deprogram such as "I'm sickly," "Children should be seen and not heard," "I'm a disappointment," or "I must criticize my partner and kids or they will never improve."

Then, take a big breath. These powerful messages can cause suffering. Don't reinforce them. They are not reality. Instead, tell yourself, "I will always gravitate to where the love is. I will not let my parents' shaming criticisms take up psychic space in my head." To counter the old scripts, write new affirmations in your journal such as "I am intelligent, caring, and strong" and "My life is important." Overriding hurtful beliefs with loving thoughts will help deprogram early brainwashing.

**SET YOUR INTENTION**
I am not my mother. I am not my father.
I will choose positive beliefs over any
negative ones they transmitted to me.

# Cultivate Courage

Courage neutralizes fear. It imparts the clarity and strength you need to surmount obstacles. Courage puts you intuitively "in the zone" and in touch with greatness. This doesn't necessarily mean that you're without fear, but rather, that you feel the fear and proceed anyway.

To conjure courage, it helps to remember brave people whom you admire. I focus on Nelson Mandela, Martin Luther King, Jr., and His Holiness the Dalai Lama. Their courage fortifies me. I agree with music icon Joni Mitchell when she says she's drawn to people who aren't afraid. You, too, can identify people from whom you can gain strength.

Reflect on a situation in which you were courageous. Perhaps you followed your intuition and chose a job that intrigued you despite others' opinions. Or you stood up for a friend in need. Maybe you just got yourself to go to work when you were feeling down. All courageous acts matter. Keep cultivating courage and rejecting fear. Spirit is always there to support you.

---

**SET YOUR INTENTION**
I am strong. I am capable. When I am unsure
of myself, I will pray to experience courage and
gain strength from role models who embody it.

# Stop Beating Yourself Up

As a psychiatrist, I know how hard we can all be on ourselves. My Taoist teacher says that spiritual progress occurs when you stop beating yourself up a little bit less each day. Gradually, replace harsh thoughts with kind ones. Focus on what you have to be grateful for rather than what is lacking.

We are all works in progress. What makes humanity so beautiful is when we strive to achieve compassion and goodness in all we do. Many times, it's easier to be kind to other people than ourselves. That is human nature. However, be inspired to shower yourself with more gentleness each day. For instance, say "I did a great job in a difficult situation," or "I paced myself today because I felt tired." Being hard on yourself only saps your vitality. The miracle of kindness is that it will uplift your spirit and be a balm for what ails you in a multitude of ways.

Loving oneself isn't always easy, but it is a worthy goal. With self-compassion, you can thrive as a sensitive person and enjoy your gifts.

---

**SET YOUR INTENTION**
I will be aware when I am beating myself
up. I will gently and lovingly reframe
my focus to what I have done well.

# Listen to the Goose Bumps

Experiencing goose bumps is a form of intuition. It's your body's way of saying, "Yes, this inspires me and feels right" or "This makes my gut uncomfortable." Always notice when you get waves of goose bumps. They occur when you have a strong positive or negative reaction to something and are associated with the fight-or-flight response. They tell you to pay attention to what is going on.

When I interviewed music great Quincy Jones for my book *Positive Energy*, he said, "I live by goose bumps. I get them everytime something really touches me. Then I know I've got the right take. Nothing to talk about unless I get the goose bumps!"

Stay alert if you experience them too. Then ask yourself, "What just happened? What meaning does it have for me?" For instance, you may have goose bumps after hearing a moving song. Leonard Cohen singing "Hallelujah" always does it for me. A stressful or fear-inducing situation can also set them off. Consider goose bumps an intuitive sign relaying important information about how to proceed. They are your body's wisdom directly communicating a message to you.

## SET YOUR INTENTION
I will be aware of when I have goose bumps
and evaluate the intuitive message they
convey. I will listen to my body's messages.

# Déjà Vu

Have you ever experienced a strong sense of familiarity with someone, even though you've never met before? Or in the midst of a situation, have you felt as if you've already gone through these exact circumstances? If so, this is an intuition known as "déjà vu," which comes from the French expression meaning "already seen."

Train yourself to be aware of experiencing a déjà vu, which can happen within seconds of meeting someone. This knowing is easy to miss or disregard if you are busy or distracted. But slowing down to explore it can be incredibly meaningful. You might meet a soul friend, a devoted ally for life. You can talk to them about anything, and they will understand. Or you might need to pay closer attention to a specific situation, such as a business venture or a health concern, to make the best decision. Recognizing a déjà vu draws you closer to the mystery of life.

**SET YOUR INTENTION**
If I have a déjà vu experience, I will take special
notice and examine the message it is conveying.
I will not second-guess myself or be too busy
to pay attention to this experience.

# Stargazing

My favorite kind of night life is stargazing, as opposed to going to clubs or noisy restaurants. It is awe-inspiring to watch the twinkling stars and planets—some of them millions of light years away. Since I was a little girl, they've always felt like friends to me. As a sensitive child, sometimes I preferred the company of the moon and stars to people.

Like me, you might love stargazing and feeling a sense of the eternal in the night sky. The magic of shooting stars and meteor showers (such as the Perseids, which occur in midsummer) can lift stresses. Also, learning to recognize planets and constellations is fascinating. From beneficent Jupiter to the mystical Pleiades, you can find endless wonder by observing the night sky. Ancient cultures paid homage to the heavens and built structures such as the pyramids in Egypt and Machu Picchu in Peru to architecturally align with the phases of the moon, the sun, and the solstices.

As physicist Stephen Hawking said, "Look up at the stars and not down at your feet." So gaze at the heavens. Knowing that we are just a speck in the universe allows us to experience the depth of existence.

**SET YOUR INTENTION**
I will spend some open-ended time watching
stars tonight. I will take a deep breath
and feel the vastness of the universe.

# Keeping Cool

Empaths can be sensitive to temperature and intense light. In the summer, you may react to the heat and brighter sunshine. Hot weather can energize some people, but it drains others, at times to the point of exhaustion or being unable to think clearly.

If you become depleted by the summer's heat, glare, and humidity, plan to keep cool and minimize light exposure as part of your self-care regimen. Experiment with different ways of doing this. For instance, you can wear a hat, sunglasses, and white, light-weight clothing, which reflects the heat (rather than darker colors, which absorb it). Frequent cool showers help. Swimming in pools, lakes, or the ocean lets you exercise without getting overheated. Indoors you may have air conditioning. If not, draw your shades and curtains to block the sun during the day. Be sure to drink at least five eight-ounce glasses of water daily and avoid dehydrating beverages such as excessive coffee. Cold drinks and cold food can keep you cooler too.

**SET YOUR INTENTION**
If I am uncomfortable in the heat, I will make
summer a meditation on self-care and keeping
cool by listening to my body's needs.

# Commune with Plants

Many native cultures believe that there are spirits in all of nature, including plants, and that we must pay them respect. Some sensitive people are plant empaths: they can commune with trees, shrubs, flowers, and all of nature. If you are one, you may be so tuned in, you can actually sense a plant's life force and needs.

Spend time with green growing things and flowers. You can admire their beauty but also stretch your senses to feel their essence. Plants emit joy, even ecstasy. Many native cultures honor plant medicine—the medicinal and spiritual healing properties of plants.

See what you intuitively feel when you sit or stand beside them. Gently rest your palm on a tree's trunk to feel the stability there. Observe the sensual movements of its branches and leaves. Trees and plants playfully dance with the air currents and also sing their own unique songs. Their movements and life force are healing. Listen carefully to this plant magic, which pervades forests, gardens, and wild places everywhere.

**SET YOUR INTENTION**
I will honor the trees, the plants, and the
flowers. I will pay attention to the natural
world and allow it to energize me.

# Ocean and Tides

Sensitive people often gravitate to the ocean. You may too. The primordial sound of the surf can feel reassuring and vibrate deep in your soul. Our Earth is blessed with many stunning bodies of water that support planetary life.

When you are burned out or just need to be calmed, visit the ocean and absorb the health-giving negative ions it produces. Though some of us are blessed to live near the sea, if you are located inland, you can enjoy photos, audios, and videos of soothing ocean sights and sounds too.

The tide is the rhythmic rise and fall of the ocean caused by the moon's gravitational forces. There are two high tides and two low tides each day. You can feel the power of the tides when you slow down and intuitively tune in. With your sensitivities, this will come naturally. Feeling the age-old sensual movement of the sea can restore you.

**SET YOUR INTENTION**
I will turn to the ocean to revive myself.
I will allow the healing energy of the waves
and tides to replenish my being.

# Dream Empaths

I am so in love with dreams because I am totally present in them, not thinking about the past or future, as I tend to do in the waking state. Ordinary time doesn't exist, and we are transported to nonlinear, intuitive states known by aboriginal and native cultures as "dreamtime."

As a dream empath since childhood, I have always been drawn to dreams and record their details in a daily journal upon awakening. Perhaps you are this kind of empath too. You are intrigued by the messages you receive and let them direct your life.

Summer is a fantastic time to remember your dreams. There is magic in the air. Shakespeare demonstrated this in *A Midsummer Night's Dream*, his comedy about young lovers and actors who are touched by the enchantment of fairies in the forest.

If you would like to remember and interpret your dreams, follow the instructions I gave on March 30. Recording your dreams every day for a week will train you to recall them.

---

**SET YOUR INTENTION**
I will turn to my dreams for guidance. The
answers they offer can help me gain greater insight
into my daily life, well-being, and self-care.

# A Little Bit of Chocolate

Chocolate can quickly transform and elevate your mood. It increases serotonin, your body's natural antidepressant, so you don't become as mired in negative thoughts. Chocolate also heightens your energy when you've absorbed emotions or stress from others.

The type of chocolate you choose makes a difference. Dark chocolate has more caffeine, which may be overstimulating, but it has less dairy and sugar. Milk chocolate, which is made with dairy and refined sugar, can increase inflammation.

A great alternative to chocolate is raw organic cacao. It is considered a superfood because it contains high amounts of plant-based iron and antioxidants, without artificial sweeteners. Cacao comes from the original bean before it is heated and processed to form chocolate, a method that destroys many nutrients.

A small amount of chocolate or organic cacao (about one to three squares or a few cacao nibs) is a good energy booster for sensitive people. More can cause the exhausting mood swings of sugar highs and crashes. So when you're stressed, turn to a bit of chocolate or cacao as a special treat and mood stabilizer.

**SET YOUR INTENTION**
When I'm tired or irritable, I will consume a small amount of chocolate or organic cacao to balance my system. I will avoid synthetic processed sugars.

# Touch Your Temples

If you feel anxious, tired, or stressed, get in the habit of pressing or massaging your temples to release tension and still your mind. This simple technique relaxes your temporal muscles, relieves headaches, and increases circulation in the area. It can also break obsessive thoughts, mind chatter, and fears that may be triggered by emotional pain and overload. Here's how to do it:

*Before bed or at any point during the day, take a few deep, calming breaths to settle your awareness into your body. Then place two or three fingers on both temples, which are located on either side of your face, between your eyebrow and hairline, and apply light to medium pressure as long as it feels good. This technique is meant to be gentle and regenerative. So take a long exhale, let go, and enjoy the experience.*

**SET YOUR INTENTION**
As part of my self-care regimen, I will get
in the habit of pressing or massaging my
temples to relax and center myself.

# Harness Your Willpower

Willpower often gets a bad rap. Of course, it is often wise advice to get out of your head and into your heart, but willpower can also give you the mental fortitude to fight off an overwhelming wave of negativity that's coming your way. At those times, focus your mind like a sword. Tell yourself, "I have the ability to deflect this threat. It cannot hurt me." Then willpower becomes your ally.

Courage arises from your heart but also from your mind. It's useful to call on both resources to repel other people's or the world's negativity and stress. With a directed will, you become like Teflon, a material to which nothing sticks. Unkind words, critical comments, and toxic energy will slide right off you and have no effect. Learning to harness your will is a basic part of a sensitive person's tool kit.

**SET YOUR INTENTION**
I will develop a strong mind and heart as
part of being a balanced empath. I will
activate my willpower when I need it.

# Nourishment

Nourishment comes in many forms. It is not only the food you eat. It is also what you listen to and watch, and who your friends are. Be mindful of what you take into your system on every level.

Physical nourishment means taking good care of your body through diet, exercise, and adequate sleep. Also, regular massage and other types of body work, such as Reiki or acupuncture, can release tension and trapped emotions that have lodged in your muscles.

On an emotional level, you get fed by the caring and positivity of others, their friendship and sense of family. Nourishment also comes from within. The more you realize that most of the fear-based stories that you concoct in your head are not reality, the more content you will feel.

Spiritual nourishment comes from the connection to your heart, a higher power, and drinking from the well of compassion. Meditation will help you deepen this link.

Today ask yourself, "What can I do to nourish myself?" Then choose one action such as resting, meditating, being with a good friend, or walking in nature. Learning to nourish yourself is a key aspect of self-care that will increase your energy and comfort level.

---

**SET YOUR INTENTION**
I will nourish my body, mind, and spirit
every day. I will grow strong from tapping into
the forces of positivity and compassion.

# My Thoughts Are Draining Me!

Your negative, stressful thoughts can be addictive. It may be hard to stop thinking them. They are obsessive and repetitive and can keep replaying in your mind relentlessly throughout the day. This can drain you! That's why you must step in and take control.

These thoughts are a form of self-inflicted suffering. Don't let them define the way you see yourself and the world because they are not reality. You must ask yourself, "How would my life change if I knew these thoughts weren't real?" Take some time to journal about it. If you continue to believe the false messages these thoughts send, you will likely be tired and unhappy. Instead, take control by saying to them, "You are a just a figment of the matrix of delusion. I can see beyond you into the realms of truth and understanding." As John Lennon has expressed, the only reality is love, and that's what we must focus on. Let "love" be your mantra as you banish punitive voices that keep you small.

**SET YOUR INTENTION**
I will not let my thoughts drain me or put
me down. I will be kind to myself when
I encounter stress and obstacles.

# Visualization of Stones

When you are feeling overwhelmed or if your thoughts are scattered, practice this visualization to center yourself:

*Take a few deep breaths. Relax your body. If thoughts intrude, keep breathing deeply and let them float by like clouds in the sky. Do not attach to them. Let the rhythm of your breathing help you completely settle into your body.*

*Picture yourself walking in a huge, majestic, red rock canyon filled with all shapes and sizes of noble stones and boulders. Some are thousands of years old, strong, wise, and omnipresent. It's a beautiful day with the perfect temperature, just right for you to wander around this enchanted place. Notice which rock formations you are drawn to. Then place your palms or your entire body on them. Feel their strength and let them ground you. You can also sit on a boulder to feel its stability, warmth, and substance. Let the grounding life force of this canyon and all its natural stone formations bring you back to center and in touch with your highest, clearest self.*

**SET YOUR INTENTION**
I will visualize this red rock canyon of wonder when I want to ground myself. I can go there whenever I like. It always welcomes my return.

# Raising Butterflies

I receive great joy from raising monarch butterflies and watching their mind-blowing transformations. They change form from fat caterpillars, to an oozing liquid substance housed in a tiny green chrysalis with golden beads, to stunning newborns.

Summer is an ideal time to raise butterflies. Simply buy a milkweed plant at a nursery and place it outdoors. Monarchs will find it. Milkweed is the only food that the caterpillars eat. I keep mine in a large screened container. At first, I leave it open to attract adult monarchs who lay their eggs there. Then I close the door and watch tiny caterpillars quickly appear, devour the leaves, and grow fat. Then they form chrysalises. Two weeks later, fully developed monarchs push their way out and are born. It takes a few hours for the newborns' wings to dry. Then I set these lovely creatures free, and they soar high into the sky, fulfilling their destiny.

Butterflies symbolize radical transformation for us too. In Christianity, they represent resurrection. To Native Americans, they signify change and hope. In the spirit of transformation, you can raise monarchs or simply watch and learn from their beautiful existence.

**SET YOUR INTENTION**
I will meditate on the symbol of the butterfly.
I will be inspired by its journey of freedom and change.

# Define Your Personal Space

We each have an invisible energetic border that determines our comfort level—our personal space. When this is violated, you can feel drained or anxious. Honoring this space protects you from becoming overwhelmed and will safeguard you from absorbing unwanted emotions and sensations.

Mapping out your personal space can protect you from taking on other people's physical or emotional stress. Think about the number of inches or feet you prefer to keep during conversations or when you're near another person. Personal space can vary with situations, upbringing, and culture. My ideal distance to maintain in public, such as in airports or waiting rooms, is about two feet. With friends, it's about half that. What are your personal space requirements? What feels comfortable for you? This is important information to know about yourself.

**SET YOUR INTENTION**
I will determine my ideal personal space needs
in different situations. I will do my best to
maintain these so I can feel at ease.

# Chronic Talkers

Have you ever been cornered at a gathering by someone who starts recounting their life story or who just won't stop talking? The person doesn't even take a breath for you to get a word in edgewise. Although you appear fidgety or restless, these talkers don't respond to nonverbal cues. Sensitive people are commonly overly polite because they don't want to offend others. Like them, you may endure the long tirade, but afterward, you feel exhausted and need a nap.

Identify the chronic talkers in your life. Is it your mother-in-law, friend, coworker, or hairstylist? Identify who they are and note the environments in which they tend to take you captive: at family dinners, on your lunch break, or on the phone?

To empower your relationships, develop a strategy to prevent chronic talkers from ambushing you. With a smile say, "I'm sorry, but I must interrupt. I'm late for an appointment." Another socially acceptable exit strategy that I use is, "Please excuse me. I need to go to the bathroom." You are not a victim. You have the right to set boundaries with chronic talkers.

---

**SET YOUR INTENTION**

I will practice interrupting a chronic talker with
kindness. Doing this will preserve my energy and spare
me from being trapped by a barrage of draining words.

# Drama Queens and Kings

These people wear you out with their intense highs and lows. They turn everyday incidents into crises. What signs give them away? They often start sentences with, "Oh my God, you'll never believe what just happened!" Or if their boss doesn't instantly compliment their work, they frantically tell everyone they are being fired. Their flare for exaggeration can put you on overload and burn you out.

Never ask drama queens or kings how they are doing—you don't want to know! The moment they start to rev up, take a breath to center yourself. Gazing intently into their eyes invites them to continue their story, so limit eye contact. This subliminally indicates you are busy. If you encounter them at work or during a gathering, you also can use body language that signifies "I am not interested." Intentionally pointing your body away from them, discourages further interaction.

**SET YOUR INTENTION**
In the presence of a drama queen or king, I will take a few breaths to center myself. I will take charge of how I respond to this situation. I will not feed into their drama.

# Holding Space

When you're with someone you care about who is going through a hard time or is expressing joy, it is a beautiful skill to hold space for them. This means that you choose to be totally present with that person. (Holding space is not something you offer everyone in need.) Your mind is still: You're not overly involved. You're not thinking about how to change or fix them. You're not focused on your own emotions, which may be getting triggered. Instead, you're looking at them with love, listening with your heart, and holding a positive, nonjudgmental space for this person to just *be*.

Holding space is a gift that you have to offer. I often do this for my patients and with friends. You're creating an aura of love that extends from you to them. Never underestimate the power of holding space for someone. It can be a vehicle for deep healing.

**SET YOUR INTENTION**
I will hold a loving space for someone today.
I will be completely present for them.

# Am I More Than My Body?

To the linear mind, it may seem that the body and this material world are all there is. But from a spiritual and energetic perspective, you are so much more than your physical self. Our essence is energy. The goodness that you develop in your life is what stays with you on your soul's journey.

I believe the main purpose of being alive is to grow spiritually. This planet is but one place to do this—there are also many others. The more we work through our fears and increasingly free ourselves from suffering, the more radiant we become.

Your spirit is timeless. What lies beyond this life? My Taoist teacher says, "The soul's work continues." But if you use your intuition to sense the enormity of your spirit and the universe, you can know that your evolution continues beyond time and space into the Mystery.

**SET YOUR INTENTION**
I know I am more than my body. I will intuitively
sense how large and timeless my spirit is.
I will sense the expansiveness of my being.

# The Purpose of Earth School

I consider Earth to be a school where our souls have an opportunity to evolve in a physical body. Here, we have a special chance to heal difficult emotions and learn to strengthen ourselves in the midst of adversity. Buddha says, "Life is suffering." It is also a chance to learn compassion for our own struggles and have empathy for others. Everyone is doing the best they can. You may not see the burdens people are carrying, but they are there. We all have challenges to contend with.

The Earth is not an enlightened planet. It is a place of both darkness and light. We can use the alchemy of self-healing to transcend suffering. When you are dedicated to opening your heart and accepting your empathic gifts, you become an alchemist who can heal your shadow side, including your fears. Do bad things happen on Earth? Of course they do. However, you can be the one to create more light, to heal deeply and not fixate on fear. By developing empathy and believing in the superpower of goodness, you can transform yourself and the world.

### SET YOUR INTENTION
I will consider all of my life's experience as
part of my education in Earth school where
I can grow more compassionate and wise.

# Overcoming Obstacles

Obstacles are part of life. How you deal with them will determine how easily you conquer these challenges. Learning to address roadblocks without clenching or fighting is key to your well-being.

When encountering an obstacle, be Zen-like in your approach. Pushing is not the answer. Instead of trying to force or resist it, take a step back and breathe. Mindfully consider what the impediment is and what actions you must take to overcome it. Life's inevitable stumbling blocks can be signals that you need to wake up and pay attention to what is going on.

Obstacles have secret meanings that will ultimately benefit you. For instance, being rejected can be Spirit protecting you from a painful situation. Or feeling too tired or ill to proceed with a goal is your body's way of saying, "Please take care of me and rest." When confronting an impasse, always ask yourself, "What is the meaning for me? Am I being asked to be courageous and find a new solution? Is it time to stop and regroup?" Your intuition can advise you on how best to proceed.

---

**SET YOUR INTENTION**
I will view obstacles as teachers.
I will ask myself, "What can I learn from them?"
They are cues for me to listen to my intuition
to find the right action (or nonaction) to take.

# Rejuvenate Yourself with Sleep

A simple, potent truth to live by is to rest when you are tired. Even short power naps can revive you and prevent you from getting run-down. If you don't take these mini breaks you leave yourself open to sensory overload and burnout. Life can wear you out, even if you appreciate every moment. You need regular repairs for daily stresses.

Sleep refreshes your body. Shakespeare's Macbeth calls it "the nourisher in life's feast." It is as vital as oxygen, food, and water. While asleep, stress recedes. Your metabolism slows, your senses quiet, and your body heals itself. Sleep recharges the emotional center of your brain. It increases your memory and learning abilities and elevates your mood. It also keeps you youthful as skin cells regenerate and damage is repaired from aging and ultraviolet radiation.

Getting adequate sleep is a necessary part of self-care. Know your own physical and emotional limits so you don't suffer from fatigue and overstimulation. Resting doesn't mean quitting. It gives you a breather so you can be clear and invigorated.

**SET YOUR INTENTION**
I will plan to get more high-quality sleep
and schedule short naps during a busy day.
I am the sacred guardian of my energy level.

# Faith in Goodness

Goodness means being good and doing good. You are kind and giving to others in healthy ways, and you are also good to yourself by practicing self-care. This firm and persistent belief in the power of love is one of our most enlightened qualities.

Goodness is so appealing to me because it is a pure, open, and vulnerable state. Good people have high integrity. When you value goodness, your presence becomes heartfelt, safe, and healing to others. Still, good people are not naive. They consciously choose to reject arrogance, greed, or harming others and our planet. If you prioritize goodness, you have no cause to feel inferior to those who have compromised their integrity to achieve "success" (even if your income is less than theirs). The karmic price for such a breach of integrity is large. My Taoist teacher says that the highest form of spirituality is being a good person.

**SET YOUR INTENTION**
I will value the goodness in myself
and others as an esteemed quality. I will stay
true to my integrity in all my decisions.

# Experience Pleasure

Today, place your attention on exploring pleasure. This is the ability to feel good and to let in positive sensations, ideas, beauty, and pleasing experiences. Sometimes it's easier to focus on pain than pleasure because that pattern is part of your early conditioning. But for now, focus on what feels terrific and what makes you happy.

The luxuries of summer include longer days, more play time, and a lightness of being. Take in the sweet scent of night-blooming jasmine, roses, or other fragrant flowers. Watch the butterflies, hummingbirds, or fireflies. Allow the breeze to caress your body during a walk. Take in the colors of dusk. At night, observe the summer's moon transit through her elegant cycles. Explore the pleasures of this season and feel enlivened by summer's sense of whimsy and play.

**SET YOUR INTENTION**
I will devote today to exploring pleasure. I will
discover different kinds and bask in their nurturing.

# Laughter

Laughter is good medicine. This is especially true for sensitive people, since we tend to be on the overly serious, intense side. I prescribe laughter to many of my patients. On a physical level, it decreases muscular tension and helps you release pent-up negativity, anxiety, and depression. It also enhances your immune response and increases the flow of endorphins, your body's natural painkillers. On an emotional level, laughter gives you a break from tensions, fears, and concerns to focus on what's whimsical and funny about being alive. Journalist Norman Cousins, the father of laugh therapy, treated his own pain from a debilitating joint disease with a ten-minute dose of daily laughter by watching *I Love Lucy* and other comedies on television. When you can find something to giggle about, you move out of your head and into your heart, a great relief.

**SET YOUR INTENTION**
I will look for something in daily life to smile at today or watch a funny movie. For now, I will set aside my cares and allow myself to laugh freely.

# Rediscover Your Playful Self

There are many aspects to yourself that deserve fulfillment. Mostly, we operate out of our adult self, the dedicated, goal-oriented persona that pays the bills, goes to work, and has conscious relationships with others (all of which can also be gratifying).

However, no matter your chronological age, you have an adorable playful child within you too. If this aspect is cordoned off from the rest of you, life may seem like drudgery.

So invite your playful self out today. Perhaps look at a picture of yourself as a little girl or boy to evoke this memory. Even if you've turned forty, fifty, sixty, or more, this playful part of you is still alive. In meditation or while you are journaling, you can inwardly ask this part of you, "How would you like to express yourself? Do you want to take some time off to go to the park or ocean? Would you like to make jewelry or paint? How about a swim?" Listen carefully to the response and document it in your journal. Set your playful side free. Let yourself laugh and have fun.

### SET YOUR INTENTION

I don't have to constantly be a grown-up without breaks. Too much seriousness is hazardous to my well-being. I will invite my inner child out to play and be lighthearted for a while.

# Growing Younger

Having abundant energy is a gift at any age. Though it is typically associated with youth, I have numerous patients in their thirties and forties who are fatigued from pushing themselves too hard and seventy-something patients who say they've never felt better.

Self-care is a secret to growing more youthful in your younger years as well as in your older ones. Still, it's never too late to start. Physically, your lifestyle choices matter. How much you sleep, exercise, and meditate and how many healthy foods you eat make a huge difference in how you feel. Emotionally, your attitude matters too. Stay focused on the present moment. Don't let your mind create scary stories about aging or the future.

To counteract the energy shifts that may occur with age, realize that there is a fire within you that most people are unaware of. It is known as Kundalini energy. During meditation or in quiet moments, picture this fire growing at the base of your spine. Feel its warmth, wildness, and power. Let it move naturally up your back. Surrender to the feeling. This is your vital life force that keeps you vibrant at any age.

**SET YOUR INTENTION**
I will focus on feeling healthy and optimistic.
I will ignite my inner fire. I will experience my
life force growing brighter and stronger.

# Feeling Seen

Many sensitive children do not feel seen by their parents, teachers, or family. Their sensitivities are treated more like aberrations from the norm than precious and unique abilities. Many of us are told as children, "Get a thicker skin" or "Toughen up," suggesting that something is wrong with our empathic nature.

On the other hand, feeling seen, with a capital S, is liberating. It means that others accept you completely for who you are. You are not judged, blamed, or minimalized. In my psychotherapy practice, "seeing" someone is a crucial aspect of what I offer my patients. When you are seen — really seen — you can breathe a sigh of relief. You don't have to change. You don't have to do anything differently. You are authentically and unapologetically who you are, including your gifts and areas in need of growth. It's a marvelous feeling to be unconditionally accepted.

---

**SET YOUR INTENTION**
Today, I will see myself with loving eyes.
I will be with others who can see me too.

# A Small Dose of People

I enjoy being with people but usually in small doses. I also prefer being with one or just a few people rather than participating in large gatherings. Clarifying how much people time is optimal for you versus how much quiet time you require can enhance your quality of life.

Give yourself permission to limit the time you spend socializing with others. It helps to specify your needs by saying something such as, "It would be great if you could come over for about an hour or two for tea this weekend." That way, you are realistically defining the expectations that your friends may have. With trusted intimates, you can tell them directly, "I am an empath. I love seeing you, but I get tired after a certain amount of time." Then people close to you won't think they have done something wrong if you leave an interaction early. An added benefit is that you are sharing more of your authentic self with them.

**SET YOUR INTENTION**
I will give myself permission to be with people in small doses. I will not pressure myself to socialize with others for more time than I feel comfortable.

# Me Time

Today ask yourself, "What are my self-care requirements, and how can I meet them?" Then listen closely to your inner voice and act on what you hear. Such astute inner listening can allow you to be your best self. Whenever you are reluctant to take me time, repeat this affirmation as frequently as you like.

I am nurturing myself when I take me time.
I am not selfish.
I am not self-absorbed.
I am practicing self-care.
I need quiet.
I need rest.
I need to be in or near water.
I need a hug.
I need nutritious food.
I need to meditate.
I need to sing.
I need to share love.
I need to give.
I need to sleep.
I need to pray.
Thank you, Spirit, for hearing my needs.

**SET YOUR INTENTION**
I will identify and respect my own empathic
needs, which may differ every day. I will enjoy
the me time I create and will be happy that
I am taking such good care of myself.

# Wish on a Star

Summer is a special time to observe the night sky. Tonight, when you look at the glowing universe above, find a star you are most drawn to and focus on it. See how it sparkles and sings. It is talking to you and connecting. It is spreading joy. Then, with your hand on your heart, make a wish to that star. You can do this aloud or silently. It could be, "I wish for health" or "I wish for a caring companion in my life" or "I wish to find a job that's a good fit for my sensitivities." Don't hesitate to ask for your deepest desire. Be sure to make just one wish so it can shoot as straight as an arrow into the matrix of universal love. Be like a child again. Temporarily suspend any disbelief and connect with the enchanted forces all around you. This star is a friend that can grant your wish in the most beautiful way.

**SET YOUR INTENTION**
I will make a wish on a star. I will stay open to
all the invisible helping forces that can intervene.
I am grateful for the loving assistance.

# The Marriage of Logic and Intuition

Empaths tend to be highly intuitive and in touch with their emotions. These are extraordinary qualities. But to be balanced, it's important to also value logic and common sense. Logic is the power of knowing when A+B=C. Following linear reasoning is a valuable skill to call on at the proper times. However, always weigh this along with the guidance that your inner voice offers.

Consider a decision you are currently facing. Then journal about it. In a column labeled "Logic" write down the rational solutions to clarify the options. Then make a separate column labeled "Intuition." Spend some time tuning in to what feels right about the choice. Be aware of any images, knowings, "ah-has!" or body signals that you receive. Also write these down. Then review both columns to see how each type of guidance can inform your choices. If both are in sync, great. However, if a solution seems logically correct but your intuition is saying, "Slow down" or "Something isn't right," pay attention to that too. Intuitive input can add beneficial nuances to how your resolve your dilemma.

### SET YOUR INTENTION
I will consult all forms of my inner wisdom — my logic and intuition — when making choices. I will explore how they can work together to improve my life.

# A Love Letter to Yourself

Set aside some time today to write a love letter to yourself. You can do this in your journal or on special letterhead. Begin with "Dear ____" and fill in your name. Then share all the qualities you appreciate about yourself and your sensitivities. For instance, you could write: "I love my eyes. I love that I am available to connect with people. I am a good friend and devoted partner. I take time for self-care. I want to learn and grow. I have a meditation practice." As you review all the aspects of yourself that you love, also acknowledge the challenges you have faced in your life and how you have overcome them. For instance, "I persevered and found a great job after a long search" or "Even though I was afraid of rejection, I expressed my empathic needs and my mate understood."

This exercise has nothing to do with reaching "perfection" but rather with embracing the totality of who you are. Showering yourself with self-love is a balm for weariness that will reboot your system with mercy and understanding.

**SET YOUR INTENTION**
I will put care and tenderness into a love letter to myself.
I will banish any negative voices that intrude. I will focus
only on an unconditional understanding of my journey.

# I'm Sorry You Were Hurt

You may have been hurt by others' callousness or insensitivity. Perhaps your parents didn't support your empathic nature or talents. They might have discouraged you from pursuing an artistic career and pushed you toward law school instead. Or perhaps your heart was broken by romantic partners who caused you much pain. Maybe friends disappointed you or treated you disrespectfully.

On behalf of everyone who has ever hurt you (especially if they were incapable of making amends themselves), I apologize. I am sorry you were hurt. I am sorry that people did not understand you in a heartfelt way. I am sorry that your feelings were disregarded. I am sorry you were shamed. Please accept my apology and know that you are a sensitive, loving person. I admire you. I honor you. I respect you.

**SET YOUR INTENTION**
I am willing to heal, to grow, and to release
the hurts of the past. I want to be empowered.
I will let my empathic gifts flourish.

# Trusting Again

A Yiddish saying that moves me is: "The most open heart is a broken heart." Still, it can be hard to trust again when you've felt betrayed or rejected. Particularly after romantic heartbreaks, I've seen some of my patients just shut down. For them, it felt too painful to be vulnerable with a new person. They ask, "Why should I open up if I will be hurt again?"

Empaths, especially, feel such penetrating sorrow from break-ups and loss. I know how painful this is and how long it takes to grieve. But I also know that I want to be strong enough to fight for love and stay open to it. True, you may get hurt again and be disappointed. Such is the nature of life. But you also may love again and flourish.

Be discerning with whom you trust. Go slowly in relationships to see if someone is kind, responsible, caring, and consistent. There is no rush. Let them earn your trust. But while you keep observing, stay receptive. Be daring. Give love another chance. With your self-care and grounding tools in place, you are in the best position to stay in your power so that your relationships thrive.

---

**SET YOUR INTENTION**
I won't allow my heart to shut down permanently.
When I'm ready, I will be open to trusting
again with the right person or situation.

# Observe Someone's Behavior, Not Just Their Words

Pay attention to how a person treats others when you're deciding if they will make a trustworthy, loving friend or mate. People may say all kinds of impressive things about themselves such as how spiritually evolved they are, but the way they behave with a food server, their coworkers, children, or the disabled is a true indicator of the way they will ultimately act toward you.

Watch for how considerate someone is when they think no one is watching, or if they have nothing to gain from their kindness. Do they wait patiently for an older woman pushing a walker as she slowly navigates a crosswalk? Do they hold the elevator for someone rushing to get in? Do they support the health of our planet? These are all telling signs of who a person really is.

---

**SET YOUR INTENTION**
I will see the whole person and not idealize anyone.
I will notice if someone's actions back up their words.

# Find an Empath Friend

You might be so accustomed to functioning on your own and feeling misunderstood that it may be hard to reach out. But doing so is a brave step in finding like-minded people.

Emotional support lets you feel at ease and grow without fear of being criticized. A good place to start is finding one empath friend to whom you can talk. Then you won't feel alone. This person can be on your wavelength without your needing to justify your sensitivities.

How do you find a friend? Look for other sensitive people in your circle and at work. Then, perhaps, bring up the topic by asking whether they've read anything about introverts or empaths. At parties, you can easily spot empaths. They are often by themselves in a corner or talking to one person. Even if it feels awkward, go over and say, "Hi."

I also encourage you to connect with empath support groups near you or online, such as the one I offer on Facebook called Dr. Orloff's Empath Support Community. Empath friends are invaluable. Communicate frequently to benefit from the strength of mutual support.

**SET YOUR INTENTION**
I will appreciate my empath friends
and stay open to finding new ones even
if reaching out feels awkward to me.

# Is It Hard to Ask for Help?

Are you afraid that you will burden others if you ask for help? Are you more comfortable with giving than receiving? It's a rewarding practice to balance these two abilities.

Growing up, many of us felt unsafe when we requested assistance. Why? Perhaps you didn't want to add to your parents' distress, or you believed your needs were unimportant. But now, experiment with moving beyond your comfort level and allow loving people to give to you. Let a neighbor pick up some fruit for you at the market. Ask your son to water the roses. Request emotional support from your partner when you're sad. Receiving also means taking in the energy of nature and Spirit. It will be a joy for you once you get used to it.

Finding your voice to ask for support is equivalent to finding your power. Otherwise you may become exhausted, anxious, or feel like a doormat when your basic needs remain unmet.

**SET YOUR INTENTION**
I will practice reaching out for help, even if I am
reluctant to do so. I will allow myself to receive.
I want my relationships to be balanced and whole.

# Pause When Agitated

When you become rattled or overwhelmed, you may lose your center and overreact or blurt out hurtful words that you will later regret. Your neurological system is highly responsive. Other people's anger or frustration can feel like an unwanted, disturbing intrusion that agitates and drains you.

In tense situations, and particularly if you're feeling anxious, it's important to pause. To offset the adrenaline rush of agitation, keep your center by taking a time-out. This means refraining from calling, talking, or sending emails and texts until you have calmed down. You may need to say in a neutral tone, "Let me think about this. I'll get back to you." Or excuse yourself and go to a different location such as your office or another room. Decreasing stimulation will recenter you too. Dim the lights, listen to soothing music, or meditate. When you put space around the conflict, it stops you from absorbing other people's distress. It also allows you to regroup and be your best self if you choose to respond.

**SET YOUR INTENTION**
I will count to ten when I am agitated. I will not
impulsively do or say anything that I might regret.

# I Will Not Lose Myself in a Relationship

Do you get so involved with your partner's problems or life that you start neglecting your own? Do you defer to their needs? Are you becoming distant with friends because you are devoting so much time to this relationship?

These are common challenges for empaths in love. You want to be caring, but you may lose your independence and sense of balance. You want a cherished companion and romantic partner, but you give away too much of yourself. This can wear at you, and, at some point, you may end up feeling trapped, restless, or suffocated.

Stay aware of meeting your own needs as well as giving to your partner. Journal about how you can balance friend time, me time, work, and quality time with your mate. Though this takes ongoing mindfulness and good communication between you both, the results are gratifying. When your mutual needs are met, you can be in a loving relationship and be your empowered self too.

**SET YOUR INTENTION**
I will maintain my identity and power in a
relationship. If I notice that I'm losing myself,
I will regroup to find my center and clarity.

# Fear of Abandonment

If you came from a family that didn't "see" you, or if you experienced neglect, abuse, or early loss or had narcissistic parents, you could have grown up feeling abandoned. This painful fear can run deep and affect your adult relationships. So much so that you might remain with an abusive partner or friend for far too long, just to avoid reactivating that feeling.

Ask yourself honestly, "Do I have a fear of abandonment? If so, what situations trigger it?" Ask yourself, "How does this fear manifest in my life?" For instance, does it arise when you think about being single again or leaving your job or setting a boundary with your family? Do you react with over-the-top anger to anything that resembles abandonment such as a boyfriend forgetting to call or a friend canceling plans at the last minute?

The next step is to turn the fear around. Consider: "What would my life be like without it?" Picture the serenity and ease in relationships that you will experience. You can also ask Spirit to lift the fear. Even if you can't do it yourself, Spirit can help you. At those moments of panic or even terror, when psychological insights are insufficient to console you, joining forces with Spirit gives you the strength and courage to shift your perception.

---

**SET YOUR INTENTION**
I will be aware of my fear of abandonment and slowly but surely begin to heal it. If this fear gets triggered, I will immediately calm myself and reach out for support rather than panicking.

# I Am Not Alone

At those moments when you feel afraid, lonely, or without the support you need, repeat this affirmation to regain your confidence:

I am not alone.
I am being watched over.
A loving force surrounds me.
When my heart is in pain,
I will reach out to Spirit.
When my fears overcome me,
I will open to the divine forces of universal compassion.
I am held in the arms of love.
All is well.

**SET YOUR INTENTION**
I can handle any emotion. I am larger than
my fear. I am connected to an ever-present
spiritual force of love that protects me.

# Morning Meditation

It is a centering practice to begin the day with a short morning meditation. Upon awakening, I head straight to my sacred space and meditate for about five minutes. This helps me gently transition from the sleep state to my adventures in the material world. I sit quietly, breathing slowing, focusing on my heart. I look at my statue of Quan Yin, the goddess of compassion, and ask for her blessing. I thank Spirit for the gift of life and for the opportunity to learn and grow another day.

For the next week, experiment with meditating each morning. It can be short—five to ten minutes is sufficient. This is your chance to start the day from your heart, connected to Spirit rather than darting out of bed obsessing about your to-do list and its accompanying anxieties. Your scheduled tasks will come later, following the meditation. This allows you to approach the day from a truly grounded place.

**SET YOUR INTENTION**
Today, I will meditate immediately after I awaken.
I will begin the day with optimism and serenity.
I will observe how this increases my
well-being throughout the day.

# Walking Through Fear

Courage or fear is a choice. Being on a spiritual path and seeking to learn and become more awake every day doesn't mean that you are immune to fear. But whether to respond to this emotion with courage or dread is a choice we can all make. Many times in my life I have felt afraid, but I have also summoned the faith within to move forward anyway. Freedom comes from making brave choices. Deciding to be strong and walk through the fear is an exercise in courage. All that's necessary is that you draw on a positive force of good that is larger than fear to regroup when this primal emotion shrinks your emotional IQ and intuition.

To deactivate fear, take a few deep breaths and calm yourself. Close your eyes and repeat this mantra: "I am not just my fear. I am larger." Then feel your soul expand and your strength returning. The situation might be intimidating, but you are more confident about conquering it to achieve your goal.

There is an old Cherokee teaching about two wolves that are always battling within you. One is mean-spirited. The other is benevolent and good. Which one will win? The one you feed. Remember: fear only becomes more powerful when you fuel it.

---

**SET YOUR INTENTION**
Though my fears may be strong, I will not feed them.
Fear is a part of life that I will gain mastery over.
I won't allow it to stop me from achieving my dreams.

# Downtime

Plan some time off today. Focus on anything but constant work and obligations. Take a breath. Take a swim. Take a walk. Push the pause button. Let your mind roam free. Imagine open space with nothing to fill it. No worries. No concerns. You are light and carefree. You have time to yourself! No one to talk to. No decisions to make. Nothing to do but relax. Breathe deeply during your break. Feel the tension releasing from your shoulders and back. Wiggle your toes. Reach your arms up into the air. Stretch. Release stress and smile. Feel your energy and optimism returning.

---

**SET YOUR INTENTION**
I will rejuvenate myself by taking some downtime,
no matter what I have planned. When I can
do this regularly, it relieves pressure so I won't
have to live in a pressure cooker of stress.

# Timelessness

Our material reality is measured by space and time. Every day, practicing fierce time management helps you guard your sensitivities, improves the quality of your life, and defines the breathing room you need.

It's also inspiring to remember that other realms of awareness exist that have nothing to do with minutes, hours, or years. They are timeless, free-and-easy places where your intuition and spirit can roam. You get there through meditation, immersing yourself in nature or a creative project, floating into a trance during a relaxing bath, or getting lost in daydreaming. Like artists who are in a flow state, you are so involved in what you're doing that you aren't concentrating on time at all. Surrendering to the moment is a timeless experience.

**SET YOUR INTENTION**
I will lose track of time for a while. I will
let my imagination travel to timeless places
that ignite my creativity. I will be free.

# Awakening

Awakening is a process of seeing more clearly from your heart so that you can experience greater inner peace. Today, pay special attention to your intuition to perceive the world from your most enlightened, tuned in, and empathic self. A sense of awakening may come in flashes: a moment of clarity or a sudden sense of unconditional love, expansion, or heavenly bliss. You may also feel a oneness with all humankind rather than perceiving division or separation. Appreciate these glimpses and the longer periods of insight too. Practice the following affirmation to acknowledge the sacred unfolding of your awakening.

I am awake.
I am aware.
My heart is open.
I feel the light
and compassion
of the universe.
I will open myself to bliss.
I will allow myself to be happy.
I can see.
I can know.
I can love.

---

**SET YOUR INTENTION**
Today, I will witness the light in myself and in all
beings everywhere. I am grateful to be awakening
my consciousness to oneness and love.

# Spiritual Bypassing

Spiritual bypassing occurs when one uses spiritual ideas and practices to avoid facing unresolved emotional issues or the necessary challenges of intimacy. It's a defensive maneuver to cover up trauma or conflict that may feel too painful to face. But the truth is, you can't heal from grief without grieving. You can't release anger without expressing why you are mad. You can't keep your fears inside and expect to be at peace.

Some of my patients don't even realize they are engaging in spiritual bypassing until I gently point it out. As you would when healing any defense mechanism, approach this one with understanding. No one is happy all the time. We all have a shadow side. When you avoid it, you can become numb and seem saccharine or inauthentic.

Honestly pinpoint any issues that you may be spiritually bypassing. Is it anger at your spouse or parents? Fear of abandonment or feelings of inferiority? Then slowly and compassionately write about your difficult feelings that are masked beneath your smile or a false persona that conveys, "Everything is fine and I am so spiritual." We humans are multifaceted with both light and dark emotional sides. Exploring these nuances will make you more interesting, whole, and capable of greater intimacy.

---

**SET YOUR INTENTION**
Being on a spiritual path means staying aware of
both my positive and more difficult feelings. I will
be mindful of not spiritually bypassing any emotions
that I need to heal. I will be brave and address them.

# A Hidden Source of Strength

Just when you feel too tired to take care of one more problem.

Or too sad to have hope.

Or too overwhelmed to love.

Or are letting fear get the best of you.

Stop trying to *do* anything and just let go. Give yourself permission to breathe, to cry, to sleep, to hide under the covers, or to be alone. Curl up in the comforting cave deep within your being where no one can find you until you are ready.

In this state of utter release, a spark will reignite. By relaxing and not trying to be so efficient or perfect, you can return to yourself. Your strength will start building. As Buddha says, "There is no external refuge." Finding the refuge in your soul is your hidden source of strength. This has been within you all along and is your safe place of retreat and renewal.

---

**SET YOUR INTENTION**
My safe haven is within me. I will go
there to tap my inner well of strength
and compassion and to restore my spirit.

# Dopamine

Dopamine is a neurotransmitter associated with pleasure. Research has shown that introverts need less of it to feel happy, so they don't require the dopamine rush that extroverts obtain from attending large, lively events. This helps to explain why introverted empaths are often happiest alone or at small gatherings—compared to extroverts who thrive on the sense of well-being generated by the dopamine rush from say, going to a Rolling Stones concert or busy, crowded restaurants. Though some empaths are extroverts who enjoy socializing, afterward, they too need to replenish themselves with solitude and quiet activities to decrease their stimulation level.

Today, boost your dopamine. Create some alone time or meet a friend for a walk in the woods if that gives you pleasure. Or socialize on a larger scale if that meets your dopamine needs. Pleasure comes in different ways that you can regulate once you know what makes you the happiest and most comfortable.

---

**SET YOUR INTENTION**
I will be aware of what types of dopamine-
boosting activities I require. I will seek the
level of socializing that feels pleasurable rather
than deferring to other people's needs.

# Empathy: The Great Healer

Your empathy is a huge asset. It allows you to feel what is going on in other people so you can have more compassion for them. You can go from "me" to "we" because it allows you to see that we all come from the same human family and have so much in common. Our life and the world can undergo healing when we all show empathy for each other, even if values or cultures differ.

Today, experiment with having empathy for everyone you meet—not just the people you like or know well. Even if someone does something to annoy you, such as cutting in front of you in the grocery store line, try to sense the stress or panic that was driving them. Your understanding doesn't excuse this person's actions—certainly they were insensitive and rude—but try to go deeper. This is a compassionate exercise to learn about human nature and the emotional forces that compel us.

**SET YOUR INTENTION**
I will see everyone through the eyes
of empathy. Even if I don't like someone,
I will try to understand their motivations.

# Emotional Honesty

As a sensitive person, you may feel so many emotions each day it is hard to keep track of them. Or you might try to ignore or squash your feelings if you're afraid that no one will understand. You may be concerned that you're "too intense" for your spouse or friends, so you'd better tone down your reactions. Since that was my fear for many years, I wasn't always my authentic self in intimate relationships.

Emotional honesty means that you can accept your true feelings and respect them. Start with yourself. Ask, "What were five dominant feelings I experienced today? Joy, fear, happiness, anxiety, or even panic?" Whatever came up, it is okay. There is no shame in feeling intensely. You have an open heart. You are free-flowing and not as guarded as other people.

Acknowledge your emotions rather than shutting them down. Cry, laugh, pound a pillow. If your partner or friends are able to hold a loving space for you, communicate your feelings to them. Let emotional expression be an integral part of your life.

---

**SET YOUR INTENTION**
I accept that I feel things intensely. I will
be honest with myself about my emotions
and share them with supportive others.

# Sunshine

In many ancient healing traditions, the sun represented the life force, strength, and power. It was worshipped as a spiritual entity, even as a god in Egypt. As part of my Taoist practice, I put my meditation altar on the eastern wall of a room to tap the energy of the rising sun, a new beginning each morning as the daylight and our inner illumination increases.

All of nature is solar powered, including our bodies. There is no food without the sun. It is also a primary source of Vitamin D, which is called the "sunshine vitamin." Your body uses this natural form more efficiently than the kind it gets from fortified food or supplements. As little as five to fifteen minutes of exposure daily can meet your requirements and avoid the potential health hazards of getting too much sun. Solar power also provides a clean source of energy that helps further the health of our bodies, air quality, the climate, and our planet.

On this summer's day, give special thanks for our closest star—the energy and light it offers, the way it sustains human and planetary existence. Watch the glory of the dawn or dusk. Appreciate the life-giving aspects of sunlight.

---

**SET YOUR INTENTION**
I am grateful for the sun's gifts. I will be aware
of how its healing powers influence my mind,
body, and spirit as well as the Earth.

# The Joy of Being a Grown-Up

The pleasures of being a grown-up are many. When you've lived a while, you become more discerning and savvy about your relationships, work, and other choices. You've accumulated wisdom along the way that makes navigating the world as an empath much easier. You grow into your gifts and become more comfortable with them and yourself. You better know what your needs are and how to express them. You can still nurture your playful inner child, but you don't allow "his or her majesty, the baby" inside of you to wreak havoc in your life or relationships.

Growing up doesn't have to be boring, overbearing, or just filled with obligation and no play. Nor is it necessary to feel hemmed in or trapped in a lifestyle that doesn't suit you. Growing up means having choices about who you are that aren't possible for the perpetual Peter Pan "I'll-never-grow-up" type of adults. You are ever-emerging, ever-changing, and increasingly capable of more empathy and compassion.

### SET YOUR INTENTION
I will appreciate my areas of wisdom and maturity.
I will thank the years for the self-knowledge, growth
opportunities, and the love that they have offered me.

# Feeling Free

What does feeling free mean to you? Is it being your authentic self? Ignoring phone calls and emails for a while? Having enough money to be comfortable? Immersing yourself in art? Traveling to a sacred site? Hiking in the mountains? How about experiencing the peace of a long meditation? Perhaps you love the freedom of taking a bath without anyone bothering you? Follow your bliss to become your best self.

Feeling free can be a part of your daily mind-set during summer and throughout the year. It's not something you just experience once in a while. Freeing your mind from the prison of fear is paramount to expanding your lightness of being. As I've emphasized before, use your breath to expand your awareness into your larger self:

> *Breathe in a feeling of calm.*
> *Breathe out fear, worry, and any notions of scarcity.*
> *Breathe in tranquility.*
> *Breathe out old judgments about yourself.*
> *Breathe in a sense of spaciousness and that anything is possible.*
> *Breathe out any feelings of constriction or limitation.*

Each day, practice breathing in this way for a few minutes to catalyze your sense of inner freedom.

---

**SET YOUR INTENTION**
I will focus on feeling free and participating
in activities that support my happiness.
I will inhabit my largest, most expansive self.

# Shifting Gears

What's exciting and maybe a bit unsettling about life is that everything is constantly changing: our lives, our bodies, our emotions, the seasons. So in these final weeks of summer, we enter a transition phase. For many, the coming of autumn signals back to work and school as well as a revving up of one's pace and busyness. You shift gears from a more open-ended focus of light-filled summer days to concentrating on work, achievements, and aspirations.

Meditate on the gifts that summer gave you and the promise of fall. Be mindful of the ongoing movement of time and the Earth's shifting mood and colors. The days are beginning to grow shorter as the Earth's axis increasingly tips farther away from the sun. Evaluate your growth so far this year and welcome changes that are yet to come. Hold great hope for the next chapter of your empath journey.

---

**SET YOUR INTENTION**
I accept that the only constant in life is change. I will be mindful of transitional times of the year and shift gears from one season to another with awareness and ease.

# The Witness State

Finding neutrality helps you stay centered during conflicts. It can rewire the circuitry in your brain so you approach life more calmly. Instead of being stuck in a difficult emotion or situation, gain some distance by taking a few steps back and witnessing yourself. For instance, when your mother criticizes you or your partner disappoints you, visualize yourself observing the situation rather than being consumed by the emotions you experience. From this wider perspective, you are better able to detach from fear, anxiety, anger, or any specific issue that arises.

When you notice yourself becoming stressed or overwhelmed, tell yourself, "I am not this emotion. I can lovingly witness my feelings and state of overwhelm as an observer." Realizing that no emotion defines you gives you the freedom to shift your mind-set to connect with your inner wisdom.

**SET YOUR INTENTION**
I have a choice about how I deal with emotions.
When I am frustrated or upset, I will witness my feelings
so that I don't simply react when my buttons get pushed.

# It's None of My Business

Many of my empathic patients sacrifice too much of their vital energy trying to solve the problems of others or take away their pain. So to maximize your energy, keep your eyes on yourself rather than getting overly involved in other people's business. Even though you have a big heart and empathize with the intense emotional trials that people go through, your own self-care involves making wise choices about where to channel your energy. So be kind to yourself and use your reserves well.

I smile at the saying, "There are three kinds of business: my business, your business, and none of my business." (And also monkey business!) Keep discovering the differences among these. If you aren't sure, it's wise to do nothing until you are clearer about the right action. Also, realize that everyone has their own path and a higher power to guide them. Simply do your best and let Spirit take over.

**SET YOUR INTENTION**
I will not be a busybody who meddles where I don't belong. I will keep focusing on myself, help if it's appropriate, and stop minding other people's business.

# Delegating

Do you feel that if you don't do something yourself it won't be done correctly? Are you afraid to ask others for help or to give up control? Are you exhausted from constantly tackling too much?

All good leaders know the importance of delegating. It frees you up from micromanaging or being overly responsible and allows others to shine. To avoid burnout, think about how you can delegate your tasks more effectively. If this is new for you, start with smaller duties to lessen your anxiety about turning over control. Take your vehicle to a car wash instead of cleaning it yourself. Ask your partner to load the dishwasher. If you can, hire someone to clean your home. Seek the help of a professional organizer. Let a friend drive instead of always picking them up.

Once you get used to this, approach larger issues. Let coworkers do their part of a project instead of you picking up the slack. Ask friends for support if you are going through a health challenge. Even if they approach tasks differently or more slowly than you, focus on being grateful for their help.

Delegating is a liberating way of lightening your load and relieving a burdensome sense of responsibility for the world's inefficiencies and woes.

---

**SET YOUR INTENTION**
To create a more balanced life, I will
practice delegating some responsibility
to others. I will allow people to assist me.

# Making Mistakes

We all make mistakes. None of us is perfect. Sometimes people try their best, but still, the situation turns out poorly. Others may not put their all into a project, and an error occurs.

When dealing with others' slipups, evaluate each situation individually to determine the right response. My Taoist teacher says that when people make mistakes, lift them up rather than berating them. Getting angry with someone or putting them down will most likely cause them to feel shamed and unmotivated to please you. If you are truly seeking a remedy, be kind and work with the person so they give you what you need. Be solution oriented. Don't hold a grudge. It tells you a lot about someone's character when they take responsibility for a blunder and want to correct it. However, if they just give excuses, become hostile and defensive, or slough off the problem, perhaps you will need to lower your expectations or simply refrain from engaging with them in the future.

If you make a misstep, remedy it with actions and amends but always be compassionate with yourself. In a more cosmic sense, how you treat yourself is more important than the error you made. If you view mistakes as spiritual lessons, they can offer you opportunities to grow more generous in spirit and to learn compassion.

---

**SET YOUR INTENTION**
I will have mercy on myself if I make a mistake
and give others a chance to remedy their own errors.

# Healthy Communication

Successful communication is based on mutual respect. Regularly express appreciation and admiration for others, particularly loved ones. Look for what they do right instead of what they do wrong. Seeing what's positive in someone helps bring out the best in them. If you always point out their flaws or how they can improve, it just makes them feel diminished. Treating people with gratitude for who they are and what they add to your life paves the way for raising more difficult issues.

When addressing a conflict, speak in "I" statements with a solution attached. For instance, with a spouse or friend say, "I feel hurt when you get too busy and ignore me. Let's plan some quality time together." Compare that to saying in an accusatory tone, "You are so inconsiderate for treating me this way." Your inner child may truly feel neglected. But if you communicate in a more empowered, solution-oriented way, you will have a better chance of being heard and getting your needs met.

---

**SET YOUR INTENTION**
I will show others appreciation and speak in "I"
statements when expressing my feelings and
needs. I will not blame or shame anyone.

# Pick Your Battles

As a sensitive person, you may react strongly to behavior that upsets you. Letting something pass can be difficult because the uneasy feelings remain in your body. However, the wisdom of self-care includes consciously prioritizing which situations warrant asserting yourself and which don't.

Choose your battles carefully. Ask yourself, "Is it worth getting into this with my spouse or coworker? What will I gain or lose?" In intimate relationships, potentially triggering issues can arise daily. Ask yourself, "Which is the most important to address? Where will I make the greatest headway?" You might find it useful to journal about the conflict. Also, you'll communicate more effectively by limiting yourself to one problem at a time and not piling on other complaints in the same interaction. Start with a lesser issue and work up to larger ones at a later date. Avoid overwhelming others with a laundry list of needs and assert yourself firmly but with kindness.

**SET YOUR INTENTION**
I will pick my battles and realize that I can't
solve everything at once. I will not overwhelm
people with too much information or by raising
multiple issues in the same conversation.

# Fulfilling Work

You deserve to have work that gratifies you. Since you may spend eight hours a day or more at a job, it can greatly affect your attitude and energy. As a sensitive person, you may be less guarded against stress than others, so it's more difficult to recover if your occupation exhausts you.

You will thrive in the right environment that is in sync with your needs. Empaths often enjoy working in a home office rather than a corporate setting. You may do well in the creative arts — writing, acting, film, or design. Also, once you learn protection techniques, you can flourish in the helping professions such as psychology, nursing, medicine, or teaching.

Today, evaluate your work situation. Journal about the positives and negatives. Think about ways you can improve or reinvent some aspects of your job to enhance your creativity. Or perhaps imagine a job that might be more satisfying. Though medical insurance and retirement packages are important considerations, it is also unhealthy to stay trapped in a job that you dislike. If you decide to stay, you have control over your attitude so you can create the most positive environment possible. But if you are considering leaving, start brainstorming about the steps necessary to reach that goal.

---

**SET YOUR INTENTION**
I will explore how I can thrive in my current work
situation or consider finding another job that better
suits me. It is never too late to consider a change.

# Healing Workaholism

Do you work excessively or feel anxious when you have time off? Do you define yourself by your job title and does your self-esteem depend on it? If so, you may be a workaholic.

Sensitive people want to do a good job and please their bosses and colleagues. It's admirable to be passionate about your work and give your all, but it is unhealthy to neglect fatigue or tolerate chronic sensory overload.

Just as any addiction can drain your life force and dominate your time, being a workaholic can take a physical and emotional toll. Working compulsively may become an excuse to ignore the rest of your life and your innermost feelings. If you're always focusing on your job, it's hard to have intimate relationships.

The solution is balance. Block out time for recreation and replenishment. Mark specific spots in your schedule. Wise time management can help break the workaholism cycle. When you calm your neurological system regularly, you will feel healthier, happier, and reenergized at the office and elsewhere.

---

**SET YOUR INTENTION**

I am more than my work. I am a whole human being
who is worthy of the happiness of a well-rounded life.

# Set Limits with Coworkers

Do your coworkers share all their problems with you? Do you overpromise or overgive to make them happy? Since empaths are such caring listeners, it's little wonder that your peers often gravitate to you to confess their woes.

Although you may want to be of service, it is essential to your self-care that you set limits with coworkers so you're not drained. Once you can protect yourself, work becomes a safer, more nourishing environment.

Give yourself permission to say no with kindness to coworkers. Your tone and delivery are everything. You can nicely say, "I'm so sorry, I'm swamped. I can't take on any extra work." Or another option is, "I'm happy to be present for you, but I only have a few minutes to listen since I'm on a deadline." In both cases you are communicating healthy boundaries. You don't have to make excuses or get into long explanations. Simply set the limit, send the person some love, and continue focusing on your own tasks.

**SET YOUR INTENTION**
I have the right to set kind but firm limits with
coworkers. I will practice this necessary skill when
they ask something of me that I am unable to give.

# Protective Bubbles

Whenever you're feeling overloaded or drained or are absorbing stress and negative emotions from others, practice this visualization at work or in any other distressing situation.

*Sit quietly and take a few long, deep breaths. Relax your body and mind. Then picture yourself sitting in the safety of a clear, round or oval protective bubble that extends inches or a foot above your skin. You can see outside, and there's plenty of room. This bubble deflects any toxic or unpleasant emotions or sensations but allows positive energy to enter. Use this bubble as much as you like. Once you are in a healthier environment or don't need it anymore, simply request that it disappear. You can create a new one whenever the need arises. Your protective bubble can be your safe place if external circumstances are overwhelming.*

**SET YOUR INTENTION**
When I want to protect myself, I will visualize
a protective bubble around me to keep out
stress or others' unwanted emotions.

# Spirituality and Money

Money is neither inherently spiritual nor unspiritual. How you use it makes all the difference.

Financial security can create comfort and offer opportunities for a good education. It allows you to purchase top quality health care and wholesome food. Knowing that you have a financial buffer in the bank lessens the fear of being unable to pay the bills each month. Financial security also provides resources so you can travel to visit loved ones if they are far away.

In addition, money is a vehicle to help others and create good in the world. However, when hoarded or used to stoke greed or to harm others and the planet, monetary wealth creates destruction and negativity.

So your attitude toward money defines the effect it has. You deserve the advantages that abundance offers. If your spirituality means coming from your heart with generosity, apply this to money. Using it well creates good karma and supports collective abundance. If you are generous with what you have, it is a beautiful form of giving. But don't ever let affluence (or lack of it) define your ultimate "success" as a person. Appreciate money's downside, including greed, as well as all its advantages. It can be an expression of your spiritual values if you allow it to be.

---

**SET YOUR INTENTION**
I am worthy of financial abundance.
I will always use money for good and as
an expression of heart-based values.

# Prosperity and Charity

What goes around comes around. Generosity is a way to spread prosperity. Tithing a portion of your earnings (whatever you can afford) to charities and worthy causes channels money in a positive way.

You want to keep money flowing. Unfortunately, some wealthy people are miserly and donate little to others. This clogs up the flow in their lives. Such stinginess may stem from fear of scarcity, low self-esteem, greed, or feeling a lack of power no matter what financial resources they have. These individuals simply want to accumulate "more" and don't realize that the emotional hole inside will never be filled by wealth or the things it buys.

Generosity means giving from your heart. It creates joy, lets you help those less fortunate, and contributes to the health of the Earth. Giving feels good. I particularly love anonymous gifts. Sometimes I leave a small amount of money — from one to five dollars — in a public place like a bathroom or waiting area. Then people can find it and feel lucky. You may also want to try this. Paying it forward is contagious. You do it and others will do it too.

**SET YOUR INTENTION**
I will donate what I can afford to a worthy cause
or financially give in other ways that appeal to me.
I will enjoy the positive energy that this act generates.

# Harvesting Success

When success grows from within, your outer achievements can also enhance your happiness. However, if you feel bad about yourself, no amount of accomplishment in your career or anywhere else will ultimately fulfill you. So focus on being a good person and living in such a way that you like yourself. This doesn't mean being perfect—we are all works in progress. But if you are on a self-healing path and value integrity in your endeavors, you're headed in a positive direction. Gradually liberating yourself from fear makes succeeding in the world even more gratifying.

As we approach the time of the harvest, reflect on your internal and external triumphs this year. Perhaps you've become more creative in your job or expanded your company or found a work environment that better supports your empathic needs. Or perhaps you've learned to have more compassion for yourself in daily life. Be grateful for your progress and open your arms and heart to continuing abundance.

**SET YOUR INTENTION**
I will acknowledge the rewards of my labors.
I will be thankful for my successes on all levels.

# Downsizing

Some sensitive people choose to be downwardly mobile instead of spending decades climbing the competitive, demanding ladder of "success." They don't need mansions, fancy cars, or exotic vacations with the debt these extravagances can entail. Instead, they choose smaller living spaces, aim for fewer expenses, and live simply on a lower income.

A less lavish lifestyle may be a choice to consider. You can do this at any age or at any time. There's even a contemporary movement among some people toward a more nomadic way of life. They have home offices in their RVs so they are free to move to different locations.

You don't have to conform to some artificial cultural norm of a stressful, expensive standard of living. Empaths are pioneers of new ways of being that support their sensitivities. Free yourself of the pressure of societal expectations. Forge your own path and explore lifestyles that best suit your needs.

**SET YOUR INTENTION**
I don't have to get caught in the hamster
wheel of striving for success. I can have
a simpler, more satisfying lifestyle.

# Contact Highs

Some people are so positive it's contagious. Their energy can actually transfer to you. You can learn from their outlook, behavior, and the good vibes they emanate. Whenever I want to develop or deepen a skill such as setting healthy boundaries, I will spend time with people who excel at this. They become models for me. I observe them. I feel them. I imprint on their behavior and how they hold their energy, so I can do it too.

Find at least one person who embodies a quality you admire such as creativity or passion. Let them spark your own enthusiasm. You can also get a contact high by visiting an uplifting location or sacred site such as Stonehenge in England or the healing waters of Lourdes in France. The positive energy in these places will rub off on you. Take it in. One of my patients goes to an observatory to watch the stars. Another walks to a Chumash ritual site in the canyons to increase her connection to the earth. Others meditate at the ocean or in a cathedral to gain closer contact to their spirituality. Choose a location that feeds your soul and soak up all the good energy there.

---

**SET YOUR INTENTION**
I will seek out positive people and places. I will enjoy
the contact high I receive from their inspirational vibes.

# The Proper Attitude to Have When Climbing a Steep Hill

When life is an uphill climb, the best way to ascend gracefully and with the least pain is to not overthink the problem. If your mind is obsessing on an issue and fueling the flames of fear, your journey will be more difficult. My Taoist teacher says that climbing a mountain will become much harder if you keep thinking about tomorrow.

In your life, hills will inevitably appear that you must learn to climb. But your attitude can lessen your suffering. Say to yourself, "I know about hills. I've climbed them before. I will not make the journey worse by dwelling on the hardships." Instead, keep breathing slowly. Stay focused on where you are, not on the far-away mountaintop. Look for the delicate, little flowers growing among the rocks and boulders you are navigating. Sing a song you love aloud or inwardly. Mountain goats make slow but sure progress on their climb to the top. Learn from their scrappiness, poise, and patience on your path up a steep hill.

**SET YOUR INTENTION**
I will approach adversity with lightness, not worry. I will not aggravate a stressful situation by dwelling on my fears of the future.

# Calming Anxiety

The secret to soothing anxiety is to prevent it from gathering momentum. As soon as this emotion hits, use conscious breathing. Take a few deep, slow breaths to expel tension so it doesn't settle in your body. Then practice positive self-talk. Tell yourself, "This is a transient situation. I will find the best way of handling it. Everything will be okay." Do not let panicked inner voices get in the way of consoling yourself with kindness.

Then take a few steps back from the feelings. When you notice yourself becoming anxious, put your hand on your heart center and tell yourself, "I will center myself and lovingly detach from my state of overwhelm. This too shall pass." Refocusing on your heart will relax you and bring a helpful perspective.

---

**SET YOUR INTENTION**
I have power over my anxious thoughts and feelings.
I will use my breath and thoughts to quiet my mind.

# Make Wise Choices

The most informed decisions are based on multiple sources of wisdom, including intuition and logic. Sometimes, you can request expert advice or logically analyze the pros and cons of a situation. This gives you a good sense of the positives and negatives to make the proper choice.

In other cases, though, logic is insufficient. You've reviewed the same arguments many times, and still a decision doesn't resonate. Now, you must listen to your inner voice. It will reveal a deeper truth about where you stand. Does a job option feel right? Is a relationship a good match? Does a health treatment feel like the best intervention for your body? Instead of overthinking, notice what intuitive flashes arise. This may be a wave of goose bumps, a body knowing, or a moment of clarity. The answers will arrive when you are humble, patient, and sincere. Use the following affirmation as much as you like to gain more confidence in your choices.

I am a strong, powerful person.
I will honor my intuition.
I will listen to logic.
I will blend many sources of wisdom
to make the right choices
for my mind, body, and soul.

**SET YOUR INTENTION**
I will make wise decisions that intuitively
feel right. I will not force a choice
because I am anxious or impatient.

# Release Regrets

Life offers a series of teachings. Looking back, you may regret how you or another behaved or a path not taken. Breakups, lay-offs, betrayals, and missed opportunities may be difficult for our tender dispositions. Still, do not use them as excuses to berate yourself, lose faith in love, or withdraw from the world.

In your journal, identify what regrets you may have. Was it not pursuing your first love? Turning down a dream job because you lacked self-confidence? Failing to assert boundaries with others because you feared rejection? Identifying regrets can lend added insight into how you would approach similar issues differently today.

Regrets are natural, but they are draining if you cling to them. Be merciful with yourself and others. Forgive your own or another's shortcomings. Make amends whenever possible. See missed opportunities as reasons to grow and accept the gifts that are offered to you now. You are not a victim. Rather, you are a beautiful soul developing and learning along the way.

**SET YOUR INTENTION**
I will not hold on to regrets. I will learn
from them to create more fulfilling
opportunities and relationships now.

# Be the Mountain: A Time for Inaction

Warriors wait for the right time to act rather than rushing into battle. They do not force an outcome. The I Ching, the Chinese Book of Changes, describes a hexagram named Keeping Still, Mountain, which teaches the wisdom of nonaction. During certain phases of your life, the wisest choice is to stop and wait. It is not the moment to move forward, no matter how much you want to pursue a goal. In fact, it would be a waste of time to do so. Instead, be the mountain and put a goal or decision on pause. This is not laziness. It is great wisdom to know when to act and when to be still.

So in the meantime, concentrate your power. See what naturally comes to you. My Taoist teacher says, "Opportunities that present themselves can be more potent than those you seek." However, if there is no activity, find peace with that too. As the cycle shifts and the flow returns, you can resume your quest with renewed freshness and integrity.

### SET YOUR INTENTION
When life is not flowing, I will be the Keeping Still, Mountain. I will have faith in myself and simply wait.

# AUTUMN

## Harvest, Change, and Letting Go

Autumn is a time to harvest the fruits of your work and your life. It's a period of transformation and letting go symbolized by the earth element, a stabilizing force during this season's dramatic shifts.

Autumn offers a special gift from the trees: the splendor of transforming foliage. A light show of blazing red, orange, and golden leaves enchants many locations, a feast for an empath's senses. In the spirit of the leaves, celebrate the progress you have made this year.

Autumn is also a teacher of change. School and work resume, and soon the year begins to wind down. Following the harvest, the growing season ends, and we enter a period of decline. The equinox—when day and night are of equal length—is a perfect time to meditate on balance. As days become colder and darker, leaves stop making chlorophyll, their green color, which triggers them to age and decay.

Empaths can be uncomfortable with aging and the unknown. We feel safe in what's predictable. A part of us may resist change because we fear it. But that's not nature's way. Self-care helps us accept our inner shifts and growth.

Autumn invites you to reflect on your priorities. It's an opportunity for metamorphosis, a chance to liberate yourself from outdated beliefs, resentments, or relationships. Ask yourself, "What are my burdens? How can I release them?" Autumn offers a deeper experience of your own transformation and spirituality.

# The Challenge of Change

As the autumn wind begins to blow and leaves drift from the trees, nature prepares for her metamorphosis. Nature doesn't resist change. It is a dynamic part of her dormancy and rebirth cycles. You, too, are shedding what's extraneous. Then, when spring comes, you will prepare for your own rebirth.

During the autumn equinox, when day and night are of equal length, nature lets you experience harmony. On the evening of the equinox, plan to meditate on balancing your mind, body, and soul. In quiet moments, thank each part of yourself for making you the interesting, sensitive person you are. Feel your logical and intuitive selves coming together in a balanced way. You can turn to each form of wisdom whenever you choose. The experience of equanimity is within you. Meditating on this will center you and help you flow with the upcoming seasons of dormancy and change.

**SET YOUR INTENTION**
I am connected to the cycles of nature and light. I will feel the sublimely perfect alignment of my body with the universal forces.

# Radiant Aging

Aging is not a disease. It is an organic unfolding that we can optimize when we learn to tap into our vital energies and release fears.

How you age is more in your control than you may think. Research has shown that illness doesn't have to be associated with age. If you follow a healthy lifestyle and diet, utilize preventive services, and engage with family and friends in a positive way, you are more likely to remain fit and have fewer medical issues. No matter your age, you can create positive changes in your body.

If you view aging from a spiritual perspective, your outlook shifts. Then you see that there is more to you than the material world or ego. You are consoled by knowing that your soul lives in a realm beyond time and space.

I believe that after we reach fifty-five, we should stop assigning people any ages and simply graduate into the wondrous "realm of discovery." I would love to stop using the word "aging" entirely and substitute "evolving" instead. Though it's difficult to release our society's shaming stereotypes about becoming an elder, as sensitive people on a spiritual path, we can more constructively approach this process.

**SET YOUR INTENTION**
I will not fear aging. I will reject outmoded
stereotypes about getting older and vow to age
and evolve in a radiant, compassionate way.

# Humility

Humility is one of the highest spiritual qualities. It is a form of strength, not of low self-esteem. It is the opposite of narcissism or arrogance. Humility means that you pay homage to your tiny but indispensable place in the universe and know that you are but a speck in the cosmic matrix of love. Through your actions, work, and behavior, you can contribute to that love, which is a noble purpose. Humility and empathy are wedded to each other. Humble people care about others and realize that we are all on the same level. No one is more important than anyone else.

Humility allows you to admit when you are wrong and to be open to other people's needs. It makes you flexible, not rigid. When your ego tries to intrude, notice it, but decline its unevolved (though often tempting) propositions such as the need to be right. Be humble and caring as much as you can. Confucius said, "Humility is the solid foundation of all virtues."

---

**SET YOUR INTENTION**
I will practice humility in my life and contribute
good to the world. I will not be seduced by ego
or greed or put myself above or below anyone.

# Cleansing Tears

Tears are a sign of courage, strength, and authenticity for both men and women. In my medical practice, I've repeatedly witnessed their healing power. They are your body's release from stress, sadness, depression, grief, anxiety, and frustration. You also may cry tears of happiness when a child is born or tears of relief when a difficulty has passed.

I am grateful when I cry. It feels cleansing—a way to purge pent-up emotions so they don't lodge in my body as empathic stress symptoms such as fatigue or pain.

To stay vibrant and let go of stress, I encourage you to cry. Your tears have numerous health benefits. Like the ocean, they are composed of salt water. While they protect your eyes by lubricating them and removing irritants, they also eliminate stress hormones, and they contain antibodies that fight pathogens.

Cry when you feel like it. Whether you've absorbed distress from other people or are working through your own emotions, tears will help you heal more quickly. If they are not forthcoming, invite them in by focusing on something that upsets you. Being aware of your feelings lets you quickly release pain when you cry. In happy situations, allow tears to be a spontaneous expression of your joy.

---

**SET YOUR INTENTION**
I will see tears as an expression of my inner
power and authenticity. I will not hold them
back but will let them flow freely.

# I Am a Spiritual Being

Everything you go through, everyone you meet is destined to teach you something. In the most positive sense, you came here on your own, and you will depart from this plane on your own. In the meantime, during this period called "life," you can build your heartfulness and love. These are qualities that you will take with you on your continuing spiritual journey.

Focus on being a good person, which is often harder than it sounds. This entails being kind and generous to yourself and others. But be careful not to overly identify with the material world or your physical form. Nevertheless, learning from both of them and from all your life experiences enables you to become a good person—a noteworthy spiritual accomplishment. Every moment of every day, let your light shine brighter. Allow your spirituality and love to emerge in stronger, more confident ways.

---

**SET YOUR INTENTION**
I am a spiritual being having a human experience.
I accept my challenges and vow to be a good person.
I will always develop loving-kindness in myself.

# I Am Accountable

Emotional maturity means being humbly accountable for your actions and emotions. In Judaism, Yom Kippur — the Day of Atonement — is observed around this time. The tradition is that you search your heart to admit when you have wronged someone and then take responsibility for your part of a situation. You compassionately review where you might have fallen short, been uncaring, or even intentionally caused harm. The raw honesty of these admissions will help free you from carrying the burden of these acts. In addition, you can make amends whenever possible. So in this spirit of clearing bad karma, review your previous year and be courageously accountable. For instance, you can say inwardly or aloud or write in your journal:

- I am accountable.
- I have hurt people.
- I have caused harm.
- I have been self-absorbed.
- I have been miserly.
- I have not loved with all my might.

Feel free to fill in whatever statements apply to you. Taking responsibility can help you release negativity and set a compassionate tone for the year ahead.

---

**SET YOUR INTENTION**
I am accountable for the hurt I might have caused
others. I will admit my shortcomings and stay
mindful of how my actions affect others. I want
to become a more loving and aware person.

# Make Amends

The liberating process of making amends involves being accountable for your actions. It lets you clean the slate so that negative feelings don't linger in your relationships. The sooner you do this, the faster you can release old hurts.

An amend is when you apologize for a behavior that may have harmed or disturbed someone, as long as it doesn't inflict more pain on others. Perhaps you were snippy to a friend because you were in a hurry. Or you made an unkind remark to your mate. Perhaps you gossiped and bad-mouthed people. Or you dismissed your sensitive child's emotional needs. Larger, more concrete "living" amends can entail repaying a financial debt, offering to help a friend in need when you weren't available to assist before, or returning someone's belongings. You can sincerely say, "I am sorry that I hurt you or I wasn't as present for you or I was financially irresponsible."

Amends are energetically cleansing for you and others. Sometimes you can't reverse the hurt you caused, but you can do your best to own your part in it and repair a situation.

Every evening for the next week, reflect on any amends that you need to make for that day or from the past. Come from a humble place to clear the air with someone.

---

**SET YOUR INTENTION**
Even if my ego resists, I will make amends
to those whom I have hurt or was insensitive
to. I will approach them with humility.

# Let Go of Resentments

A resentment is a grudge that you hold after you've felt hurt or mistreated. It's easy to fixate on all the situations that angered you, from a coworker who snubbed you to a spouse who betrayed you. If you asked your friends, you'd probably get a lot of them on your side about your right to stay resentful. Yes, someone wronged you. You are entitled to be angry and hurt. But is that the bitter person you want to be? Instead, try to release resentments and let compassion purify them.

Buddha says that holding onto resentments, is like "grasping a hot coal with the intent of throwing it at someone else, but you are the one who gets burned." Resentments only damage you and keep you obsessed on misery or even revenge. It's helpful to list your resentments in your journal. Once you know what they are, releasing them increases your energy and clarity. The relief of letting go of a resentment is that you can focus on your current life without being stuck in your past or becoming a broken record of complaints. You are free to enjoy the spaciousness of love, kindness, and community.

---

**SET YOUR INTENTION**
I will choose one resentment and pray to let
it go so I can move on. With no attachment
or ego, I can feel this hindrance disappear.

# Passionate Presence

Every step you take to deepen your empathy and love makes your presence more vibrant and passionate. Your devotion to releasing stagnant parts of yourself will make your presence more compelling. Imagine shedding your regrets, your resentments, and old ideas that keep you small. Imagine how radiant you will feel. The emotional baggage you carry in your mind can weigh you down. It will serve you to release it.

On your empath journey, you are kindling a flame of compassion that is strong and bright. It will attract others and convey hope. It is also a kind of protection that makes you better able to deflect the world's negativity and stress. As you embody more light, your loving-kindness will grow, and others can feel it. You will emanate a sense of passionate presence.

**SET YOUR INTENTION**
I will be aware of how my presence is
becoming more powerful and heartfelt as I feel
increasingly at home with my sensitivities.

# Meditate on the Harvest Moon

The harvest full moon is a special night in autumn that typically happens around the September equinox or a bit later. The moon rises soon after sunset, and you can see the abundance of moonlight in the evening. Traditionally, this illumination of land and sky has helped farmers harvest their summer crops. This moon is a heavenly sight to witness since it is larger and even more radiant than many other full moons.

Similarly, during this time, you can reap what you have sown and harvest the fruits of your labors. Reflect on the following questions:

- What goals have I aimed for this year?
- What benefits have resulted from my hard work?
- What areas involving success would I like to further expand?
- How would I like to deepen my relationships?
- How have I grown as an empath?

Consider ways you can conclude unfinished business and enter the last quarter of the year with a fresh mind and optimism.

---

**SET YOUR INTENTION**
I will appreciate the rewards I have received
from my work and my relationships and
in my evolution as an empath this year.

# Leave Me Alone. I'm Meditating!

Meditation is a sacred time that must not be disturbed. When you are meditating, shut off your phone, close the door, and ask those in your vicinity not to intrude. Shifting from your everyday consciousness to a clearer, quieter state takes some focus. You don't want to be interrupted once you've settled into being still. During meditation, inhale and exhale slowly to help you relax and attune to the rhythm of the breath. Then allow your inner flow to take you where you need to go. Your intuition opens and you become a channel for new insights and revelations.

When I meditate, I place a "Do Not Disturb" sign on my bedroom door. The only exception is an emergency. If meditating is new for you, you may need to educate those nearby about how to support you. Frame your request by making them your champion in protecting your private time. For instance, say, "You are such a thoughtful partner to help me with this." Then rally their support in claiming this special time for yourself.

### SET YOUR INTENTION
I will create quiet, protected time to meditate. I will communicate with others on how they can support me in carving out these intervals of stillness for myself.

# Flow with Conflict

Conflict is a natural part of the ebb and flow of interacting with people. Expect disputes to arise. In fact, some periods are fraught with them — at work, at home, or elsewhere — while other phases run more smoothly. As an empath, you may take to heart disagreements and feel upset by even temporary discord. You want to please others, yet you also must assert your own needs. So it's important to find balance.

If you experience a conflict, first take a breath. Stay calm. Do not tense your body, react impulsively, or say something you will later regret. Avoid making someone else "the enemy," which is especially easy to do with loved ones. Simply realize you have reached a temporary impasse. Be patient. Do not force a resolution. Try to hear the other person's perspective without judging it. Then you will better understand how they feel.

Successful conflict resolution comes from empathy and understanding. The Taoist philosophy values the principle of harmony. So try to harmonize with the situation instead of futilely butting heads. Be open to compromise and always approach the other individual with respect. Most situations can be resolved, but for those that can't, you either agree to disagree or accept that there is limited potential moving forward.

---

**SET YOUR INTENTION**
I will approach conflicts in a relaxed, nondefensive way.
I will not feed into any drama or force a resolution.

# Healing and Illness

If you experience illness, consider it a spiritual teaching. You are dealing with an imbalance in your body and psyche that requires loving attention. Kindness is central to healing. You have not done anything wrong. It is not your fault. Do not buy into any notions that you have fallen short on your spiritual path.

Illness is a time to rest, meditate, and tune in to your body's wisdom and needs. It may mean tolerating pain or discomfort. Tensing up increases suffering, so the more you can relax and breathe through it, the easier this passage will be. You want to keep exhaling and softening your body and mind. If negative or fearful thoughts enter, such as, "Why am I not healing faster?" or "I'll never be well," do not indulge them.

For speedy healing, reject any scary stories you might tell yourself, hear from others, or read on the internet. Instead focus on a positive outcome and stay in the Now. The reality that matters most is the present moment and your quality of self-compassion. Healing takes patience and respect for your inner rhythms. Befriend your body during times of illness and health. Keep optimistic people around you. Leave adequate time to rest and rejuvenate yourself. Keep envisioning a healthy, robust, and happy future.

**SET YOUR INTENTION**
I will view illness with compassion and patience.
I will use it as an opportunity to love myself
and practice self-care. I will hold a vision of
wellness, not illness, now and for the future.

# Empath or Hypochondriac?

Many mainstream medical practitioners don't know how to correctly diagnose empaths, so they often label them as hypochondriacs or "neurotic." In fact, empaths are frequently confused with hypochondriacs because their symptoms may have no obvious cause.

As an emotional sponge, your porous system is continually processing energy from your environment and other people (especially when you are tired or upset). This translates into very real physical and emotional symptoms.

In contrast, hypochondriacs are mainly obsessed with their health and potential threats to it—they don't usually absorb other people's distress. Their experience is more a function of fear-based thoughts than an energetic phenomenon. Also, hypochondriacs don't respond as readily as empaths do to self-care techniques such as shielding, meditation, and boundary setting. When empaths practice these, the discomfort that they take in from the world will diminish. As a result, their energy increases, and they are less prone to fatigue, adrenal burnout, or other types of "dis-ease."

**SET YOUR INTENTION**
If I obsess about my health, I will shift my mind-set
and visualize feeling vibrant and well. I will listen to the
wisdom of my body's signals and prioritize self-care.

# Staying Conscious

A danger of denial and unconsciousness is that you will ignore your intuition and lose the benefits of an accurate inner guidance system. But when you stay awake and aware, you can experience the many passions of life. You're not too busy to marvel at the tiny flowers on your path or too tired to enjoy the gifts of nature, spirituality, and play.

A regular meditation practice helps you remain conscious. It trains you to drop deep within yourself to connect with your essence and, even more, to the essence of life. When you practice conscious breathing, you are exhaling stress and emotional sludge from your body.

How can you stay more conscious? Gently and slowly inhale and exhale with mindfulness. Sip your water slowly and feel the miracle of its life-sustaining properties. Listen to your inner voice. Slow down time to see — *really see* — the beauty that is all around you. Then you can benefit from the ecstatic loving energies of life with a crystal-clear and compassionate vision.

---

**SET YOUR INTENTION**
I will stay awake and consciously aware of
myself, my relationships, and the greater
world. If I slip into unconsciousness or denial,
I will catch it quickly and reemerge.

# Empathic Role Models

You can learn so much about how to be an empowered empath from positive role models. Stay aware of the empathic, caring people whom you admire, especially those who are dedicated to self-care.

See how they find satisfaction and joy. Observe how they give to others without giving themselves away. Notice how much alone time they plan as well as the recreation breaks they take in nature or other rejuvenating locations. Talk to them about the difficulties they have encountered as an empath and how they have overcome them. Discuss any issues about their sensitivities that they are still processing. Becoming an empowered empath is an ongoing exploration with new teachings along the way.

If you lack a specific person in your life to model, look to public figures, heroes, or historical icons who have exemplified empathy, freedom, and tolerance. Consider Martin Luther King, Jr., Saint Francis of Assisi, Eleanor Roosevelt, or Mahatma Gandhi. One of my role models is Carl Jung, who pioneered the role of intuition in psychiatry. Read about these people and emulate their dedication to integrity, caring, empathy, and doing good in the world.

**SET YOUR INTENTION**
I will identify my empathic role models. I will
learn from them about how to express my
empathy more fully, proudly, and wisely.

# Taming the Ego

The ego has light and dark aspects. On the positive side, it gives you a strong sense of self and the confidence you need to pursue your dreams. When your ego is weak, you may lack the determination to create a life you love. However, an out-of-control ego can make you self-absorbed, grandiose, and arrogant. It always needs to feel important and to be right. This turns people off and limits the empathy you can offer others. You don't want an overblown ego to run your life or block out the voice of Spirit.

Your goal is to tame the ego. This means that you tap into its positive attributes, but you also take a step back to observe when it grows too large. If your ego starts to inflate, train it to back off. On my Taoist path, taming the ego is a mindful practice of observing it, noticing what triggers it, and always returning to the heart through meditation or introspection. Remember, the ego comes from your head, with all of its insecurities and fears, whereas humility comes from your heart.

**SET YOUR INTENTION**
I will not let my ego control my life. I will
keep a loving eye on my ego and tame
it if it starts to get out of control.

# Integrity

Integrity means staying true to values such as honesty, empathy, compassion, and spirituality. When you are faced with a choice, you take the higher road rather than compromising your beliefs, even if you lose a friendship or a job or experience some other untoward consequence.

The reward of integrity is integrity. The gratification of staying true to yourself over a lifetime is that you'll feel good about yourself. You don't want to sell yourself out or betray your values or sensitivities because you fear rejection or loss. Rather, you want to look back and be proud of how you behaved, even if there was a cost.

Being an empath with integrity allows you to use your abilities well and stay humble about your gifts. You will listen to your intuition and respect your body's needs. The integrity of empathy impels you to want to understand other people's perspective instead of making them wrong. Staying true to your empathic heart lets you love yourself and others more fully.

---

**SET YOUR INTENTION**
I will practice integrity in my life. I will value
my integrity and not compromise my values or
behave in ways that are incongruent with love.

# The Serenity Prayer

Acceptance is key to feeling more peaceful and balanced in your relationships. If you judge someone's behavior or a situation as wrong or needing correction, you will always have a reason to be unhappy. But when you accept each person, event, and emotion as exactly how it is meant to be at that moment, you will experience fewer struggles and less energy drain.

Instead of concentrating on others' perceived flaws, focus on what attitudes you can change in yourself. No matter what you decide, you can come from a calmer position. You may choose to set boundaries with a friend's behavior, end a relationship, or modify your job. However, you can make wise decisions based on accepting others as they are, rather than engaging in blame or drama. Though you can't always alter a situation, you can control how you feel about it and the actions you take.

When practicing acceptance, you can pause and inwardly repeat the Serenity Prayer:

> Grant me the serenity
> to accept the things I cannot change,
> courage to change the things I can,
> and wisdom to know the difference.

---

**SET YOUR INTENTION**
I will practice acceptance instead of fighting
what is. I will have realistic expectations of
other people. I will not attempt to change them
or situations that are beyond my control.

# Dealing with Loss

Love is a high stakes endeavor. When you love deeply, you risk everything, including the pain of loss and grief. Some sensitive people withdraw from loving because the agony of losing someone seems unbearable. So they pass up a promising new relationship or they decline to rescue an adorable animal from the shelter in an attempt to avoid ultimately letting go of yet another beloved. I understand the fear. But I also know that love is all there is and that loving illuminates our hearts and the world.

Fear of loss need not be your primary motivator. Even so, choosing to keep an open heart while also knowing that you will grieve and begin to heal your pain is an incomplete consolation. Still, I hope you choose love. No one says loss is easy. But grieving, too, can be liberating and may take you to a higher spiritual and healing state. You grieve in full devotion to the person you lost. And, yet, despite everything, you keep remaining open to ongoing intimacies in your life.

**SET YOUR INTENTION**
I am resilient enough to deal with the pain
of loss. I am strong enough to go through
the grief process and to risk loving again.

# Tolerance

Tolerance is the philosophy of "live and let live." It makes you curious about different opinions, cultures, spiritual beliefs, or lifestyles. Tolerance gives others room to be who they are. It means holding space for diversity without creating an us-versus-them mentality. Also, practicing acceptance for our own and others' human failings is crucial when learning compassion.

Cultivate tolerance on an energetic level too. For example, don't send bad vibes to the guy who is talking loudly in the gym or the teenager who is tailgating you. This doesn't mean you're condoning their behavior, but you won't waste your energy resenting what you can't control.

Instead, experiment with being more tolerant and less quick to condemn others (except, of course, if it's a matter of abuse). Everyone is dealing with some hardship that may be invisible to you. In India, the greeting *namaste* means, "the soul in me sees the soul in you." You don't have to agree with or even like someone, but you can show them respect.

---

**SET YOUR INTENTION**
I will be more tolerant of people and view them
through the lens of my heart. Most people are
doing the best they can with their challenges.

# Fight, Flight, or Freeze

Anxiety triggers an automatic physiological stress cycle in your body called the "fight-flight-freeze response." When confronting danger, your instincts may be to fight with someone, flee the situation, or freeze (you are emotionally paralyzed or too frightened or overloaded to even move). Though these impulses can help you survive, empaths on chronic sensory overload often live in this hyperaroused state constantly, which is exhausting and unhealthy.

The fight-flight-freeze response may be a protective mechanism too. You verbally lash out when you think your mate is trying to hurt you. By pushing them away, you don't have to risk being vulnerable and open. Also if someone is aggressive, you meet force with force rather than dealing with the situation more empathically. Or you simply avoid a confrontation, or you freeze.

Identify the incidents that set off your fight-flight-freeze response. You don't want to be taken by surprise. Is it when your boss reprimands you? When your kids are screaming? When you're feeling claustrophobic in a crowded mall? Knowing your triggers allows you to plan self-care strategies to more effectively protect your sensitivities and react from a centered place in these situations.

**SET YOUR INTENTION**
I will be mindful of the stressful circumstances that
trigger my body's fight-flight-freeze response. I will take
steps to quickly calm my system and regain my center.

# Healing Touch

Too many people are touch or "vitamin T" (as I call it) deprived and are craving genuine connection. Caring touch can send positive energy throughout your system. Sensitive people respond to the right kind of touch, which transmits good vibes: a friend's hug, intimacy with their partner, a supportive colleague's pat on the back.

In addition, therapeutic massage such as Swedish, deep tissue, or shiatsu allows you to experience the power of healing touch. Depending on your preference, light or intense massage can be relaxing. It quiets your biochemical stress response and cleanses the lymph system. During your treatment, you may release emotions that have become stuck in vulnerable parts of your body such as your lower back or shoulders. Let those feelings flow. As part of your self-care, I recommend getting regular massages for pleasure and to clear any unwanted stress or emotions you've absorbed from the world.

**SET YOUR INTENTION**
I will fulfill the vitamin T requirements in my life. I will explore ways to experience healing touch, including massage and hugging friends and loved ones.

# Forest Bathing

Research has shown that the average American spends over 90 percent of their time indoors. Instead, go out in nature. Being in the presence of trees is healing. Plant empaths — people who have a special affinity for green, growing things — know this well.

When you need to recharge yourself or simply want to be touched by the serenity of trees, let yourself experience "forest bathing." This is the Japanese healing tradition of *shinrin-yoku*, the rejuvenation that comes from simply being in the woods. Forest bathing has become a health prescription and part of preventative therapies in Japanese medicine.

If you live close to the forest or even a grove of trees in a park, spend regular time there. Open your senses — your sight, hearing, smell, and touch. Be aware of the myriad of sounds in the forest, such as birds singing and the rushing of water in creeks. Savor the fragrance of pine needles or eucalyptus, the colors of leaves, and light dancing on the branches. Inhale the pure oxygen that plants so generously share. Let yourself daydream and experience the spirits of the trees.

**SET YOUR INTENTION**
I will soak up the healing atmosphere of the
forest or even of a single tree. I will let it
help me relax and think more clearly.

# After a Long Day at Work

As an empath, you may encounter a common dilemma: your partner, children, or roommates pounce on you with demands or the details of their day just as you walk in the door. Even if your job is your passion, you could still be tired. Your body needs a rest. Your mind needs some space and peace.

The solution is to establish some clear boundaries that will protect you when you come home after a long day at work. I suggest establishing a Ten-Minute Rule (or longer, if you like) to allow time for you to acclimate to being home without having to talk or address any issues. (This rule can apply to others in your household coming home too.) Go to your room and close the door. Rest, listen to music, meditate, change into comfortable clothes, or simply do nothing. Then, after decompressing, you will be better equipped to approach others from a more centered place.

**SET YOUR INTENTION**
I will set a healthy boundary with loved ones such
as the Ten-Minute Rule that establishes a period to
unwind when I come home from work. I will take this
quiet time for myself before I interact with others.

# Rejection Is God's Protection

No one likes being rejected. It hurts and makes you feel unappreciated or possibly discarded. Many people fear rejection, anticipate and avoid it, and even have nightmares about it. Some empaths become people pleasers and hide their true needs just to avoid this possibility.

That's why it's important to view rejection from a spiritual context so you don't deny your true self out of fear. Ask yourself, "What is the greater meaning of this rejection for me? Is it to enhance my self-esteem? To stay strong during difficulties? To avoid danger? To believe in the integrity of my life's path?" Journal about your thoughts.

Consider this: Many times, I've seen personally and with patients how rejection can be the universe protecting you from harm. Even though you may passionately want a romantic relationship or a certain job to work out, in the long run it might not be the best choice for you. It takes faith to have this belief, but when it has proven true, time and again, you will see its wisdom. There is a greater force in charge that is always watching over you.

---

**SET YOUR INTENTION**
I will consider the greater meaning of rejection.
I will view it as a form of divine protection
at those times when my strong desires or
willfulness cloud the bigger picture.

# In Good Time

I love the verse from Ecclesiastes that says, "To every thing there is a season, and a time to every purpose under heaven." Listening to your intuition keeps you in touch with divine timing. If you try to rush what is not yet ready to occur, you will create an impossible expectation and a deep sense of frustration. But if you practice patience, the art of waiting, listening, and knowing when to act, each day will unfold naturally.

The timetable for your life is unique to you. Perhaps you marry for the first time at seventy or change careers at fifty. Or you awaken as an empath at nine or at ninety. There is no right or wrong. Your internal readiness for change is the catalyst. As they say, when you are ready, the teacher will come in the form of a person or an experience. Everything happens in its own perfect time, a truth to depend on.

**SET YOUR INTENTION**
I will practice patience and follow my intuition
instead of trying to push a door that's not ready
to open. I will have faith that my life's purpose
and lessons will reveal themselves in good time.

# Soften Resistance

Throughout the day, be mindful of when you are flowing with life and when you are resisting it. Flowing feels energizing, fun, joyful, even effortless. Resistance feels tense, tight, and stressful, as if you are pushing a giant boulder up a steep hill.

When you encounter inner or outer resistance, pause to evaluate. Perhaps you've reached a stopping point on a project, yet you're still trying to force it to proceed. Or you're convincing yourself to go on a date with someone to whom you're really not drawn, though your friends are all crazy about this person. Or you've had a disagreement with a colleague: you keep making a point, but they resist it, and you get nowhere.

Compassionately evaluate resistance in yourself or others. Consider the wisdom it imparts. To find its greater meaning, practice softening around it instead of becoming rigid. Then notice any new, intuitive insights about your resistance such as the timing isn't right for a circumstance to manifest.

Physical movement also lessens resistance. Journal about ways you can exercise, including stretching, breathing, yoga, meditating, or walking by water — then go do it. If a relationship feels stuck, giving it some space can help dissolve blocks and conflicts when communication resumes again. Softening resistance will bring clarity and prevent you from trying to remove obstacles in frantic, unwise ways.

---

**SET YOUR INTENTION**
I will keep breathing, releasing my rigidity
and stubbornness, and be gentle with myself
when I am experiencing resistance.

# The Power of Showing Up

Some of the qualities I look for in friends and in my partner are whether their behavior backs their words and if they are available for intimacy. A good way to tell is if they consistently show up. Intimate relationships require trust before you can feel safe to reveal your more vulnerable parts. Dependability creates that sense of comfort.

When someone shows up for you, they are communicating, "I care" and "I value our time together." Whether they celebrate your birthday or provide moral support when you are down or simply take in a movie with you, they are demonstrating that you can rely on them. True, sometimes people get overwhelmed in their own lives and are simply unable to be there for you. But, for the most part, true friends don't keep canceling plans or perpetually send notes such as "I'll be there in spirit" when they live only a mile away. Close friends are there for each other during the highs and lows of life, which instills deepening trust.

**SET YOUR INTENTION**
I will seek relationships with those who are available
to show up for me. I also will show up for them. I will
avoid flaky people who can't keep time commitments.

# Baby Steps

The world is in such a hurry. Many of my high-achieving patients want and expect instant gratification for their efforts. When they don't get it, they become restless, irritable, and self-critical—a setup for low self-esteem and burnout.

As an empath, I see things differently. Being in a hurry exhausts me. It also causes me to make mistakes. I know how wonderful it feels to be comfortable with my measured pace. A little stone turtle totem sits on my desk to remind me of the virtues of being slow but sure, perseverant but patient. Mindful baby steps make golden footprints in the sand. They are purposeful, forward moving, and wise.

The happiest, most successful people often say they have attained their goals in increments by making one positive choice after another. Building on your smaller victories can create great, enduring achievements.

---

**SET YOUR INTENTION**
I will go at a healthy pace in my life and avoid
rushing. I will value the baby steps I take each
day as part of my consistent path of progress.

# I Am Enough

We all have periods when we question ourselves. At those points of self-doubt when you may not feel attractive enough or smart enough or successful enough or even spiritual enough, repeat the following affirmation. Then be ready to shed your fears and recognize the caring, worthy person that you are. Eleanor Roosevelt said, "No one can make you feel inferior but yourself."

I am enough.
I don't have to prove my worth to anyone.
I don't have to be someone I'm not.
I don't have to pretend I'm not sensitive
or smile when I'm unhappy.
I am pleased with myself.
I love myself.
I am grateful for the opportunity of my life.

**SET YOUR INTENTION**
I will keep awakening to my best self. I will
not see myself as inferior or superior to
anyone. I am enough by simply being me.

# Being Happy or Being Right

Set your priorities in your relationships. Do you want harmony or drama? Empathy or blame? Can you compromise or do you always need to be right? If you come off as a know-it-all, you may face strong pushback. But if you opt for the high road, your communication will improve.

Your ego can get in the way. To sidestep it (even if you know you are correct) ask yourself, "Would I rather be happy or right?" You have a choice. You can keep pounding the other person with why they should agree with you even when they are unyielding, or you can, at least temporarily, let go of the issue or agree to disagree.

In lesser disputes, I actually enjoy letting someone "win" their point. It feels liberating to me and to them. For instance, when a friend insists that "it takes an hour to get there," but I know the trip is much shorter, I don't keep arguing.

People are thrilled when you let them be right. It's a gift you can give them. You don't have to become a doormat or ignore larger issues. Rather, you become mindful of when pushing your point gets you nowhere or creates more problems than it solves.

---

**SET YOUR INTENTION**
I don't always have to have all the answers or
the last word. Sometimes, I will allow people to
be right and notice how happy it makes them.

# Your Buddha Nature

Everyone has a higher self, their Buddha Nature, which is a luminous expanse of awareness. This actually *is* the real you—the part that is beyond any attachments to fear, anger, or insecurities. Because many people cling to their finite, smaller selves, they may not connect with their Buddha Nature, which is already enlightened. Your spiritual path becomes about removing all the obstacles to knowing this.

My Taoist teacher says, "There is an angel and demon inside the Buddha." So remain vigilant about dealing with your darker side and also feed your own goodness and compassion. If you stay awake, doing this becomes a conscious choice. You are in charge of the kind of person you want to be—and whether you can refuse fear-based thinking by saying yes to love. By patiently peeling away all the layers of unconsciousness and fear that keep you from knowing your Buddha Nature, your inner light will be as radiant as the sun.

**SET YOUR INTENTION**
I will meditate on my Buddha Nature. I can choose
to nurture those aspects of myself I respect.
I will feed the compassion and clarity within.

# Vulnerable and Strong

A gift of being an empowered empath is that you can be both vulnerable and strong. I want to dispel the misguided notion that we can only be one way or another, that we are incapable of holding many seemingly opposite qualities at once. It takes tremendous strength to shed the armor that protects you from the intensity of your true emotions and to deal courageously with fear, anxiety, or depression head-on.

Though it's healthy to develop protection strategies to deflect stress and toxic energy, don't sacrifice your vulnerability by becoming overly defended. Many times each day, you must intuitively access the energy of your interactions to know when to remain open with others and when to protect yourself. It's admirable to be fluid so you're able to decide whether to become vulnerable or protected in a situation.

**SET YOUR INTENTION**
I am vulnerable and strong. I will practice
discernment in my decisions and utilize my
intuition as my internal guidance system.

# Keeping Your Edge

Your edge makes you interesting. It's your wild, creative side that keeps you true to your emotions. When you are in touch with your edge, you neither sugarcoat your ideas nor become obsessed with what others think of you. You express your natural talents and personality.

Over the years, I've seen many empathic patients lose their edge when they give away too much of themselves. They sacrifice their free spirits by trying to please everyone else: their mates, parents, bosses, and children. They become overly sweet, compliant, even passive. But they need their edge to be free thinkers—to be quirky and creative. So they end up feeling trapped and angry, fearing that a part of themselves has been lost.

Your edge is a vital aspect of being an empath, and you can always reclaim it. Reflect on what it looks and feels like. What does this part of you long to say? Does it feel stifled? Does it want to be less constrained? How can you liberate it? It's fine to be an agreeable person, but you also can keep your edge alive at the same time.

---

**SET YOUR INTENTION**
I will be my authentic self and not sacrifice my
edge because I'm afraid that people won't approve
of me. I will value my edge and my free spirit.

# Pain Is Different from Suffering

Pain refers to uncomfortable physical or emotional sensations. Chinese medical practitioners say that pain is a blockage of chi, your vital life force. Suffering, on the other hand, is your response to pain, how you think and feel about the sensations.

A certain amount of pain is unavoidable in life, but as the saying goes, "Suffering is optional." It is amplified by the stories you tell yourself regarding the pain. Your fearful untrue thoughts can be your worst enemy. For instance, "My back pain will never improve" as compared to "This is just a temporary setback, and I will be better than ever when I recover." Suffering is also intensified by resisting painful sensations. Tensing up makes it worse. But doing your best to relax and breathe into the pain will lessen your suffering.

So the more you can still your mind and surrender to Spirit, the less discomfort you will experience. Here's a formula to remember: Overcontrol + Overthinking = Pain in your physical and emotional body. So let go and think less to minimize the suffering you experience.

---

**SET YOUR INTENTION**
When I'm in pain, I will be gentle with myself. I will
not focus on fear or imagine the worst in a situation.
I will keep a peaceful mind to limit my suffering.

# Detach from the Ten Thousand Things

Both Buddhism and Taoism talk about the "Ten Thousand Things." It refers to the multiple ways the mind can distract you from your inner voice and spiritual path. These can range from worrying about your to-do list, to obsessing about a painful conversation, to fixating on the world's suffering. If your mind attaches to even one of the Ten Thousand Things, your clarity can be thrown off.

You want to outsmart these distractions by stilling the mind. However, instead of trying to force it to be quiet (which only makes it angry), assign your mind a task. Counting your breaths works well. Here's how:

*Inhale to a count of four, and hold it for four counts.*
*Next, exhale to a count of four and rest for four counts.*
*Do three rounds of this breathing exercise in one sitting.*
*Then meditate for at least ten minutes.*

When your mind is occupied, it won't be tempted to pay attention to the Ten Thousand Things.

### SET YOUR INTENTION
I will count my breaths to calm my mind during meditation. I will not allow myself to be distracted by anything. I will be calm and clear as an open sky.

# Healing Trauma

Empathic children may experience varying levels of trauma while growing up. Sources can include being yelled at, hearing your parents or siblings argue, or being shamed or blamed or abused or bullied. Even being subjected to intense household noise and chaos can be traumatic. An empathic child's highly sensitive system may absorb more stress than others would in these situations.

Your past can still affect you now. When you are exposed to a similar stimulus as an adult such as a disagreement with your partner, you may have an exaggerated emotional response because you are flashing back to the original trauma. (This is similar to a veteran who misreads a car backfiring as an exploding bomb.) With post-traumatic stress, your system can't fully return to its calmer state before the upset or even the initial incident. You are never quite at rest and remain ever vigilant to protect yourself from further threats.

Journal about causes of any early trauma you experienced (none are "too small" to count). Then notice post-traumatic stress reactions to your spouse, coworkers, or others, so you can keep them in perspective rather than panicking. Also seek the help of a therapist to work through the original trauma and get regular massage or energy work to clear any remnants of it that are lodged in your body.

---

**SET YOUR INTENTION**
I will identify my early traumas. I will notice how my reactions to them may be repeating in my relationships today. I am capable of healing from these wounds.

# Release Shame

Shame is a painful sense of humiliation that comes from feeling defective or inferior. You judge yourself harshly because you're afraid you're not living up to your own or another's standards.

Shame often originates in childhood. Your parents or teachers may have scolded you in private, or worse, in public—or you might have suffered abuse or bullying from classmates. Perhaps others said, "You are stupid for doing that!" or "You're aren't good for much of anything." When I was a teenager, my mother used to say in front of her friends, "Judith, you'd be so beautiful if it weren't for your clothes and wild hair." Naturally, I felt belittled and embarrassed. Being shamed in public leaves an indelible mark. Unless you consciously heal the tenacious effects of shame with compassion, it can stick in your consciousness and taint your adult choices and relationships.

Journal about areas in which you've been shamed such as your appearance or intelligence or financial status or acute sensitivity. Identify those who shamed you. Then have your empowered self tell the wounded part of you, "None of this is true. Those people were being cruel." Use loving-kindness to counter feelings of toxic shame.

**SET YOUR INTENTION**
I am worthy of success on all levels. When I
feel shame about some aspect of myself, I will
substitute it with a kind thought. I will heal
and release old shame from my past.

# Embrace Your Unique Magic

You have your own allure and magic. The holidays of Halloween and Día de los Muertos, or Day of the Dead (observed from the evening of October 31 through November 2), are perfect times to tap into and express your enchanted and intuitive self. On these days, pay special attention to your gut feelings, dreams, or any creative flashes and follow them. You can wear masks and costumes. Or, in a private ritual, you can simply honor loved ones who have passed on. (One such Latin American custom is to spread golden marigold petals on altars next to candles and photos of deceased relatives.)

Also, if you're fortunate to have little children come by trick-or-treating, allow their cuteness and innocence to delight you. Their sweet voices and imaginative costumes can spark your sense of playfulness and experimentation. Or, if you prefer not to socialize tonight, go inward. Meditate on listening to your intuition or remembering those in the Great Beyond.

---

**SET YOUR INTENTION**
I will recognize that I'm a mystical being. I will know
that I am full of wonder, surprises, and intuition.
I vow to never lose sight of my own personal magic.

# I Don't Want to Leave Home!

As days grow colder and darker, you may instinctually want to hunker down at home and become a hermit. It feels safe and warm inside. You can stock up on your favorite foods, books, and music and have an internet connection. You can be at peace in your meditation space and play with your animals. Also, if you are able to work remotely, you're spared the stress of commuting and office politics.

However, along with the advantages of staying home, there also can be a downside. Like many empaths, you may tend to isolate socially and then feel lonely if you've withdrawn for too long. While you can better control your stimulation level at home, you may also lack the positive energy of human contact, except for those you live with. So if you become lonely when you're in your cave indefinitely, seek balance in the fall and winter months. Respect your desire to hibernate but also reap the benefits of the world of people and be sparked by the electricity of life.

**SET YOUR INTENTION**
I will give myself the alone time I need, but I will not go to extremes. I will balance my desire to hibernate with my need to connect with people.

# Bundling Up

A fun part of colder weather is that you can wear warm, cozy clothes. During summer, some empaths feel overexposed and vulnerable in light clothing. In contrast, the fall and winter seasons let you bundle up in coats with hoods, scarves, down vests, and gloves lined with soft fleece or natural fibers. At night you can wear flannel pajamas and sleep on warm flannel sheets. During snowstorms or icy temperatures, you can keep your legs and feet warm and protected in thick cashmere or cotton socks, leggings, and sturdy boots.

Like many empaths, you may be intolerant of certain fabrics. You may dislike the scratchiness of rough wool or feel constricted by turtleneck sweaters that are too tight around the neck. But soft cotton, silk, or flannel feels pleasing. Clarify your preferences, so your clothes feel good on your body.

**SET YOUR INTENTION**
I will take pleasure in bundling up in outfits that keep me safe from the cold. I will let myself be held in the secure embrace of cozy clothes in chilly climates.

# The Groundless Ground

Life is full of flux and change. If too much is coming at you too fast, it can feel overwhelming and trigger sensory overload. Some days your emotions can swirl wildly and intensely. *Even so, you are never given more than you can handle.* Your anxious mind might say, "I can't cope with all this!" Still, realize that on a deeper level, you are fully capable of growing from all the difficult emotions and situations you experience.

As Buddhists say, there is always a groundless ground that supports you. In the midst of a traumatic event or when you are inundated with excessive stimulation, the groundless ground is there. When you are called to draw on a reservoir of inner strength that you don't think you have, an invisible, loving spiritual support structure is available to protect you. In meditation, spend time intuitively sensing this divine safety net so you can be consoled by the reality of its existence. Though the nature of life is impermanent, the groundless ground is infinite and eternal.

**SET YOUR INTENTION**
There is always a groundless ground
beneath me. I will trust that I am cradled
by an ever-present network of love.

# Depression as a Teacher and Healer

Healing depression is holy work and an opportunity for your spiritual transformation. It's a wake-up call to examine possible changes you might want to make in your life. However, since feeling depressed can be so profoundly unsettling, it's often labeled as "darkness."

Still, I believe, as do many spiritual paths, that depression is the "dark night of the soul," a term used by mystic priest Saint John of the Cross describing his journey from despair to wholeness. It is a potentially revelatory stage in your spiritual development. I suggest that you view depression in this way, especially if it is severe. You are not merely experiencing a biochemical deficiency of serotonin, your body's natural antidepressant, as some neuropsychiatrists define this "mood disorder." Depression presents the strenuous but worthy challenge of having faith in yourself even when all may seem lost, of finding light in darkness.

**SET YOUR INTENTION**
If I feel depressed, I will stay in the Now, seek
help from a therapist and friends, and practice
loving self-care. I have not done anything wrong,
nor is the depression my fault. I will stay open
to the spiritual lessons of this experience.

# The Heart Knows When It Has Had Enough

When you have reached the end of the road with a painful relationship or a negative emotional pattern, your heart knows when it has had enough.

If you feel too tired to go on, or you need to back off from helping someone who doesn't want assistance, your heart knows when it has had enough.

When you are working too much and brutally pushing yourself, your heart knows when it has had enough.

When you keep beating yourself up for not getting the promotion you deserve, your heart knows when it has had enough.

Some of us are addicted to pain. Letting go of this, or any unhealthy habit or person, can feel wrenching and sad. You need to grieve the loss or be resolved to wait for a possible future opening in which to intervene. But for now, the door is shut. If you can't accept this and keep returning to a futile situation or mindset, you will only experience more pain or frustration. Respecting the holy closure of what is complete, of what is over, can help you heal and move on.

**SET YOUR INTENTION**
I realize that some relationships or situations
must come to an end. I will listen to the messages
of my heart to know how to care for myself
and release what no longer serves me.

# Sabbath

Take a day of rest each week or at least several hours if that's what is possible. Plan a time that will be most convenient, which may be Saturday or Sunday, as is traditionally observed in Judaism and Christianity. This is the sacred pause when you let go of worldly concerns and focus on replenishing your mind, body, and spirit.

The Book of Genesis defines the Sabbath as a period of holy rest on the seventh day, as Spirit rested from creation. One of the Ten Commandments states, "Remember the Sabbath and keep it holy. Six days you shall labor and do your work, but the seventh day is Sabbath."

In the spirit of this ancient rite, you too can incorporate the practice of Sabbath in your life to avoid burnout. It's exhausting to be constantly busy or working all the time. You are temporarily letting go of your inner taskmaster, no matter how much it tries to seduce you back into stressful activities. Sabbath is a time to take a big exhale and temporarily cease all efforts to further your goals.

**SET YOUR INTENTION**
I will plan regular periods for Sabbath in my life
to restore and re-create myself. I will simply rest,
meditate, and nurture the essence of my being.

# The Clock Yoga Pose

To relax and unwind, practice this gentle yoga pose in which you make your body into a clock.

*Start by lying on your right side with both knees pulled toward your chest. Next, extend both arms out straight in front of you, one resting upon the other. Let this be the position of nine o'clock. Then, keeping your right arm straight in front of you, let your left arm begin to slowly rotate around your body like the second hand of a clock. Tick. Tick. Tick. Let it go on to the position of ten o'clock, then eleven, then midnight. When you arrive at one o'clock, let the increased stretch naturally open your chest and heart area. Your body will gently turn as it follows the lead of your arm. Go at your own pace. Continue moving your left arm around the numbers of the clock until you reach the position of nine again. Do three rounds of this routine.*

*When you've finished, repeat the same activity on your left side but now start by pointing your arms toward three o'clock.*

This yoga pose lets you experience your body as part of the process of time. It also opens your chest and shoulder areas to release stress and blocked emotions.

---

**SET YOUR INTENTION**
I will experiment with yoga as a form of self-care
that allows me to more fully inhabit my physical self.
I will create a clock with my body to stretch and relax.

# The Empathy Quotient

Just as there is an intelligence quotient (IQ), I have developed an empathy quotient (EQ) to measure the degree of empathy someone shows. To gauge a coworker, friend, or loved one's EQ, ask yourself, "Do they genuinely care about others? Can they put themselves in other people's shoes to see where they are coming from? Do they listen with their hearts, not just their heads? Can they hold a loving space for others to express their emotions without needing to immediately fix their problems?"

If a person fulfills all these criteria, they have a high EQ. If they fulfill only a few or none, their capacity for empathy may be more limited or even lacking. Though empathy can be developed through mindful awareness and focused listening skills, it's also useful to determine how capable of empathy someone is right now. Keep a person's EQ in mind when forming close relationships and in choosing coworkers or friends to confide in.

The world needs more empathic leaders, parents, and people in every profession and area of life. Empathy allows you to understand where others are coming from even if you don't agree with them. It bridges differences and opens communication with others.

---

**SET YOUR INTENTION**
I will choose empathic, loving people in my life.
I will be aware of a person's EQ to gain a realistic
grasp of how caring and supportive they are.

# Boost Your Immune System

A basic strategy to boost your immune system is to get sufficient rest and alone time, which reduces sensory overload. When you experience excessive stimulation, your immune function can be compromised by your biochemical stress response. This, in turn, taxes your adrenal glands and may lead to autoimmune disorders. Self-care techniques such as regular meditation and exercise help you stay calm and happy so that you're not as susceptible to adrenal burnout.

As the fall and winter cold and flu season is getting under way, it's a good practice to follow a healthy diet that includes vegetables, fruits, nuts, and seeds as well as vitamin C supplements. You can also take probiotics to balance your gut's bacterial flora and eat medicinal mushrooms like shiitakes, which enhance immunity. Washing your hands frequently also limits your exposure to germs. Lowering your stress level by calming your thoughts, avoiding being in a rush, and minimizing contact with draining people will enhance your ability to fight off illness too.

### SET YOUR INTENTION

I will boost my immune system by participating in healthy, positive activities. I will not allow negative, fear-based thinking about illness to dominate my mind.

# Feeling Good

Focus on feeling good today. Enjoy the pleasures of walking, seeing, smelling, and hearing the creative expressions of life. Raise your arms high in celebration. Place your awareness on the areas of your body that are at ease rather than obsessing about aches, pains, or limitations. Eat slowly and enjoy the sensuality of different foods. Mindfully drink a glass of water. Choose to have positive, hopeful thoughts and not feed any negative or fearful feelings that intrude on your serenity. By shifting your awareness to feeling good, you can choose your mind-set to emphasize what is healthy, inspirational, and in sync with your greatest sense of well-being.

---

**SET YOUR INTENTION**
I will be in charge of what sensations and thoughts
I focus on. I will give myself permission to feel good,
to be positive, and experience unobstructed happiness.

# The Security of Structure

Creating a daily routine can provide a safe container for your life. As a sensitive person, you may experience many emotions, thoughts, and inspirations during the course of a day. It is centering to have a stable environment. For instance, waking up at a certain hour, eating regular meals, and allotting time for work, play, exercise, and meditation each week provides a framework that doesn't have to feel constraining. On the other hand, if your schedule is chaotic, or if you spend too much time either socializing or alone, this can cause inner turmoil and insecurity.

When I'm writing a book, I'm living in a timeless, altered state. That's why I prefer having a daily structure that is pretty much the same. I like to go to sleep early, eat at the same times, and work in the same spot. This structure lets me stay open to creative impulses and limits distractions.

Spend time journaling about a daily structure that feels good to you. Are you an "early to bed, early to rise" person? When do you prefer having meals? When do you work most efficiently? Do you enjoy meditating at night or in the afternoon or morning? Knowing these preferences can feel both comfortable and liberating.

**SET YOUR INTENTION**
I will not overschedule my days. Rather, I will create a daily routine that satisfies my need for structure yet allows for spontaneity too.

# A Happy Home Life

Let yourself focus on being happy with the people you live with (including yourself) rather than on their imperfections. Be grateful for companionship, laughter, and the gift of human contact. Don't take anyone or anything for granted. There's a sacredness to sharing meals, discussing your day, or even talking about nothing particularly important. Looking back on your life, the smaller moments will have such significance. The fabric of our days is made up of them woven together with luminous threads. Let every smile, every time your partner says, "Good night sweetheart" or "I'll see you later after work" make you feel loved and content.

Also be happy with yourself: The way you move, the way you eat, the way you look, the way you relate to others. It's too easy to slip into self-criticism or focus on a glass being half full. Recognize that temptation and choose to reject it in favor of acknowledging blessings. Life is so amazing. Seeing yourself and others through appreciative eyes generates a sense of contentment with yourself and your home life.

---

**SET YOUR INTENTION**
Today, I will be happy with my home and its inhabitants,
including myself. Home is where the heart is.

# Don't Look Back

The past is part of your personal history. It has helped shape you into the person you are. However, the present is your current reality. Too many people get bogged down in their past, as if sucked under by quicksand. Be careful not to let that happen to you.

Instead, keep moving forward in your life. Don't let yourself get fixated on your previous disappointments, pain, betrayals, and hard times. Learn from them and don't repeat the same mistakes but keep progressing onward. Also be careful not to place former lovers, mentors, or friends on a pedestal, so no one in your present can possibly live up to this ideal. Keep living and learning while acknowledging the teachings of past happiness and pain.

The light is clear and bright in the moment. Your future is yet to unfold. Keep your eyes on the red-tailed hawk soaring in the sky or the freshly fallen snow. Listen to the wind whistling in the trees. Stay aware. See those who love you smiling at you — a blessed event. Feel the light shining from their eyes and from their hearts.

**SET YOUR INTENTION**
I will not get seduced by the pain or pleasure of my
past. I will stay focused on the treasure of the moment.

# Go Where the Light Is

As a general philosophy of life, always go to where the love and light are. With your intuition, you can spot them easily. They are the situations that feel positive and nurturing to your soul. They are the people who care about you, who are considerate and show up for you rather than being unavailable.

At times, you will be at a crossroads. You can either choose the path of love and light or the path of pain and struggle. The problem is that the latter may appear more exciting, sexier, even dangerous. So you opt for difficulties and the wilder side rather than the simpler (and also sexy) yet often subtler path of love. Bad-boy or bad-girl types can seem alluring at times, but eventually, you will be impacted by their limitations and wounds. One path is not better than another, though some choices may be more painful. You are accountable for your decisions. Whatever path you choose, learn from everything, including your suffering. Love is always there for you when you are ready.

**SET YOUR INTENTION**
I am the master of my destiny. The path I take is
up to me. I will choose to move toward the light.

# Minimize Smaller Frustrations

There's an art to playing down smaller frustrations, especially those you cannot remedy. No one is perfect. People will make unintentional mistakes that may complicate everything. Still, it's up to you how you deal with them. Do you really want to use up your vital energy on being upset about why the car door was dinged in the parking lot or that your partner forgot to stop at the market?

When you can prioritize what is truly important and worthy of your energy, you will be smarter about how to respond. There are ongoing annoyances in daily life. You can either fight them or flow with them. But you don't want to turn a frustrating ten minutes into a frustrating day. Learn to minimize the smaller irritations and deal with the larger ones from a grounded place.

**SET YOUR INTENTION**
I can choose what I get upset about. I will not
let minor frustrations sap my energy, throw
me off-center, or steal joy from my day.

# Emotional Weather

Your sensitive nature opens you to experiencing a range of emotions. It's important to flow with them. The key is to stay attuned to your emotional weather — the fluctuations of your feelings from anxiety to happiness — and allow them to pass through your system.

Like terrestrial conditions, your emotional weather changes from sunshine to rain, to darkness, to cool quiet mist, to light peeking through the clouds. At other times, your mood can be icy or hot. My partner often asks me, "Judith, what is your emotional weather report today?" and I share it with him. Since my feelings often shift subtly and sometimes dramatically, this gives him a better sense of where I'm coming from. He values this information because he cares about my feelings. You can also plan a check-in like this in your relationships.

When you embrace the organic flow of your moods as part of the nuanced being that you are, they begin to feel natural and nurturing. Whenever strong emotions throw you off, remember to bring your focus back to your heart and your center.

---

**SET YOUR INTENTION**
I will stay aware of my emotions and moods. I will
track my emotional weather to better harmonize
with my inner atmosphere. I will communicate
my emotional changes to supportive others.

# Empathy Deficit Disorder

Research has shown that some people demonstrate a lack of empathy. Full-blown narcissists, sociopaths, and psychopaths fall into this category. Sadly, their compassion hasn't developed, or it has been inhibited from early trauma such as abuse or from having been raised by narcissistic parents. Scientific research now postulates that their neurological systems are wired differently than people that do have empathy.

Though these individuals may initially seem charming or caring, this is simply a facade that will soon crumble when you oppose them. Hard as it may be to comprehend, people with empathy deficit disorder have little insight into their unconscionable actions, nor do they regret them.

Take an honest accounting of your relationships to identify people in your life who may lack empathy. Then either lower your expectations or limit contact. Do not confide your deepest feelings to them. Instead, seek intimacy from those who are capable of reciprocating empathy with kindness.

---

### SET YOUR INTENTION
I will not have false expectations of people who
have narcissistic tendencies. I will not open my
heart to anyone who lacks empathy, no matter how
seductively understanding they may first appear.

# Create "Safe" Words and Signals

A useful communication strategy with your partner, colleagues, or friends is to agree on "safe" words or signals that convey a message during an awkward conversation. For instance, if your partner tends to tell long stories in social situations, agree on a hand signal, such as touching your left ear or flashing the peace sign, to remind them to wrap it up. Or you may pick a word such as *antelope*, *sunset*, or *mercy* that a friend can use with you in social situations when she is ready to go home. Deciding on this strategy beforehand helps you prevent embarrassing moments and preserves the health of a relationship.

**SET YOUR INTENTION**
I will select "safe" words or signals to use
with others to avoid unskillful or hurtful
communication. This strategy will caution me
to avoid going down a counterproductive path.

# Managing Your To-Do List

Your attitude toward your to-do list can have a big effect on your stress level. Realize that daily demands are endless. Though occasionally you might actually reach the end, your list will just keep growing again.

If your to-do list is the first thing you think about upon awakening — a sure way to start your day with stress — shift your perspective. You want to wake up slowly, not with your heart pounding or your mind obsessing on what you have to accomplish. Surrender the notion that you can do it all. You can't. None of us can. So relax. Each day you are alive is a blessing. True, there are many practical necessities to address, so mindfully complete them one task at a time. Prioritize items that are essential and leave the rest for later.

Think of your to-do list as a spiritual teacher imparting the lessons of compassion, healthy pacing, and staying in the moment. This relieves the tension of having to achieve what is too much for anyone.

**SET YOUR INTENTION**
I will not let the length of my to-do list upset
me. I will not keep pressuring myself about
completing tasks. I will make continual progress
with this list — and that is good enough.

# Relax Your Eyes

Your eyes offer you the miracle of visual perception. You want to take good care of them. So be mindful not to overstrain them while working long hours on your computer or while trying to decipher small print on text messages and phones. To soothe tired eyes, practice the following exercise one or more times throughout the day.

*Take a few minutes to quiet yourself and be still. Sit in a comfortable position. Then close your eyes and gently cup one palm over each eye. You are giving your eyes a rest from light and movement so they can relax naturally. While you're doing this, turn your focus to your heart energy in your mid-chest. Allow the sense of bliss and healing it conveys to flow up your arms and out your palms to caress your eyes. This is comforting and will release any stress you are holding in this area.*

**SET YOUR INTENTION**
I will be proactive about keeping my eyes healthy. I will periodically rest them from stress and ongoing overuse.

# A Small Circle of Friends

Over the holidays (and during the year), you may prefer being with a small group of friends rather than attending larger gatherings. If you feel more comfortable with just one or a few people, honor that need. Or if you prefer hibernating alone, that's also fine. (One of my friends, with her husband's support, takes periods of silence over the holidays.) If you do attend large gatherings, sit next to someone you like and take a few short rest breaks to center yourself. Look for attendees whom you can laugh with and relate to. Create your own fun. If you are an extroverted empath, you might love socializing with larger groups but also allow downtime afterward to regroup and decompress.

**SET YOUR INTENTION**
I will not succumb to social pressure to attend large gatherings unless I like them or they are unavoidable. I give myself permission to be with a few people or alone if that's what I need.

# Don't Overcommit Yourself

If you tend to be a people pleaser, you may feel exhausted because you have a difficult time saying no. You end up overcommitting to holiday office parties, family dinners, or other events so you begin to feel the malaise of being overscheduled. But paradoxically, the holiday season is an excellent opportunity to reel in your codependent tendencies so you don't burn yourself out trying to make everyone happy at the expense of your own energy.

Scrutinize your schedule so that you don't plan too many events. Also, as a compromise, make short appearances at gatherings rather than staying for hours. If you feel guilty about saying no or haven't come to terms with the reality that sometimes you will disappoint others, take more time to contemplate this truth and see if you can feel it more deeply. It is not your job to constantly satisfy other people's needs. During the holiday season and afterward, give yourself permission not to overcommit yourself.

### SET YOUR INTENTION
I will practice self-care by not overcommitting
myself to social events. I will relax more as the
year winds down and leave some unstructured
time for self-reflection and rejuvenation.

# Beware of Energy Vampires

The quality of your relationships affects your well-being. Some people will increase your energy, whereas others, whom I call "energy vampires," will sap it. Staying mindful of draining people who suck you dry is part of your self-care during the more social holiday season and always.

How do you know you've encountered an energy vampire? Your eyelids grow heavy, and you suddenly need a nap. Your mood takes a nosedive—you may become agitated, depressed, or angry—when you were fine before. Or you feel attacked, criticized, or blamed. Train yourself to be aware of these telltale signs.

Be ready for energy vampires and proceed accordingly. Avoid sitting next to a chronic complainer or nonstop talker at a holiday dinner. Do not let yourself be triggered by a friend's judgmental comments. Take regular bathroom breaks to decompress and center yourself. Or utilize the "protective bubble" technique I discussed on September 11 to safeguard your energy. It's also helpful to journal about the energy vampires in your life and strategies for dealing with them. When you practice self-care around these people, you will protect yourself from being depleted.

---

**SET YOUR INTENTION**
I will be aware of the energy vampires in my life
and not give away my power to them. I deserve
to have gratifying and energizing relationships.

# Giving Thanks

This is an ideal time of year to be grateful for your blessings. Gratitude is a spiritual act. You are sending a message to loved ones, colleagues, and Spirit that you are thankful for them. Even if you perceive your life as lacking, just for today, humbly focus on your blessings.

Ask yourself, "What am I grateful for? My health? Physical mobility? Clarity of mind? Or the capacity to love, despite all the challenges I've faced?" What about your friends, family, and animal companions? Or your home, car, job, and healthy food?

Then inwardly declare, "I am grateful for my life. I am grateful for everyone who loves me, and whom I love. I am grateful for the Earth, the birds, the sky, and the oceans." Feel free to add to this list in any way that applies to you. In addition, you can express your gratitude directly to others by saying, "Thank you for being in my life. You have enhanced it more than you could know." A simple expression of appreciation means so much.

This time of year — and really every day — is a sacred opportunity for thanksgiving.

---

**SET YOUR INTENTION**
I will focus on all I have to be grateful for
and allow my heart to feel content and full.
I will be thankful for the love in my life.

# Recovery Time

After socializing or being in public for an extended duration, give yourself some downtime to recover. Even if you had fun with the increased stimulation of people contact, you may develop an emotional hangover later that day or the day after. Also you may notice that you have absorbed unwanted emotions from others. Empaths frequently don't feel well going from one activity to the next without having some recovery time. Do not plan anything else right now. Make time to be quiet and still to shake the emotional hangover. Breathe out any stress you might have absorbed. Take a long, luxurious bath to let the water wash away your cares. Immerse yourself in meditation to cleanse your subtle energy body. Or go to sleep early. Talk less, rest, and spend quiet recovery time alone to return to your center of gravity.

**SET YOUR INTENTION**
I will not plan back-to-back activities without
a break. I will allow recovery time after the
higher stimulation of social contact.

# All My Relations

You are interconnected with all of life, including your own lineage. Vital energy infuses everything in our world. For our intuition, this is a cellular truth. Though you are a separate being, it is also respectful to honor all of your relations from humans to the natural world. In my life this means: The spirit of the river is important to me. I want her water to be fresh and clean. I bow to the holiness of Father Sky and Mother Earth. I care about the stranger and all those who are suffering in the world, though I do not take on their pain. I acknowledge the wisdom of my elders and the purity of children.

Your life is important to me. Though we may have never met, I am delighted with your happiness. My wish is that you be well and flourish. And if you grieve, my heart goes out to you. We are all bonded through the intricate web of existence. In that spirit, I embrace all my relations, the entirety of life, and the infinity of the unknowable.

### SET YOUR INTENTION
I will remain aware that I belong to the intimate energy
network of all sentient beings. I will remain aware that
I am connected to my human family and to the Earth.

# The Earth Speaks

Some say that if you travel far enough into the open desert you will hear the ancient hum of the Earth called the "Sonora." She emanates a primal sound that you can detect if you get quiet enough, if you go deep enough, if the stillness of nature allows you to be privy to its existence.

Researchers claim that our planet's constant hum originates at the bottom of the ocean, and that it is the native sound of the Earth. Its frequency is lower than humans can ordinarily hear. Yet there are ancient ones and current-day sensitives who have heard the hum in places like Taos, New Mexico, and the Anza-Borrego Desert in Southern California. They say it feels satisfying, compelling, and mysterious. It seems that this hum would be in harmony with the sand dunes that sing when the wind is just right and with the moon when she chants on the solstice. In your quiet moments, listen for this sound to connect you with the vibration of life.

**SET YOUR INTENTION**
I will remember that there is more to the universe
than what science deems possible. I will stretch
my intuition to sense the mystery of life.

# Am I an Energy Vampire?

We all can become draining at times. That's why it's essential to be honestly and nondefensively accountable for your behavior. You may not intend to deplete others, yet, still you lapse into a period of complaining, of ungratefulness, or of being critical. If so, no blame.

Simply take stock and begin to quickly shift your behavior. Be compassionate with yourself. It's okay to fall into old emotional patterns that you thought were behind you. Perhaps you recognize the slip and self-correct without external feedback. If others have the courage to kindly mention your behavior to you, it's affirming when you can respond, "Wow, thank you for pointing this out. I will stay more aware of it." The problem with becoming an energy vampire is if you remain unconscious of your behavior and continue to inflict it on others. So the key is to stay self-aware. Genuinely powerful and secure people are able to recognize and own their behavior. They set aside their egos in service to conscious, loving communication.

**SET YOUR INTENTION**
If I become an energy vampire, I will stay open
to considerate feedback from others about my
actions. I will be aware of my behavior and make
an effort to shift to a more positive state.

# Small Acts of Service

Giving is the language of love. It's exciting to be of service to others and the world. What you give, you get back a thousandfold. Giving from your heart creates radiance around you. Small acts are magnificent. Many opportunities will cross your path. Even when you are in a hurry, hold the elevator door open for an elderly person with a walker or a harried mother with a small child. Allow the stranger in the bank line who is late for work to step in front of you. Pick up litter on the street. Tell your partner or coworker, "You look fantastic today."

Orient your life to being of service every day in healthy ways without overgiving (which is exhausting). It's our holy duty to be of service to each other and to the Earth. Don't worry that you are doing too little. I'm in love with small acts of service, minute bursts of light, and smiles between strangers who have lent each other a helping hand. When you give just the right amount — and your body's signals and energy level will tell you this — you will feel good about yourself and become the human angel that Spirit intended.

**SET YOUR INTENTION**
Actions speak louder than words. I will
experience the joy of being of service to
another. I will do something helpful to ease
the burdens or responsibilities of a loved one.

# Gestating

Gestation is a creative period of growth and development from within, just as a fetus gestates in a womb. Sometimes you may be overly aggressive about furthering your goals, so you don't allow enough time for your visions, relationships, or projects to incubate. However, the I Ching says that the darker seasons lend themselves to learning from hibernation and gestation, preparing for your renewal in spring. Shorter days and longer nights are conducive to deep meditative practice, grounding in the earth, and locating your own center.

You are called to withdraw within to find answers. You talk less and listen more to the sounds of silence. Creative impulses arise out of nothingness when your active mind can step aside to allow revelations to surface. Simply stay receptive and still. You don't have to try to manifest anything. Letting go to the mystery of life as the darkness builds naturally leads to discovering the light within.

**SET YOUR INTENTION**
I will support my own inner process
of gestation by allowing time for inspiration
to take form in the stillness of my soul.

# First Snow

One frosty day, you can see the first flurries of pure white snow-flakes drifting from the sky. Like tiny pieces of cotton and light as feathers, they soften the edges of the landscape with change. The sky is bedazzled as a serene layer of snow adorns the wanting, bare trees, meadows, and concrete cities. If the weather gets cold enough, snow turns into icicles, a stunning transmutation of the water element.

The first snow offers another kind of new beginning. Nature is saying, "Start again in a different phase. Be fresh, be renewed, be enchanted." The snow may be so deep that all footprints disappear so your new path is totally clear. Whether you watch the first snow falling outside your window, in nature, or see it in the news, pause for a moment. Snow is a purifier and cleanses the environment. Appreciate its delicate beauty. Also visualize a peaceful snowfall within yourself softening your rough edges and craggy boughs.

---

**SET YOUR INTENTION**
I will pay attention to the magic of the first snowfall.
Just as the Earth is entering another creative cycle with
changing weather, I will be ready for my changes too.

# The Sacrament of Passing Time

Does it seem that time is passing too quickly? Do the days, weeks, and years go by in a flash? Time speeds up when you have an active life. Also rushing, overthinking, and being too busy separate you from the slower, more organic rhythms of life.

Be aware of the sacrament of passing time by concentrating your focus and developing a slow-motion gaze. Be present with what you are doing rather than having your mind wander in many directions. Pay close attention to daily events such as preparing breakfast or walking your dog. Feel how exuberant these moments are.

Planning to do less helps you retain the sacredness of the moment. Gazing at a rose for five seconds instead of one second or not at all lets you experience its essence rather than simply being just another passerby with a short attention span. Track the passage of time with your eyes, ears, and energy. Love the moment for the blessings it bestows.

### SET YOUR INTENTION
I will not simply look at the world as an observer. I will experience the brilliant life force emanating from everything. This allows me to appreciate the sacrament of passing time.

# The Comfort of Hot Water Bottles

A hot water bottle is an old-fashioned remedy that reduces pain, quells anxiety, and warms the bed. While growing up, my mother used to give me one to soothe me and ease discomfort. At some point, hot water bottles seemed to go out of style—replaced by more utilitarian electric heating pads—but recently, a friend reintroduced me to them. Mine has become a happy addition to my self-care regimen.

I love the therapeutic benefits of a hot water bottle. It makes you feel secure and snuggly, especially in the chill of winter. It can be your warm friend and pain reliever. You can place it on your feet if they are cold, and it can relieve the muscle tension of an aching back. It also relaxes children and adults before bed so they drift into sleep more peacefully. Give yourself a present of a hot water bottle. Let it provide ongoing ease.

**SET YOUR INTENTION**
I will have a hot water bottle on hand to relieve discomfort and help me relax. I will feel comforted by its heat and friendliness.

# Getting Cozy with Your Animal Friends

Spend a happy day cuddling with your animal companions. Animals have an instinct for finding just the right places on your body to comfort and heal. Your dog looks at you with unflinchingly adoring eyes. Or your cat curls up and blissfully purrs on your chest. Feel the positive energy they send so easily and willingly. They are adorable angels sent as emissaries to offer solace and care.

Animals give unconditional love. They are devoted to you, no matter how distraught or distracted you may feel. They are always present to calm your woes. If you don't have an animal at home, you might want to visit a friend's dogs or cats to bask in their playfulness and the affection they offer.

Let yourself be loved by animals. Especially on cold, blustery days, cuddle up to them and surrender to the pleasure of their company.

**SET YOUR INTENTION**
I will spend quality time with animals and soak up the sustenance of their giving. Bonding with animals is a tender way to give and receive love.

# Melting Rigidity

In Taoist philosophy, when you become rigid, it blocks your flow of energy and well-being. You may tense up as a way to protect yourself when you are physically or emotionally threatened.

In nature, rigidity has a positive function. After all, ice is simply water frozen into a solid state. The polar ice caps keep our climate stable. Polar bears need to hunt on solid ice to survive. Similarly, we must know when not to give in and when to stay firm and sure.

However, the challenge is to become less rigid without compromising your integrity—and to hold space for others' needs without sacrificing your soul. So keep examining ways to become less tight, icy, and uncompromising. Reflect on what triggers your rigidity, and how you can heal those fears. The less fear you have, the less rigid you will be. Gradually melt the tense and constricted parts of yourself.

---

**SET YOUR INTENTION**
I will be firm but not rigid. I will be flowing
but know where my limits are. I will be mindful
of those times when I become rigid and unyielding
so I can shift into a more fluid state.

# Aurora Borealis

In the northern latitudes, the aurora borealis, or northern lights, is a psychedelic light display in the sky. (The version in the southern hemisphere is called aurora australis, or southern lights.) The chances of seeing it are greater in winter. Since childhood, I have been mesmerized by pictures of the aurora. Her wavy multicolored illuminations in the sky hold such wonder for me. (In fact, "Aurora" is my chosen nickname.)

Some say that seers can view the light around the human body: dazzling blue, green, yellow, orange, and white. Imagine the aurora surrounding your body, the ever-changing rainbow being that you are. Even in harsh circumstances, or at those times when you can't access it, your light is present.

So to keep that "knowing" alive, remember the aurora borealis. You can even make a pilgrimage to parts of the Earth such as Iceland or Alaska where the aurora is visible. It's a dream of my own to fulfill one day.

**SET YOUR INTENTION**
The splendor of the aurora's light mirrors the light emanating from my body. I will meditate on the aurora borealis and feel that stunning radiance within myself.

# Holiday Cheer

There is a lightness and joy during the holiday season. The festive decorations, like candles and angels adorning shop windows, can be enchanting. Scents of cinnamon, hot chocolate with whipped cream, gingerbread, and pine trees waft through the air. Little dogs are dressed in the cutest warm sweaters. Also I am transported by the divine harmony of choral music and Gregorian chants, so medieval and mystical.

However, this season may also be stressful for sensitive people who can be overwhelmed by crowds, commercialism, noise, drinking, social demands, and expectations to "be happy." When I was single, I would see all the "happy" families or couples and feel so left out. It's easy to get lonely around the holidays. To cope, I would stick close to one or a few good friends, a strategy I suggest if you are in this position.

You can also be of service to the needy if that feels right. Or take a friend to lunch. Give in a way that feels good to you. In fact, you can tap into some truly uplifting energies this month when you focus on the power of love, giving, and the spiritual birth within you.

**SET YOUR INTENTION**
I will find happiness this holiday season and be grateful
for my blessings. I will make my own fun wherever I go.

# Overwhelmed by Crowds

During the holidays, the world becomes particularly crowded. Take special precautions to practice self-care around swarms of people. Be mindful not to become overwhelmed in crowds. Consider limiting your exposure to them. Since people's energy fields overlap when they are in close proximity, you may be vulnerable to absorbing the stress of others.

If you visit shopping malls, large stores such as Costco or Walmart, or other busy places, make sure you are rested and that you have eaten some protein beforehand to ground yourself. Keep breathing deeply to circulate unwanted energy out of your body and plan a few minutes to sit or meditate on benches or in the bathroom. Taking periodic mini breaks to replenish yourself can help you stay more centered and less prone to being drained. Then you can more easily find joy in this season's festive atmosphere while you safeguard your energy.

**SET YOUR INTENTION**
I will practice self-care in crowded locations to
avoid feeling overloaded or taking on other people's
stress. I will not go to crowded environments
unless I feel centered and ready for the task.

# The Universe Has a Plan

When the sky is dark and each day feels like a demanding uphill climb, know that the universe has a plan. When you are happy, fulfilled, and your dearest wishes manifest, know that the universe has a plan. Nothing is out of order in the perfectly orchestrated timing of your life. Nothing is random or meaningless. Nor are you ever alone. You are always being watched over and guided in every phase of your life. You need to do your part to heal and overcome obstacles, but an invisible helping hand is always there. Even when you feel lonely or depressed and can't find a solution to whatever is blocking you, know that the answers will come. That's where faith comes in. When you hold this all-inclusive view of your entire life, both the obstacles and periods of grace, you will profoundly connect with your own destiny.

**SET YOUR INTENTION**
I will accept that everything I encounter has a
divinely inspired message to help my spirit evolve.
I will have faith in my intuition and trust that I'm
on the right path, whether it is smooth or rugged.

# Longevity

Longevity commonly describes becoming an elder, but it can also refer to a long-term relationship, career, or a set of enduring beliefs. I greatly value friends, family, and my readers who have known me for decades and have witnessed my changes.

Father Winter symbolizes longevity and the colder seasons. He is an ancient pagan figure who has evolved into Santa Claus. As a messenger of the goddess riding a white horse, he delivered fruit and magical herbs to the people. Is he just a symbol for children? I think not. Watch for glimpses of him and the goodwill he bestows.

Reflect on what aspects of longevity you've experienced. Which long-term relationships or personal values have brought you comfort? Have you reached longevity in terms of years on this planet? Are there advantages to growing older, such as becoming more awake personally and spiritually? How have positive beliefs helped you stay vibrant and optimistic? You can be luminous at any age when your heart stays open and pure.

---

**SET YOUR INTENTION**
I will appreciate the various forms of longevity
in my life, including aging. I will view the
gratifying relationships and situations that have
stood the test of time with renewed gratitude.

# Walking Each Other Home

I am touched when spiritual teacher Ram Dass talks about how we are all just walking each other home. Each day, we continue on this inevitable journey of the spirit. Our stay on Earth is transient. Beyond the time-space realm, a greater mystery awaits. Some spiritual traditions call this heaven. With intuition, you can get a sense of its light and bliss and of burdens lifting. Having felt this even once, you can also create a little more heaven on Earth too.

When the time comes, we will all take the leap into the Great Beyond. No way around it. In the meantime, your beloved companions are good company here. Fellow empaths are part of your family too. Value these soul friends. They will bring solace and are like-minded people to commune with on your path. With every passing moment, we get closer to the eternal. Let's go there together as seekers who can appreciate the grandeur of it all.

### SET YOUR INTENTION
I will walk each step home with humility and awe. I am grateful for every fellow traveler who lightens my load and with whom I share love and laughter along the way.

# Moon Bathing

Bathe yourself in the moon's sublime white light and sensuality. Moonlight on the hills or on water infuses you with gentleness and the receptive "yin" energy. When it is reflected on the whiteness of snow, the night becomes even brighter. I have a large window above my tub that allows the lunar radiance to stream through. Floating in the water, I am immersed in ribbons of liquid light that move when I move.

Empaths react differently to the moon's cycles. Notice how your emotions fluctuate. The tides are regulated by the moon and our body's physiology is responsive as well. Experiment with moon bathing when the moon is full, a time when empaths may feel extra energized and emotional or sometimes even unbalanced. Also see how the new moon affects you. You may feel calmer and more still.

Moon bathing cleanses your energy and is fun. Find a place where the moon is visible and focus on her light. Walk outside. Get in your tub. Or simply watch her gracing the sky. The moon never forsakes us. She is always there to offer a kind word and gentle prayer.

**SET YOUR INTENTION**
I will practice moon bathing to clear negativity and stress. I will open to the delicate beauty of moonlight and let it bring solace to my soul.

# Stillness

Stillness is a wide-open space, a place of inactivity and quietude. It is the quintessential intuitive realm. When the chatter in your mind quiets and your mind and body are at rest, inspiration will come.

Science has shown that silence and stillness are good for your brain and that excessive noise can shorten your life span. With the intense input of the digital world, your brain has less time to switch off. You are constantly processing massive amounts of information. But if your environment has lower levels of sensory input, your brain can recover its cognitive clarity. Spending time alone in silence allows your mind to relax and release its constant focus. When you aren't rushing or overscheduled, your body will breathe a sigh of relief and become still. The noisy world can drown out creativity, but the stillness of quietude will help you make better sense of your life.

Since this time of year can be noisy and hectic, be mindful to catch the first signs of sensory overload in yourself so that you can quickly tone down your activity level and become still.

---

**SET YOUR INTENTION**

I know that excessive noise and activity may be overstimulating. I will plan still, nonverbal periods to allow my brain to physiologically recover from noise and information overload.

# Prayer

When you pray, you are calling out to the benevolence of the universe for protection, clarity, and care. By requesting assistance from a force greater than yourself, you are reaching beyond your ego and mere logic. In this humble, receptive state, your prayers will be heard. But there's no guarantee that they will be answered in the exact form you specified or hoped for. Sometimes unanswered prayers are the greatest blessings of all.

Prayer is an attitude of the heart. It reattunes you to hope, the way a tuning fork offers perfect pitch. When you're confused or tired, optimism can seem so far away. But, as silent actress Dorothy Bernard said, "Courage is fear that has said its prayers." To pray is an act of opening to Spirit and then of being filled. Poet C. K. Williams writes, "I'd empty like a cup; that would be prayer, to empty, then fill with a substance other than myself."

Rather than being more specific, pray for the highest good for yourself or others. Sometimes "good" things happen that turn out to be bad. And supposedly "bad" things happen that turn out to be good. That's why praying for the highest good allows Spirit to respond in the purest, most perfect ways. Simply become an open vessel for prayer and let the answers appear.

---

**SET YOUR INTENTION**
I will turn to prayer to reach out to the infinity of love.
I will sincerely pray for the highest good in a situation.

# Watched Over by Angels

Angels are often considered messengers from Spirit and manifestations of goodness. They help us when we are in danger or need guidance. You may not even realize when an angel intervenes. Maybe you barely avoid a terrible car accident. Or you are hired for your dream job, despite fierce competition. Or a stranger steps in to help you when you drop all your groceries.

You can call on specific angels to protect you from harm such as archangel Michael, the mighty warrior who defends against the forces of darkness. If you need assistance to handle a difficult situation, you can call on Michael or any angel for divine help. Then feel the grace that comes. Even if you might think angels are "woo-woo," that's fine too. You don't have to believe in them to be a good or spiritual person. But if you acknowledge angels as allies, they can become the celestial pillar of your empath support team.

---

**SET YOUR INTENTION**
I will be like a child again and, at least for now, set
aside my disbelief about angels or other nonphysical
kinds of spiritual aid. I will ask an angel for
guidance and act on the instructions I receive.

# Seasonal Affective Disorder

Empaths are often sensitive to changes in natural light. This makes them vulnerable to seasonal affective disorder (SAD), a type of depression that starts as the days shorten in autumn and ends in spring. Symptoms include lethargy, social isolation, low motivation, difficulty concentrating, and overeating (especially carbohydrates). Like clockwork, your mood changes in direct relationship to the available sunlight of a season.

If you suffer from SAD, light therapy can be effective. Your symptoms lessen when you sit in front of a light box for an hour every morning. This exposure to bright, artificial light replaces the decreased sunshine. Also, low vitamin D levels are associated with SAD, so some physicians suggest daily supplements. Psychotherapy and occasionally antidepressants may also be recommended by a physician.

Since SAD can intensify your usual need for alone time and low stimulation, meditating and exercising more can help boost serotonin, your body's natural antidepressant. Though you may want to isolate socially when you experience seasonal depression, do your best to stretch yourself to be with loving people too. The right kind of human contact is healing. We can be good medicine for one another.

---

**SET YOUR INTENTION**
I will give myself an extra dose of loving
self-care if I experience seasonal depression.
I will view this experience as a teacher for
cultivating deeper self-compassion.

# Closure

This month brings closure to the year. Reflect on what you have accomplished and tie up any loose ends. Consider your relationships, work, and finances. Do you still need to make amends to a friend or coworker? Are there any unexpressed or unresolved feelings? Do you want to complete a project or finalize a decision at work? Can you clear up any debts, financial obligations, or leftover paperwork? Perhaps this year a friendship or intimate relationship has ended. Or someone you loved has transitioned to the Great Beyond. Let yourself fully grieve and say goodbye. This allows for a conscious resolution rather than repressing your feelings of loss.

When one door closes, another will open. Closure allows you to find a resolution or conclusion. It means finality; that you have accepted people or circumstances exactly as they are, and you are complete with them. There is no unfinished business left unattended. No resentments. No leftover anger. Nothing more to say about an issue. You are free to go on to something new.

---

**SET YOUR INTENTION**

I will identify aspects of my life that require closure and take action to achieve it. This will bring completion to an issue or situation so I can move on with a clean slate.

# The Wisdom of Slowing Down

There comes a point when your body and soul need to rest. As we approach the winter solstice, maximum darkness cradles us in serenity and quiet. Your heart may long to go inward. It deserves a break from worry and striving. You want to daydream and gaze at the empty spaces between things.

There is tremendous wisdom in not pushing yourself so hard. You deserve a break. Though you may socialize more during the holidays, leave a resting place for your heart and your body. Mark empty periods in your schedule so nothing can intrude. Ideally, take time off from work so your metabolism can slow, your stress can decrease, and your heart and spirit can flourish in the holy emptiness of unplanned time.

---

**SET YOUR INTENTION**
I will practice the wisdom of slowing down.
I will stop pushing and striving. I will arrange
periods to decrease my pace, to hibernate and
safeguard my downtime for rest and reflection.

# Create Peace

Making peace with yourself leads to contentment at home. Seek harmony with the people you live with. Jesus said, "If two make peace with each other in a single house, they will say to the mountain, 'Move from here,' and it will move."

You have nothing to gain by clinging to resentments and bad feelings. Despite what your ego says (it always feels justified in remaining bitter), move your awareness to your heart, which is not at all invested in being right or vengeful. Look at a person who annoyed or upset you and create peace. Respect everyone in your circle of intimates, despite their shortcomings, and stretch your heart to get along.

Chaos theory advances the notion of the butterfly effect: Under the right conditions, the flap of a butterfly's wings in China can ultimately cause a tornado in North America. Similarly, your inner peace can ripple out to your environment and the greater world.

**SET YOUR INTENTION**
I will take responsibility for creating peace
and vow to heal the parts of myself that are
still at war. Peace starts from within me.

# Empathy Is the Medicine the World Needs

Empathy lets you see the world through another's eyes, even if you don't agree with them. You come from your highest self rather than from your ego-driven "lower self," which only wants to blame and lash out.

As a psychiatrist, I know that when people are hurt, they can become unkind, a symptom of their woundedness. I agree with the saying "Hurt people hurt people." When you're feeling good about yourself, you don't want to be unkind. Empathy lets you choose not to react defensively to a person's wounded self; though, of course, you can set a boundary with their behavior. Having empathy for where someone is coming from doesn't always ensure that you will get through to them, but it's your best hope.

If you want peace, you are the messenger. Be the first to say no to division and polarization and yes to understanding our human family. Choosing empathy gives peace a real chance in your life and in the world.

---

**SET YOUR INTENTION**
I will rise above my emotional wounds to feel empathy
for others. I will keep trying to win over people with
my heart rather than engaging in a confrontation.

# WINTER

## Going Inward, Sensing Truth

Winter welcomes you to quiet your mind, be still, and listen to your intuition. It is associated with the water element and its properties of conserving energy and providing tranquility. It is the season of the recluse or hermit, which suits many empaths who adore retreating into their caves. You can also gather in front of cozy fireplaces and bundle up in warm clothing outside.

During the dark of winter, icy winds blow. Trees slow their metabolism to become dormant. Bears and other animals enter the long sleep of hibernation. Similarly, you can focus on building your internal energy.

Since empaths are often light sensitive, a challenge of winter is feeling depressed—your body's response to less daylight. Also, you may isolate socially, feel lonely, or be overwhelmed by holiday crowds, gatherings, and a frenetic pace. It's vital to balance the natural rhythms of winter with a busy world.

The winter solstice marks the first day of this season. It's the darkest point of the year when the Earth tilts furthest away from the sun. As days grow longer again, there is a gradual ascent into light. Winter invites you to heal your shadow side, including fears or self-doubts.

Winter is exciting because it takes you to your depths. Reflect on your progress and areas that need growth. I love conducting this comprehensive review in December to evaluate my life and move on with more clarity to the year ahead.

# Gifts from the Shadow

In Jungian psychology, the shadow refers to the darker part of our personalities. Everyone has a shadow side. Lovingly addressing the parts of you that may be fearful, angry, or even spiteful and mean lets you tame and heal them.

Around the winter solstice, the longest night of the year, reflect on the lessons you've received from the shadow. Did you find hope during a depression? Were you kind to yourself when you felt anxious? Did you say no to an abusive relationship? Affirm your courage in facing your shadow side and the progress that you made.

The cold mood of winter can catalyze the depth of your inner journey. Just because it's dark doesn't mean your light is gone. As Albert Camus wrote, "In the midst of winter, I found there was, within me, an invincible summer." The first rays of a new dawn are about to come.

**SET YOUR INTENTION**
I will not be afraid of or avoid my shadow
side. I will explore it and acknowledge its
lessons as a way of becoming more whole.

# Igniting the Light

Illuminating the darkness is a theme for this season. In the spirit of Hanukkah, known as the Festival of Lights, Christmas, and all traditions that celebrate spiritual rebirth and the love of humankind, you can reignite your inner flame. It doesn't matter if it has temporarily gone out or if you have lost faith in yourself or in life. You can rekindle your flame now by pledging allegiance to goodness and vowing to fight darkness in all its incarnations.

Today, do something special to pay homage to the light. Build a blazing fire in your hearth. Light candles. Be grateful for the sun's illumination. Or you can burn sage or sweetgrass to purify the environment. In quiet reverence, meditate on the radiance within you, feel its warmth and bask in its glow. There is no limit to your inner brightness. Let your heart connect to it and grow stronger.

**SET YOUR INTENTION**
I can always rekindle my inner flame if it has grown
dim. I will focus on my own light and on my strengths.
I will create an abundance of light in my life.

# Soulful Giving

Soulful giving feels good. There are many gratifying ways to give. You can offer your time, your heart, or a material present over the holidays or on no special occasion at all. In addition, you can donate anonymously to a worthy cause. Or, as I do, you can leave small amounts of money in public places—by an office water cooler or in the park—so that people can find them and feel lucky. It's a fun way to give anonymously too.

For me, simple, heartfelt gifts have more meaning than extravagant ones. A journal. A small plant. Candles. Oracle cards. Moving music. A poem. You don't need to overspend or overgive to others. Just consider whether the gift resonates with the intended receiver.

I always add positive vibes to a present I'm giving someone by holding the object in my hands for a minute and sending it loving energy. The gift absorbs these good feelings so when the recipient opens it, they are washed with love. You can try this too. When you give a material present that is infused with love, it becomes a more soulful offering.

---

**SET YOUR INTENTION**
I will look at gift giving as a chance to share
love and positive energy with another person
or a cause. I will give from my heart always.

# Open to Miracles

Amazing grace is everywhere. Take time to feel and absorb it. The miraculous is right before your eyes if you can *see*. It's present in the small wonders of everyday life as well as when your larger wishes come true. Don't ever become too much of an adult or too "levelheaded" and lose your innocence. The more you believe in miracles, the more they will manifest. This is not simply naive. You're rightly recognizing the limits of the laws of physics and affirming that a surprisingly wonderful event (unexplained by science) is possible. Realizing that something greater exists beyond our mere human powers, statistical probability predictions, or physical laws is a testament to hope and the amazing grace of spiritual assistance.

**SET YOUR INTENTION**
I will be ready to receive blessings from the universe.
I will be open to miracles occurring in my life.

# The Power of Love

A belief in love is unstoppable.

Let today represent the rebirth of love. When everything falls apart, love emerges. When sadness overtakes your heart, a glimmer of hope reappears. All is not lost. Love is more powerful than hate or resentment or depression. Love is the antidote to every war waged within your heart or in the world. Love is the force that makes atoms and quarks vibrate. Everything would come to a standstill without the compassionate energy of the universe propelling it.

Awaken the love in your heart. Choose to resolve your resentments and embrace hope for a better day. Don't keep looking back. Rather, see the light and promise of your future. Begin again, always. Affirm to yourself, "I vow to love myself and spread love in the world. I am capable of rising above my fears and insecurities. My love will not be stopped."

**SET YOUR INTENTION**
I stand at the feet of love and bow to it. I will sing its praises and embody its precepts. Love is all there is.

# The Grace of Forgiveness

Forgiveness lets you compassionately release the need to punish someone or yourself for a wrongdoing. It's a state of grace, nothing you can force or pretend. When you forgive, you don't change the past. You change the future.

Begin to forgive by identifying one person (this could be yourself) whom you are angry with or who hurt you. There are no shortcuts. Journal about your authentic feelings. Don't censor your pain, rage, or disappointments. Or perhaps you've been shamed about being sensitive. Get out all your feelings. Then inwardly ask Spirit to help you experience forgiveness, which is more for your sake than another's. Holding on to blame and pain only drains you and throws you off-center.

You don't have to excuse a despicable act, but you can aim to forgive the damaged, thoughtless part of someone who committed it. This releases you from bearing the albatross of toxic emotions or grudges so you can move forward with your life.

---

**SET YOUR INTENTION**
I will not let myself be weighed down by
resentments. I will allow the healing power
of forgiveness to cleanse and renew me.

# Life Review

By taking stock of your experiences this year, you'll gain clarity and compassion on your journey as an empath.

Reflect on your progress and challenges. What were the emotional high points? Did you honor your sensitivities? Were you able to overcome low self-esteem? Did you set kind but firm boundaries with a colleague? Did you make a new friend or travel to an exotic location? Be grateful for these strides.

Then review your challenges. What losses or heartbreaks did you experience? When did you succumb to fear? When did you ignore your intuition or forget to practice self-care? Did you break a promise and still need to apologize? Everyone makes mistakes, but taking ownership of them helps clear bad karma. It also stops you from repeating these behaviors and minimizes their repercussions if you make amends. Lovingly appraise everything you've been through and set positive goals for the new year.

**SET YOUR INTENTION**
I will do a thorough life review of the past year.
I don't have to be perfect or infallible. I will learn
from my mistakes and my successes so I can grow.

# The Sensitive Will Inherit the Earth

In the end, love will be victorious. Jesus said in the Sermon on the Mount, "Blessed are the meek, for they shall inherit the Earth." (The word *meek* is also translated as "gentle" or "sensitive.") The wisdom of this passage speaks to the ultimate triumph of humility and kindness.

As an empowered empath, you are both sensitive and strong. You are firm in your beliefs, yet yielding when the occasion warrants it. Bravely, you forge your own path, even when innumerable voices pressure you to go in another direction or to stop believing in yourself. You don't heed their bad advice but instead stay loyal to your own truth.

Because of your good heart, the Earth has chosen you as her guardian. Arrogant or greedy people are simply unfit for this task. The Earth's survival is in your loving hands. There is no doubt that you will care for her well just as you tenderly care for yourself and others. Your generous nature holds the secret to our longevity as humans and of this magnificent planet Earth.

---

**SET YOUR INTENTION**
I will have faith in my empathic gifts. I will accept
the responsibility of being an emissary of love
and embodying the change I want to see.

# All Is Well (and Getting Better in Every Dimension!)

In the Buddhist tradition, *haola* (pronounced "how-la") means "all is well and getting better." You can use this mantra to release worry and fear. During quiet moments repeat *haola* inwardly or softly chant it a few times. I learned this inspiring practice from Master Mingtong Gu as he led us through the ancient movements of chi gong practice at his center in Santa Fe, New Mexico.

There is no need to worry or be afraid. Keep shedding layers of concern and anxiety. When you encounter obstacles and fear, keep breathing through them. Don't give them any power. Keep opening to your intuition and all your empathic strengths for guidance. Your growth process is underway. Be happy with your destiny and your life. All is well and getting better in every dimension.

**SET YOUR INTENTION**
I am excited about what my life will bring and my ongoing learning as an empath. I will focus on the brightness of my future and the surprises that lie ahead.

# New Year's Dreams

As an empath, what do you dream about for the coming year?

I dream of peace and quiet. I dream of adventure and also of staying at home. I love to be alone, and I love to be with you. All this can come together when I express my true needs. I don't dream of pretending to be happy when I'm falling apart. Nor do I dream of being in a noisy, frantic world where I can't hear my intuition. I dream of being comfortable in my own skin, free of worry and strain. I dream of dreaming and coming into my own.

What are your fondest dreams, the ones you have and haven't yet achieved? Let yourself imagine everything that's possible. Be propelled by love and inspiration. Don't let anything stop you from envisioning a more fulfilling way to be. Also consider what you *don't* dream about. What do you want to avoid? What habits don't you want to repeat? Express your heart and all its yearnings. Your future is wide open. New possibilities are about to unfold. Dream your way into the new year with hope, imagination, and joy.

**SET YOUR INTENTION**
I will always allow myself to dream.
My dreams are real. I will make them come true.

# Shine Brightly, Warrior Empath

You have come so far on your journey of awakening. You have grown stronger and more sure as a warrior. You can embody the power of your sensitivities. You don't have to hide your gifts anymore.

Knowing you are an empath changes everything. Notice how your life has improved from this revelation. Applaud your progress every time you listen to your intuitive voice, express your empathic needs, and practice self-care. Keep expanding ways to nurture and protect your sensitivities. Keep learning how to become more centered and confident as you navigate the world of people. Self-care is a sacred process to continue refining over a lifetime.

Our collective light as empaths synergizes each other. We are rebels, outsiders, individualists, the ones who dare to break the mold. Your gentleness and caring can penetrate our callous society. Be a role model for newer empaths and show them the way. Let's walk the road less traveled together and support each other in bringing love and understanding to our own lives and the world.

---

**SET YOUR INTENTION**
I humbly embrace the power of being sensitive.
I will shine my light brightly and be
a messenger of goodness.

# ACKNOWLEDGMENTS

I am forever grateful to the people who have supported my writing and my sensitivities: Richard Pine, the agent of my dreams. Susan Golant, my highly skilled, devoted editor. Rhonda Bryant, my trusted assistant and friend. Corey Folsom, my multitalented partner who supports me as an empath and loves me in countless ways. Berenice Glass, who helps me stretch my heart to grow. Lorin Roche and Camille Maurine, soul friends and teachers who share my passion for the ocean and the universal mysteries.

A special thanks to the extraordinary, creative team at Sounds True: Tami Simon, Jennifer Brown, Leslie Brown, Wendy Gardner, Kira Roark, Lisa Kerans, Hannah Lees, and Mitchell Clute.

In addition, I take a deep bow to my friends, family, and support team for their inspiration and devotion: Dr. Ronald Alexander, Barbara Baird, Barbara Biziou, Charles Blum, Ann Buck, Laurie Sue Brockway, Kirk Curry, Dr. Eric Dolgin, Lily and David Dulan, Felice Dunas, Berenice Glass, Susan Foxley, Victor Fuhrman, Pamela Kaplan, Cathy Lewis, Reggie Jordan, Darlene Lancer, Dr. Richard Metzner, Daoshing Ni, Liz Olson, Dean Orloff, Scott Orloff, Maxine Orloff, Meg McLaughlin-Wong, Rabbi Don Singer, Leong Tan, Jacob and Laurie Teitelbaum, Josh Touber, and Mary Williams.

And always, I have abiding appreciation for my patients, workshop participants, and readers from whom I continue to learn so much. I have disguised any identifying characteristics to protect their privacy. Finally, I want to express my admiration for the more than fourteen thousand members of Dr. Orloff's Empath Support Community on Facebook who bravely embrace the power of being an empath and spread goodness in their own lives and the world.

# ABOUT THE AUTHOR

Judith Orloff, MD, is a psychiatrist and *New York Times* best-selling author. Her books include *The Empath's Empowerment Journal* (the companion to this daybook) and *The Empath's Survival Guide*. Dr. Orloff specializes in treating empaths and highly sensitive people in her Los Angeles private practice. An empath herself, Dr. Orloff synthesizes the pearls of conventional medical wisdom with cutting-edge knowledge of intuition, spirituality, and energy medicine. She is also the author of *Emotional Freedom*, *Positive Energy*, and *Second Sight*. Her work has been featured on the *Today Show*; CNN; and PBS, in *USA Today*; the *New York Times*; and *O, The Oprah Magazine*; and at Google. To learn more about empaths, *The Empath's Survival Guide Online Course*, or to join Dr. Orloff's Empath Support Community on Facebook and newsletter visit drjudithorloff.com.

## ABOUT SOUNDS TRUE

Sounds True is a multimedia publisher whose mission is to inspire and support personal transformation and spiritual awakening. Founded in 1985 and located in Boulder, Colorado, we work with many of the leading spiritual teachers, thinkers, healers, and visionary artists of our time. We strive with every title to preserve the essential "living wisdom" of the author or artist. It is our goal to create products that not only provide information to a reader or listener, but that also embody the quality of a wisdom transmission.

For those seeking genuine transformation, Sounds True is your trusted partner. At SoundsTrue.com you will find a wealth of free resources to support your journey, including exclusive weekly audio interviews, free downloads, interactive learning tools, and other special savings on all our titles.

To learn more, please visit SoundsTrue.com/freegifts or call us toll-free at 800.333.9185.